Fictional Translators

Through close readings of select stories and novels by well-known writers from different literary traditions, *Fictional Translators* invites readers to rethink the main clichés associated with translations and shines a light on the transformative character of the translator's role and the relationships that can be established between originals and their reproductions. Arrojo expertly builds her arguments on the basis of texts such as the following:

- Cortázar's "Letter to a Young Lady in Paris"
- Walsh's "Footnote"
- Wilde's *The Picture of Dorian Gray* and Poe's "The Oval Portrait"
- Borges's "Pierre Menard, Author of the *Quixote*," "Funes, His Memory," and "Death and the Compass"
- Kafka's "The Burrow" and Kosztolányi's *Kornél Esti*
- Saramago's *The History of the Siege of Lisbon* and Babel's "Guy de Maupassant"
- Scliar's "Footnotes" and Calvino's *If on a Winter's Night a Traveler*
- Cervantes's *Don Quixote*

Fictional Translators provides stimulating material for reflection not only on the processes associated with translation as an activity that inevitably transforms meaning, but, also, on the common prejudices that have underestimated its productive role in the shaping of identities. This book is key reading for students and researchers of Literary Translation, Comparative Literature, and Translation Theory.

Rosemary Arrojo is Professor of Comparative Literature at Binghamton University, USA.

New Perspectives in Translation and Interpreting Studies

Series editors:

Michael Cronin holds a Personal Chair in the Faculty of Humanities and Social Sciences at Dublin City University.

Moira Inghilleri is Director of Translation Studies in the Comparative Literature Program at the University of Massachusetts Amherst.

The *New Perspectives in Translation and Interpreting Studies* series aims to address changing needs in the fields of translation studies and interpreting studies. The series features works by leading scholars in both disciplines, on emerging and up-to-date topics. Key features of the titles in this series are accessibility, relevance, and innovation.

These lively and highly readable texts provide an exploration into various areas of translation and interpreting studies for undergraduate and postgraduate students of translation studies, interpreting studies, and cultural studies.

Cities in Translation
Sherry Simon

Translation in the Digital Age
Michael Cronin

Translation and Geography
Federico Italiano

Translation and Rewriting in the Age of Post-Translation Studies
Edwin Gentzler

Eco-Translation
Michael Cronin

Translation and Migration
Moira Inghilleri

Fictional Translators
Rosemary Arrojo

Fictional Translators
Rethinking Translation Through Literature

Rosemary Arrojo

Taylor & Francis Group

LONDON AND NEW YORK

First published 2018
by Routledge
2 Park Square, Milton Park, Abingdon, Oxon OX14 4RN

and by Routledge
711 Third Avenue, New York, NY 10017

Routledge is an imprint of the Taylor & Francis Group, an informa business

British Library Cataloguing in Publication Data
A catalogue record for this book is available from the British Library

Library of Congress Cataloging in Publication Data
A catalog record for this book has been requested

ISBN: 978-1-138-82713-4 (hbk)
ISBN: 978-1-138-82714-1 (pbk)
ISBN: 978-1-315-73872-7 (ebk)

Typeset in Sabon
by Saxon Graphics Ltd, Derby

Printed and bound in Great Britain by
TJ International Ltd, Padstow, Cornwall

To the memory of my parents, Catharina Visconte and
Raphael Arroyo

Contents

Acknowledgments

I am grateful to all the countless colleagues, students, and friends with whom, in the last few decades, I have had the privilege of sharing my enthusiasm for critical theory and literary fiction in multiple venues and institutions not only in Brazil and the United States, but also in other countries such as Turkey, Austria, Germany, Spain, Italy, Australia, and Northern Ireland. My analyses of most of the stories and novels discussed here were developed throughout many years and I am especially thankful to the colleagues who have edited previous versions of some of the pieces that I have revisited for this book. With their careful readings, these colleagues have helped me sharpen my thinking and refine my writing: Edwin Gentzler, Maria Tymoczko, Maria Calzada Pérez, José Santaemilia, José María Rodríguez García, Carol Maier, Françoise Massardier-Kenney, Brian J. Baer, Klaus Kaindl, and Karlheinz Spitzl. I am forever indebted to Ben Van Wyke, who has been kind enough to read most of what I have written in the last decade or so and always offers me pertinent feedback and teaches me some English. I would like to thank Routledge and, more specifically, Michael Cronin, whose comments on my work have been stimulating and extremely helpful; and Laura Sandford, who has played the role of a kind, understanding publisher in the story of my life in the past two years. I am deeply grateful to my sister, Ana Maria Arrojo, whose friendship and care have been fundamental, particularly in the difficult times that coincided with the writing of most of the chapters that constitute this book.

Introduction

This book has been engendered by my long-held conviction that fictional representations of the work of translators will shine a special, often unexpected light on the scene of translation as an asymmetrical encounter between different languages, interests, and perspectives. In addition, and perhaps more importantly, these representations are likely to allow some glimpses into what might be lurking behind the prevailing clichés associated with such an encounter and, therefore, into what is often repressed, barely theorized, or even acknowledged by conventional narratives about translators and their practice, particularly when this practice involves texts highly valued like those labeled as "literary." In contrast to the usually sober discourse of scholarly studies, fictional texts focusing on issues of translation, authorship, and reading can provide a more nuanced frame of reference as they introduce us to translator characters that oftentimes reveal their inner struggles while facing the ethical conundrums associated with their work and the relationships they are expected to establish with author and/or reader figures that also have a stake in the process.

The storylines examined in this book feature intriguing versions of the all too familiar dilemmas that have informed the common discourse on questions of translation and interpretation for millennia and are mostly associated with the "suspicious" status of the translated text as the translator's potentially inaccurate replacement of somebody else's original in another language and context, a replacement that inevitably fails to repeat sameness and for that is often perceived as a threat that can unsettle the alleged authority of the original and/or its author. A critical examination of these issues is especially relevant in the context of contemporary viewpoints that recognize the interfering role of translators not as something that needs to be curtailed or penalized, but as part and parcel of the process that inevitably transforms texts across languages and whose circumstances and motivations should be carefully investigated. I am referring to the importance of post-Nietzschean thought for an understanding of interpretation, often represented by approaches associated with deconstruction, poststructuralism, gender, and postcolonial studies that challenge essentialist conceptions of language and text and underscore the interpreter's and the translator's authorial role in the shaping of meanings and identities. As the translator's visibility became the focal point of such trends within the discipline of translation studies, we started paying closer attention to the strong link that binds questions of language to power, and, therefore, to what ultimately anchors the hierarchical relationships that have defined the production and the reception of translations.

The rationale inspiring the eight chapters that constitute this book is directly associated with what has been labeled as "the fictional turn" in translation studies to signify the recognition of fiction as an appropriate source of reflection "on translation and other hermeneutical processes," a "turn" that might indeed represent "one of the main contributions to translation theory" put forth just before the close of the twentieth century (Pagano 2002: 81). As proposed by Else Vieira in the mid-1990s, "the fictional turn" reflected her interest in highlighting the pivotal role played by translation-related issues in the fiction of key Brazilian and Latin American authors such as João Guimarães Rosa, Mário de Andrade, Jorge Luis Borges, Julio Cortázar, and Gabriel Garcia Marques, as well as the dialogue that a few scholars, including myself, had been trying to establish between fictional texts by these authors and theoretical discourses associated with Western thinkers such as Jacques Derrida, Charles Peirce, and Luce Irigaray (Vieira 1995: 50; cf., also, Gentzler 2008: 109–111). Obviously, though, with the growth of translation studies as an interdiscipline and the proliferation of translator characters in world literature intensifying at the turn of the millennium, the scholarly interest in representations of translators and translation-related issues in fiction began to produce an abundance of critical material elsewhere as well.

This output, by scholars with various agendas and from multiple cultural and scholarly backgrounds, has covered mostly contemporary fiction from an array of traditions and has provided a plethora of significant insights into translation practices and concepts as well as trends and themes in world literature (see, for example, Strümper-Krobb 2003, Wakabayashi 2005, Wilson 2007, Ben-Ari 2010, Baer 2005, Goldbout 2014, Wozniak 2014, just to name a few scholars among the many who have published in English). In recent years the exploration of fictional representations of translation has expanded to motion pictures, opening up new and exciting possibilities not only for research on translation but also for its teaching (cf. Cronin 2009). The vitality of this kind of study, which is bringing much needed visibility to the ever growing role of translators in our everyday lives and calling attention to the far-reaching implications of their practice in times of intensified globalization, has also been showcased in pioneering collections of articles such as Delabastita and Grutman (2005) and Kaindl and Spitzl (2014). The latter is a direct result of the "First International Conference on Fictional Translators and Interpreters in Literature and Film," held at the University of Vienna's Centre for Translation Studies in 2011, and whose success prompted the organization of two others: "Translators and (Their) Authors," held at Tel-Aviv University, Israel, in 2013; and "The Fictions of Translation," at Concordia University in Montreal, Canada, in 2015.

In the introduction to "Fictionalizing Translation and Multilingualism," the special issue Dirk Delabastita and Rainier Grutman edited for *Linguistica Antverpiensia*, they recognize that there has been, in recent years, "a growing number of fictional representations of translation and multilingualism, as well as an upsurge in their study," and directly associate this upsurge with the view of translation "as a cultural and historical phenomenon" that many specialists have "gradually" come to accept since the 1970s (2005: 29). As they argue, such a view has led to a new interest in "older and 'pre-scientific' discourses on translation," by which they mean "anthologies and discussions of historical statements" such as Douglas Robinson's *Western Translation Theory from Herodotos to Nietzsche* (2002) (ibid.). For them, it is in this category, that is, as "statements *about* translation," that fictional representations of translation should be included and, for the examination of "historical concepts and practices of translation," both fictional and non-fictional narratives are as "worthy of research" as translations themselves (ibid.). Since it takes into account the full implications of the fact that translations as well as their theories, like everything else we know, cannot be dissociated from the cultural and historical circumstances that produce them, my perspective obviously distrusts any attempt to consider what some scholars may still view as "scientific" and "pre-scientific" translation discourses in terms of a universally accepted hierarchical opposition. Consequently, while I generally agree with Delabastita and Grutman's perceptive commentary, I do not endorse their classification of literary representations of translation as a "pre-scientific" type of discourse, particularly if that implies that fiction may not be as legitimate or relevant as "science."

The storylines studied in this book have been treated as exceptional representations of the ways in which translation and/or interpretation tends to be experienced in different contexts, revealing implicit and explicit interests and concerns that can be productively analyzed and bring significant insights into the usual conceptions found in prevalent non-fictional discourses on texts and translations as well as the relationships that produce them. If we are willing to consider the notion of theory more broadly and in terms that would be compatible with the etymology of *theoria*, that is, as a way of seeing or looking, we are likely to learn a great deal on translation and translation-related questions from fictional narratives, whose plots usually defend or side with a certain point of view and play out some of its most impacting consequences, offering unique opportunities for reflection that can be potentially more insightful than those associated with what specialists tend to classify as "real" theory. As Thomas O. Beebee has succinctly put it, in an article on Abdelkebir Khatibi's *Love in Two Languages*, if fiction "is distinguished from other forms of discourse in its propensity to 'play' with the given ideologemes of its cultural context," that is, if fiction can be freer and more creative in the ways in which it conveys or represents concepts and values, then, "the best place to trace the ideology of translation is through its fictional embodiment" (Beebee 1994: 72). Beebee's position on the reading of fiction as a space of theorization, like mine, is compatible, for instance, with Jacques Derrida's defense of literature as a privileged site for the kind of reflection generally associated with philosophy or theory. For him, "the thinking that takes place in philosophy" is not "confined to technical philosophy, or to the canonical history of philosophy," but can also be found "in many other places, in law, linguistics, and psychoanalysis. Above all, the thinking that occurs in philosophy communicates in a very special way for Derrida himself with literature" (Caputo 1997: 57–58).

In consonance with this line of argument, I have examined short stories and novels by several authors from different backgrounds, not in the position of a supposedly non-biased exegete determined to describe as faithfully as possible what they have to say, but with the explicit goal of highlighting (and learning from) the contradictions and the aspirations associated with their implicit and/or explicit views on language, texts, interpretation, authorship, and translation. In my readings of these stories and novels, I have often been confronted with the fact that what is usually described as surreal or fantastic in fiction is indeed quite similar to what allegedly sober discourses on translation are trying to defend as "rational" or "objective." At the same time, I cannot think of any scholarly text on the translator's (in)visibility, for example, that could be more eloquent, or more convincing or touching than some of the fictional plots I have examined. It is thus my belief that the chapters that follow will offer specialists, even those who may not agree with my premises, stimulating material for reflection not only on the processes associated with translation but, also, on the common prejudices and idealized expectations that have characterized it as a secondary, mostly mechanical activity that should blindly attempt to reproduce sameness. Some of the authors whose fiction is studied in the following pages are widely known among educated readers of world literature – Jorge Luis Borges, Miguel de Cervantes, Franz Kafka, Edgar Allan Poe, Oscar Wilde, Julio Cortázar, Isaac Babel, José Saramago, and Italo Calvino. Others may not be so well known worldwide, but are outstanding figures in their own national contexts – the Argentine Rodolfo Walsh, the Brazilian Moacyr Scliar, and the Hungarian Dezsö Kosztolányi. With the exception of Walsh's "Nota al pie" ("Footnote") (Walsh 2008) and Scliar's "Notas ao pé da página" ("Footnotes") (Scliar 1995), which I will be quoting from my own unpublished translations, all the fictional texts studied in the following pages are available in the English versions that constitute the actual texts I have analyzed. In the privileged company of these distinguished authors, I invite readers to follow the vicissitudes of a few writer figures, several translator characters, a proofreader, two painters/translators, and a handful of reader characters, all of them deeply involved in the pursuit of some form of textual mastery.

As these engaging storylines can obviously count on the appeal of fiction's creative resources – colorful, contradictory characters; humorous or unpredictable intrigues; surprising events and revelations; dramatic twists and turns – they are quite efficient in enticing non-specialists to begin probing some of the theoretical concerns that have defined the practice of translation and captured the attention of scholars. As I suggest in Chapter One, their use for pedagogical purposes is perfectly suited for the teaching of key theoretical notions to undergraduate or graduate students interested in a variety of fields involved with issues of language such as translation studies, comparative and world literature, classical and modern languages and literatures, philosophy, and linguistics. The use of fictional representations of translation for pedagogical purposes has been addressed by Michael Cronin in his study of film and translation in terms that are quite compatible with my own view. As he suggests, "neglecting to use cinema in translation studies is neglecting to use a highly engaging and effective medium for soliciting responses on a wide variety of topics directly related to the business of translation," topics such as "[e]quivalence, fidelity, infidelity, domestication, foreignization, control, invisibility, identity, untranslatability, positionality" (2009: xi; see also Kaindl 2014: 13).

My readings have been influenced most of all by Borges's "Pierre Menard, Author of the *Quixote*" (Borges 1998a, trans. Hurley), the quintessential story about the impossibility of translation as the repetition of the same, whose focus is an unforgettable portrait of the translator as a Quixotic figure fully invested in an absurd mission to defeat difference and the passing of time. The translator in Borges's irreverent, thought-provoking plot is the Frenchman Pierre Menard, who dedicated his life to composing, in the first decades of the twentieth century, the exact same text Cervantes had produced in his native Spanish of the early 1600s. As the story so superbly illustrates, it is impossible to separate the translator's seemingly commendable goal of being totally faithful to the original he chose to reproduce from the apparent madness that led him to consider actually *becoming* Cervantes. In only a few pages, Borges has created, as has been shrewdly observed, not only "the most acute, most concentrated commentary anyone has offered on the business of translation" (Steiner 1975: 70), but, also, a wealth of material on the dynamics of reading, which, like translation, is viewed by the story's narrator as a practice that actually produces meaning rather than merely reproduces it. As the most important source of inspiration for this project, "Pierre Menard," which can also be read as an inspiring synthesis of postmodern notions of translation and interpretation, has supplied the backbone and the main direction of my basic arguments. It also underscores some of the multiple ways in which fiction can be read as a deconstructive instrument that helps us reevaluate mainstream statements about the relationships that should be established between texts and what is routinely repressed or ignored by such statements, that is, the premises, the illusions, as well as the anxieties and the desires that often underlie the ways in which we deal with issues of language and the subject.

"Pierre Menard" has been crucial not only for this project, but for my own growth as a scholar as well. It was, for instance, the topic of my very first publication (Arrojo 1984) and the focus of a few other pieces I have written throughout the years (cf., for example, Arrojo 1986: 11–24; Arrojo 1993: 151–175; Arrojo 2004; Arrojo 2010; and Arrojo 2014), some of which have also been rethought for this book (cf. Chapters One, Four, and Eight). When I first read the story, as an inexperienced teenager used to reading more conventional forms of fiction, and, thus, long before being exposed to theory or philosophy, I found it dull and could not quite understand why Borges was such a celebrated author. However, when I reread it in the 1980s, in the wake of my early exposure to poststructuralism, I became instantly infatuated with Borges's wit and the possibilities his work seemed to offer for the reading of fiction as a form of theory. Since then, "Pierre Menard" has been a constant companion in my teaching and in the development of my own thinking about questions of literature and translation. Furthermore, these different readings can be viewed as compelling evidence of the fact that no text can be read in a vacuum. Besides exploring some of the many ways in which the story can be interpreted, my comments on "Pierre Menard" also exemplify the kind of dialogue I have tried to establish, throughout the years, between Borges's work and seminal texts by major thinkers such as Plato, Friedrich Nietzsche, Michel Foucault, Roland Barthes, Jacques Derrida, Sigmund Freud, and Jacques Lacan, texts that have played a defining role in the ways in which I read fiction and reflect on its relevance and its implications.

In my preparation of the chapters that follow, I have made sure that each of them can also be read as an individual essay. At the same time, since they all feature storylines that revolve around overlapping themes and concerns, these chapters build on one another and, together, can hopefully offer a solid reflection on the fantasies and assumptions that seem to be involved in the notions of authorship and translation that have defined mainstream views and the institutions that support them. In Chapter One, "Introducing Theory through Fiction," my main goal is to show how Borges's "Pierre Menard" can inspire students to reflect on the nonsensical positions on originals and authors, translators and readers, which are commonly taken for granted by our persistent essentialist tradition and its belief in the possibility of fixed meanings and ideally neutral, non-interfering subjects. Besides the material about "Pierre Menard," which is based on a previously published essay (Arrojo 2010), Chapter One presents a reading of Julio Cortázar's "Letter to a Young Lady in Paris" (Cortázar 1985, trans. Blackburn), another short story that never fails to captivate students and stimulate them to rethink the basic issues involving translation and how it should relate to the writing of originals. Cortázar's story is a poignant narrative in the format of a letter that turns into a suicide note addressed to Andrea, the young lady of the title. It is being written by the story's narrator, who works as a translator and tells Andrea about the ambivalence he feels towards the little rabbits he must often vomit up and that, little by little, transform and finally destroy her apartment, which can be interpreted as a compelling metaphor for the original text on which the translator is allegedly working. While in "Pierre Menard," we learn about the French translator's peculiar decision to become Cervantes in order to repeat the *Quixote*, in "Letter to a Young Lady in Paris," we are exposed to the translator's gripping narrative of his own failure to protect the author's textual space from his agency and relentless creativity. Both pieces are quite effective in getting students to ponder the issue of (in)visibility in translation and whether translators could indeed repress or ignore who they are while devoting their efforts to someone else's text. My reading of the two stories in the same chapter also intends to emphasize the value of a comparative approach, in which the interpretation of one piece illuminates and complements the interpretation of the other.

This is an approach that I have adopted in all the chapters, with the exception of Chapter Two, "Fiction as Theory and Activism," a revised version of a recently published essay (Arrojo 2016), which proposes a reading of Rodolfo Walsh's "Nota al pie" ("Footnote") (Walsh 2008), a unique, moving story that, unlike the other fictional texts studied in the book, features a narrator who openly sympathizes with the plight of the underpaid, silenced translator, and unequivocally defends his right to be visible and recognized. The focal point of Walsh's story is a suicide letter written by a translator character and intercepted by the narrator who turns it into a footnote that grows larger on every page until it literally takes over the narrative and exposes the dead translator's miserable life in the Argentina of the late 1950s. Even though I have not commented on how Walsh's story could be read together with (or against) other stories, I encourage readers to further explore the many possibilities of a comparative approach when examining all the fictional texts featured in this book. In my discussions of these pieces with students, I have explored, for instance, some of the obvious similarities between Walsh's and Cortázar's stories, beginning with the fact that Walsh's translator figure, like Cortázar's, can no longer bear to repress his agency, but is only able to express himself after deciding to take his own life. Thus, in both cases, the only acknowledged, visibly signed piece of writing they leave behind is a suicide letter.

In Chapter Three, "The Illusive Presence of Originals," readers will find a critique of the idealized conception of originals typically cultivated by tradition. It focuses on Oscar Wilde's *The Picture of Dorian Gray* (Wilde 2014) and Edgar Allan Poe's "The Oval Portrait" (Poe 1983) (the material on the latter is based on Arrojo 2003). Their well-known plots can be read as revealing explorations of the metaphor of translation as portrait painting, a metaphor that reflects the long-established hierarchy separating fetishized conceptions of the original as a fully present, reliable bearer of its author's acknowledged meanings and intentions, from its allegedly inadequate representations in other languages or media. As this metaphor is normally meant to suggest, while the original as a live model is multidimensional, but supposedly predictable and immune to change, its translations, like painted portraits, will always be lacking since they cannot possibly do justice to whatever glorified plenitude they may be required to reproduce. The conceptual frame behind this metaphor is radically challenged in both Wilde's and Poe's plots, which play with the idea that painted portraits could in fact be more authentic, and even more alive, so to speak, than the live models/originals that they are supposed to reproduce. Considering that these narratives dare to defy the customary, age-old opposition between originals and their reproductions, it seemed fitting that I preface my readings of Wilde's and Poe's pieces with a brief introduction to "Book X" from Plato's *Republic* (Plato 1991, trans. Jowett), a foundational text that famously addresses, among other issues, the relationship between the unattainable, absolutely perfect original, understood here in its broadest sense, and its reproduction in painting. Hopefully, the commentary on Plato's "Dialogue" will also help readers unfamiliar with this kind of thinking to follow the introduction to Nietzsche's philosophy featured in Chapters Four and Five.

The focus of Chapter Four, "The Translation of Philosophy into Fiction," in which I revisit and expand on previously published material (Arrojo 2014), is the exploration of what I see as a close connection between key notions from Nietzsche's philosophy and Borges's "Funes, His Memory" (Borges 1998b, trans. Hurley), the story of the young Uruguayan who became famous for his prodigious memory, and which can be read as a creative translation of *Thus Spoke Zarathustra* (Nietzsche 2006). The chapter starts with an introduction to Nietzsche's conception of language, which I find to be quite compatible with Borges's views on translation as they are represented not only in several of his stories, but also in his essays on the subject, "The Homeric Versions" (Borges 1999a, trans. Weinberger) and "The Translators of *The One Thousand and One Nights*" (Borges 1999b, trans. Allen). An important goal of the chapter is to show how the reading of Borges's fiction can be illuminated by Nietzsche's philosophy and how both can help us develop a deeper understanding of the essays just mentioned. Furthermore, while my reading of "Pierre Menard" in Chapter One sets up the context and serves as a kind of prologue to my comments on Cortázar's story, in Chapter Four it is "Funes, His Memory" that will guide me in further reflecting on "Pierre Menard." More specifically, a thorough reading of "Funes" will shine a light into the kind of ambivalent treatment the French translator receives from the story's narrator and, thus, also into Borges's complex views on the translator's visibility subtly suggested in "The Translators of *The One Thousand and One Nights*."

Chapter Five, "Texts as Private Retreats," also an expansion of previously published material (Arrojo 2002), focuses on three remarkable pieces: Kafka's "The Burrow" (Kafka 1971, trans. Muir); Borges's "Death and the Compass" (Borges 1998c, trans. Hurley); and "Gallus," a chapter from

Kosztolányi's *Kornél Esti* (Kosztolányi 2011, trans. Adams). These narratives work quite well together particularly as I read them alongside Nietzsche's concept of the "will to power" and its deconstruction of the essentialist basis of any "natural," hierarchical distinction between the writing and the interpretation of texts. In my readings of Kafka's and Borges's stories, besides taking a closer look at the profile of their bizarre authorial figures, I examine the metaphor of text, or the writing of a text, as the construction of an ever-changing labyrinth that should protect its constructor from the invasion of unwelcome intruders. The labyrinth maker in Kafka's story is presumably a burrowing animal, obsessed with the possibility of creating a flawless structure that could be definitive, perfectly closed and, hence, shielded from difference and the interference of others. The reflection I construct around Kafka's story is supplemented by a reading of Borges's "Death and the Compass," in which the unconventional author figure is Red Scharlach, an assassin who weaves a textual labyrinth to trap his arch-enemy Erik Lönnrot, the reader/detective who is determined to outsmart and arrest Scharlach. This textual labyrinth finds a fitting representation in Triste-le-Roy, the abandoned villa located in the outskirts of the city where Scharlach finally catches Lönnrot. While Kafka's and Borges's stories can be read to illustrate and even expand on some views associated with Nietzsche's concept of the will to power and its implications for writing and interpretation, it is in Kosztolányi's piece that an actual translator figure is brought to the scene. From the perspective of the Hungarian author's narrator, who introduces himself as a respected writer, Gallus, the translator, was a promising, talented young man with exceptional language skills. However, as a chronic kleptomaniac, he could not stop himself and ended up "stealing" an odd assortment of objects from a second-rate English thriller he was commissioned to translate, and which he transformed into an elegant piece of Hungarian prose. The characterization of the translator as an incurable thief provides a comical, but eloquent portrayal of the difficulty of establishing a clear-cut distinction between the author's and the translator's roles in the production of translated texts, a difficulty that is also behind the often complicated relationship authors and translators tend to establish with one another.

In Chapter Six, "Authorship as the Affirmation of Masculinity," I revisit similar versions of these distinctions, but, this time, they are anchored to the most fundamental dichotomy of all, that is, the one that reduces gender to an opposition that values males over females and is traditionally viewed as self-evident and unquestionable. The chapter proposes a reflection on gender-related stereotypes often found at the core of clichéd assumptions about authorship and translation and is organized around two pieces – José Saramago's *History of the Siege of Lisbon* (Saramago 1997, trans. Pontiero) and Isaac Babel's "Guy de Maupassant" (Babel 2002, trans. Constantine). Particularly when read comparatively, these very different texts can bring to the fore the intimate relationship often established between mainstream notions of authorship and the recurrent hierarchy that opposes literary creativity, commonly identified as a masculine attribute, to feminine or less than masculine, "reproductive" textual practices such as reading or translation (for the theoretical basis informing my commentary, I am indebted to Gilbert and Gubar 1984 and Chamberlain 2000). This opposition is emblematically illustrated in the trajectory of Raimundo Silva, Saramago's protagonist in *The History of the Siege of Lisbon*, a lonely, almost asexual proofreader in his fifties who has settled for a profession he despises until he finds the courage to change a key sentence in the history book he is proofreading about the reconquest of Lisbon in the twelfth century. As the plot associates the emergence of Raimundo's authorial voice to the reawakening of his masculinity and, thus, to the possibility of a fulfilling relationship with a loving female, it also suggests the outline of a simplistic, gender-based opposition between authorship and proofreading, according to which females (or less than aggressive males) seem to have no desire or adequate skills to create texts of their own and are, thus, meant to proofread the texts of others. A similar dynamic is suggested in Babel's "Guy de Maupassant," whose plot allows me to expand on the discussion outlined above with a focus this time on the process of translation and the figure of the translator. The story takes us to 1916 Saint Petersburg, Russia, where we get acquainted with three translator figures: Aleksei Kazantsev, a gentle male teacher and translator who has no ambition to do anything else; Raisa Bendersky, a wealthy, married woman whose hobby is to translate stories by her beloved Maupassant, but who has no talent for literature; and the oversexed young narrator who is adamant about becoming a writer and resorts to literary translation in order to pursue his dream. When the narrator is hired to revise Raisa's translations, the opportunity provides him not only with the writing exercise supplied by translation and some means to support himself, but also with the sexual initiation Raisa is willing to offer. Indeed, as the narrator manipulates and rewrites Maupassant's stories in Russian, translation allows him to temporarily take the author's place and seduce Raisa in her domestic context. If, as Saramago's and Babel's storylines seem to suggest, proofreading and translation are viewed as devalued practices pursued either by those who lack appropriate authorial skills, or those who view such practices mostly as a writing exercise that might lead to the composition of their own texts, they basically deny the actual possibility of translation and proofreading as legitimate professional activities that deserve to be taken seriously for their own sake.

Chapter Seven, on "The Gendering of Texts," based on a previously published essay (Arrojo 2005), proposes readings of Moacyr Scliar's "Notas ao pé da página" ("Footnotes") (Scliar 1995) and Italo Calvino's *If on a Winter's Night a Traveler* (Calvino 1981, trans. Weaver). These pieces have allowed me to continue probing the interface between gender and general conceptions of textual practices with a focus this time on representations of women and texts as highly prized property, and, therefore, as the objects of desire and contention that divide author and translator figures. As in the storylines examined in the previous chapter, the roles attributed to women in Calvino's and Scliar's plots revolve around simplistic, sexist stereotypes, which suggest, among other things, that texts, like women, are not to be trusted and can only be somewhat stabilized or temporarily tamed under the sway of a steady male authority figure. Scliar's story, like Walsh's, commented on above, resorts to footnotes as a persuasive representation of the translator's marginal position not simply in the process of translation, but in the very text he produces, where he may be allowed to be visible only at the bottom of the page. From the narrator/translator's five footnotes, one at the bottom of each blank page, we learn that they refer to the translation of a poet's memoir, the same poet whose work this translator/narrator had also translated, and the same poet whose mistress the translator ends up marrying. As a valuable asset that changes hands, the poet's mistress, as a sort of "belle infidèle," can be interpreted as a metaphor for the text that cannot stay the same or stand still and is thus unable to remain truly faithful to the author, or anybody else, for that matter. This trope of the woman as text, or the text as woman, can be explored in greater detail in Calvino's acclaimed novel, in which a male Reader, an impotent author figure, and a deceitful, powerful translator character, are all pursuing the attractive Ludmilla. As the female reader character, who has had an affair with the translator and has no interest in being intimate with the elderly author, but ends up married to the Reader, Ludmilla represents not only a close association between woman and text, but, also, the usual conception of reading as a "feminine," passive activity that is expected to revere the allegedly unconditional authority of the (male) author.

Considering that Calvino's and Scliar's gender-focused plots bring out weak male author figures who cannot get or keep the girl, so to speak, in sheer contrast with highly visible, empowered translator characters, it is fair to argue that they both recognize the productive nature of the translator's practice and, consequently, also the difficulty of clearly separating what belongs to the author from what belongs to the translator in the process of translation. In fact, up to a certain point, Calvino's and Scliar's pieces could be read as humorous, albeit sexist, representations of post-Nietzschean conceptions of text and authorship, with an emphasis on the "death of the author" arguments proposed by French poststructuralists. However, a closer look at Calvino's and Scliar's ambivalent treatment of the translator's visibility will also reveal a different picture. In both pieces, there is an obvious contrast between the theoretical or ideological positions implicitly represented in their plots and what they actually seem to value on a more subtle, subterranean level, as revealed, for instance, by the characterization of their translator figures as grossly unethical individuals. Such a characterization implies, of course, that in these storylines the translator's visibility is not seriously treated as the logical outcome of the fact that translators do have to make choices and reveal themselves in the translations they compose, but, rather, as a symptom of their abusive personalities or sheer lack of scruples and, hence, as something that could (and should) be potentially corrected or neutralized.

What appears to be a contradiction between the underlying motivations of Calvino's and Scliar's narratives and the notions of text, authorship, and translation identifiable in their storylines is actually one of the most valuable characteristics of the fictional pieces analyzed in this book. Because of their multiple perspectives and the different viewpoints represented, these pieces allow us not only to learn from the theoretical constructs that seem to inform their plots, but also to peek into the kind of emotional response that such constructs tend to elicit, particularly from author/narrator figures who are highly invested in shaping the textual practices that make it possible for their work to circulate. From this perspective, Calvino's and Scliar's texts, like most of the storylines examined in this book, can also be discussed in light of an argument introduced by Freud in "Creative Writers and Daydreaming," which relates the writing of fiction to its author's desire to be invulnerable (Freud 1983: 25, trans. Strachey). According to Freud, while the creative writer "creates a world of fantasy which he takes very seriously – that is, which he invests with large amounts of emotion," his ultimate goal is "to rearrange the things of his world in a new way which pleases him" (ibid.). As a consequence, this kind of fiction will always feature a "hero who is the center of interest" and whom the author "seems to place under the protection of a special Providence" (Freud 1983: 26). In Calvino's and Scliar's texts, as in most of the storylines analyzed, even though such a hero can be associated with an author or narrator figure, the very fact that his antagonist is a daring translator or reader seems to suggest that, besides being recognized, the creative power of translation or interpretation is feared as a major threat, particularly on a more personal level that could even be traced to the actual author. From this stance, it seems fair to speculate that while the translator's alleged invisibility does not reflect the actual practice that allows for texts to live on and travel across cultures and languages, its implicit idealization in fiction may be a forceful projection of the (male) author's desire to reign invulnerable within the imagined limits of his text, even after it has been rewritten by someone else in a different language and context.

Chapter Eight, "Translation as Transference," a revised version of an article that first appeared in *Diacritics* (Arrojo 2004), addresses the question of the translator's visibility from a different angle. Its main goal is to pursue some associations between Borges's own biography and his "Pierre Menard," with special emphasis on his early translation practice and the launching of his career as a poet after he falls in love with Walt Whitman's poetry. My starting point is a close look at the peculiar bond that Menard seems to have developed not only with the *Quixote*, but, more significantly, with Cervantes himself, a bond that, as I claim, can be plausibly understood in the light of the concept of transference in Lacanian psychoanalysis anchored in "the formula of the subject presumed to know" ("Le Séminaire," Lacan 1975: 64, trans. and qtd. by Felman 1987: 86). From this viewpoint, it would be feasible to consider Cervantes as "the subject presumed to know" for the French translator, who actually desires to *be* the Spanish master and do and write exactly what he did. From this perspective, it can be argued that Menard uses translation as a convenient response to transference, a response that allows him to imagine that he could (and even should) indeed take Cervantes's place and rewrite his masterpiece. Through readings of pivotal texts such as Borges's "An Autobiographical Essay" (Borges 1987), I establish some significant links between his early years as an aspiring poet and translator and the story of Pierre Menard: just as Cervantes seemed to function as "the subject presumed to know" who stimulated Menard to compose fragments from the *Quixote*, it was Borges's love for Whitman and his poetry that inspired him to publish, in 1919, "Himno del mar" ("Hymn to the Sea") (Borges 1997), his first poem, which reads like a clumsy imitation of the American poet's work. Borges's interest in Whitman also produced *Hojas de hierba* (Whitman 1969), his translation of *Leaves of Grass*, whose publication, first announced in 1927, did not take place until 1969. As I speculate, this forty-year gap between the announcement and the actual publication of *Hojas de hierba*, in addition to some of Borges's puzzling choices, could be ultimately associated with the Argentinian author's need to deal with his infatuation with the American poet and, perhaps, to feel reassured that he could indeed become a major literary figure and would not end up simply repeating Pierre Menard, the translator who never managed to overcome his obsession with one of the greatest authors of all time and left no legacy of his own. While, in previous chapters, Borges's stories are shown to destabilize the conventional distinction between fiction and theory, in Chapter Eight it is the distinction between fiction and autobiography that is found to be blurred.

Readers will probably note that the blurring of the long-established oppositions that have defined the relationship between the writing of originals and their representations, either in translations or interpretations, is indeed one of the most recurrent topics in my commentary. As my readings intend to suggest, what supposedly separates originals from their translations, texts from their readings, authors from translators and/or readers, fiction from theory, or writers from their writings can be productively rethought, particularly when examined through the creative, enriching filter provided by literature. Hence, the recognition and the exploration of what such a rethinking entails will expand and deepen our understanding not only of processes of interpretation, but also the scope and the function of literary fiction. At the same time, as the following chapters will hopefully convey, the perspective that has inspired my approach does not have to lead us to nihilism or to the chaos of a world in which anything goes. In fact, coming to terms with the provisionality and the contextualization of all allegedly clear-cut distinctions can sharpen our awareness of the fundamental roles we play – whether as authors, readers, or translators – in the construction of the meanings that matter to us. Consequently, it is likely to encourage us to confront the responsibilities involved in being true agents, rather than mere spectators, in the communities whose language practices shape us and are also shaped by our interventions. As a diligent interpreter of the fictional pieces chosen for this book, I can only hope that readers will recognize how seriously I have taken not only the authors and the texts I have chosen to write about, but, also, my role as the commentator who must interpret and, thus, rewrite their unforgettable plots.

Bibliography

Arrojo, R. (1984) "'Pierre Menard, autor del *Quijote*' – esboço de uma poética da tradução via Borges," *Tradução e Comunicação: Revista Brasileira de Tradutores* 5: 75–90.

—— (1986) *Oficina de Tradução – A Teoria na Prática*, São Paulo: Ática.

—— (1993) *Tradução, Desconstrução e Psicanálise*, Rio de Janeiro: Imago.

—— (2002) "Writing, Interpreting, and the Power Struggle for the Control of Meaning: Scenes from Kafka, Borges, and Kosztolányi," in E. Gentzler and M. Tymoczko (eds.) *Translation and Power*, Amherst: University of Massachusetts Press, 63–79.

—— (2003) "The Power of Originals and the Scandal of Translation: A Reading of Edgar Allan Poe's 'The Oval Portrait'," in M. C. Pérez (ed.) *Apropos of Ideology*, Manchester: St. Jerome, 165–180.

—— (2004) "Translation, Transference, and the Attraction to Otherness – Borges, Menard, Whitman," *Diacritics* 34(3): 31–52.

—— (2005) "The Gendering of Translation in Fiction: Translators, Authors, and Women/Texts in Scliar and Calvino," in J. Santaemilia (ed.) *Gender, Sex and Translation – The Manipulation of Identities*, Manchester: St. Jerome, 80–95.

—— (2010) "Fictional Texts as Pedagogical Tools," in C. Maier and F. Massardier-Kenney (eds.) *Literature in Translation – Teaching Issues and Reading Practices*, Kent, OH: The Kent State University Press, 53–68.

—— (2014) "The Power of Fiction as Theory: Some Exemplary Lessons on Translation from Borges's Stories," in K. Kaindl and K. Spitzl (eds.) *Transfiction – Research into the Realities of Translation Fiction*, Amsterdam: John Benjamins, 247–251.

—— (2016) "A Portrait of the Translator as Laborer: A Reflection on Rodolfo Walsh's 'Nota al pie'," in F. Massardier-Kenney, B. J. Baer, and M. Tymoczko (eds.) *Translators Writing, Writing Translators*, Kent, OH: The Kent State University Press, 39–53.

Babel, I. (2002) "Guy de Maupassant," P. Constantine (trans.), in N. Babel (ed.) *The Complete Works of Isaac Babel*, New York: W. W. Norton & Company, 679–686.

Baer, B. J. (2005) "Translating the Transition: The Translator-Detective in Post-Soviet Fiction," in D. Delabastita and R. Grutman (eds.), "Fictionalizing Translation and Multilingualism," *Linguistica Antverpiensia* 4: 243–254.

Beebee, T. O. (1994) "The Fiction of Translation: Abdelkebir Khatibi's *Love in Two Languages*," *SubStance* 23(1): 73: 63–78.

Ben-Ari, N. (2010) "Representations of Translators in Popular Culture," *Translation and Interpreting Studies* 5(2): 220–242.

Borges, J. L. (1987) "An Autobiographical Essay," in J. Alazraki (ed.) *Critical Essays on Jorge Luis Borges*, Boston, MA: G. K. Hall, 21–55.

—— (1997) "Himno del mar," in *Textos recobrados, 1919–1929*, Buenos Aires: Emecé, 24–26.

—— (1998a) "Pierre Menard, Author of the *Quixote*," A. Hurley (trans.) *Collected Fictions*, New York: Penguin, 88–95.

—— (1998b) "Funes, His Memory," A. Hurley (trans.) *Collected Fictions*, New York: Penguin, 131–137.

—— (1998c) "Death and the Compass," A. Hurley (trans.) *Collected Fictions*, New York: Penguin, 147–156.

—— (1999a) "The Homeric Versions," E. Weinberger (trans. and ed.) *Selected Non-Fictions*, New York: Penguin, 69–74.

—— (1999b) "The Translators of *The One Thousand and One Nights*," E. Allen (trans.), E. Weinberger (ed.) *Selected Non-Fictions*, New York: Penguin, 92–109.

Calvino, I. (1981) *If on a Winter's Night a Traveler*, W. Weaver (trans.), New York: Harcourt Brace and Company.

Caputo, J. D. (1997) *Deconstruction in a Nutshell – A Conversation with Jacques Derrida*, New York: Fordham University Press.

Chamberlain, L. (2000) "Gender and the Metaphorics of Translation," in L. Venuti (ed.) *The Translation Studies Reader*, London: Routledge, 314–329.

Cortázar, J. (1985) "Letter to a Young Lady in Paris," P. Blackburn (trans.) *Blow-Up and Other Stories*, New York: Pantheon, 39–50.

Cronin, M. (2009) *Translation Goes to the Movies*, London: Routledge.

Delabastita, D. and R. Grutman, (eds.) (2005) "Fictionalizing Translation and Multilingualism," *Linguistica Antverpiensia* 4.

Felman, S. (1987) *Jacques Lacan and the Adventure of Insight: Psychoanalysis in Contemporary Culture*, Cambridge, MA: Harvard University Press.

Freud, S. (1983) "Creative Writers and Daydreaming," J. Strachey (trans.), in E. Kurzweil and W. Phillips (eds.) *Literature and Psychoanalysis*, New York: Columbia University Press, 24–28.

Gentzler, E. (2008) *Translation and Identity in the Americas – New Directions in Translation Theory*, London: Routledge.

Gilbert, S. M. and S. Gubar (1984) *The Madwoman in the Attic – The Woman Writer and the Nineteenth-Century Literary Imagination*, New Haven, CT: Yale University Press.

Goldbout, P. (2014) "Fictional Translators in Quebec Novels," in K. Kaindl and K. Spitzl (eds.) *Transfiction – Research into the Realities of Translation Fiction*, Amsterdam: John Benjamins, 177–187.

Kafka, F. (1971) "The Burrow," W. and E. Muir (trans.), in N. N. Glatzer (ed.) *Franz Kafka – The Complete Stories*, New York: Schocken, 325–359.

Kaindl, K. (2014) "Going Fictional? Translators and Interpreters in Literature and Film: An Introduction," in K. Kaindl and K. Spitzl (eds.) *Transfiction – Research into the Realities of Translation Fiction*, Amsterdam: John Benjamins, 1–26.

Kaindl, K. and K. Spitzl (eds.) (2014) *Transfiction – Research into the Realities of Translation Fiction*, Amsterdam: John Benjamins.

Kosztolányi, D. (2011) *Kornél Esti – A Novel*, B. Adams (trans.), New York: New Directions.

Lacan, J. (1975) *Le Seminaire*, livre XX, Paris: Seuil.

Nietzsche, F. (2006) *Thus Spoke Zarathustra – A Book for All and None*, A. Del Caro (trans.), A. Del Caro and R. Pippin (eds.), Cambridge: Cambridge University Press.

Pagano, A. S. (2002) "Translation as Testimony: On Official Histories and Subversive Pedagogies in Cortázar," in M. Tymoczko and E. Gentzler (eds.) *Translation and Power*, Amherst: University of Massachusetts Press, 80–98.

Plato (1991) "Book X," B. Jowett (trans.) *The Republic*, New York: Vintage, 360–397.

Poe, E. A. (1983) "Life in Death [The Oval Portrait]," in *The Unabridged Edgar Allan Poe*, Philadelphia, PA: Running Press Book Publishers, 734–738.

Saramago, J. (1997) *The History of the Siege of Lisbon*, G. Pontiero (trans.), Orlando, FL: Harcourt.

Scliar, M. (1995) "Notas ao pé da página," in *Contos Reunidos*, São Paulo: Companhia das Letras, 371–375.

Steiner, G. (1975) *After Babel – Aspects of Language and Translation*, Oxford: Oxford University Press.

Strümper-Krobb, S. (2003) "The Translator in Fiction," *Language and Intercultural Communication* 3(3): 115–121.

Vieira, E. R. P. (1995) "(In)visibilidades na Tradução: Troca de Olhares Teóricos e Ficcionais," *ComTextos* 6: 50–68.

Wakabayashi, J. (2005) "Representations of Translators and Translation in Japanese Fiction," in D. Delabastita and R. Grutman (eds.), "Fictionalizing Translation and Multilingualism," *Linguistica Antverpiensia* 4: 156–169.

Walsh, R. (2008) "Nota al pie," in *Un Kilo de Oro*, Buenos Aires: Ediciones de la Flor, 69–96.

Whitman, W. (1969) *Hojas de hierba*, J. L. Borges (trans.), Buenos Aires: Juárez Editor.

Wilde, O. (2014) *The Picture of Dorian Gray*, Brooklyn, NY: Millennium Publications.

Wilson, R. (2007) "The Fiction of the Translator," *Journal of Intercultural Studies* 28(4): 381–395.

Wozniak, M. (2014) "Future Imperfect: Translation and Translators in Science-Fiction Novels and Films," in K. Kaindl and K. Spitzl (eds.) *Transfiction – Research into the Realities of Translation Fiction*, Amsterdam: John Benjamins, 345–361.

1 Introducing theory through fiction

Jorge Luis Borges's "Pierre Menard, Author of the *Quixote*" and Julio Cortázar's "Letter to a Young Lady in Paris"

I have assumed the mysterious obligation to reconstruct, word for word, the novel that for [Cervantes] was spontaneous. [...] Composing the *Quixote* in the early seventeenth century was a reasonable, necessary, perhaps even inevitable undertaking; in the early twentieth, it is virtually impossible. Not for nothing have three hundred years elapsed, freighted with the most complex events. Among those events, to mention but one, is the *Quixote* itself.

Jorge Luis Borges, "Pierre Menard,
Author of the Quixote," trans. Andrew Hurley

Don't reproach me for it, Andrea, don't blame me. Once in a while it happens that I vomit up a bunny. It's no reason not to live in whatever house, it's no reason for one to blush and isolate oneself and to walk around keeping one's mouth shut.

Julio Cortázar, "Letter to a Young Woman in Paris,"
trans. Paul Blackburn

A close look at the revealing scene of translation sketched in the fragment reproduced above from Borges's "Pierre Menard, Author of the *Quixote*" (Borges 1998, trans. Hurley), first published in Argentina in 1939, gives readers a privileged insight into the translator's "mysterious obligation" to faithfully reconstruct someone else's text at another time, in another context, for different reasons, and with different goals, an obligation that Pierre Menard diligently tries to fulfill even though he knows that it is impossible for sameness to be reproduced in difference. Borges's fragment, like the story as a whole, confronts attentive readers with the undeniable fact of difference as a constitutive element of translation and invites them to ponder the transformational character of the translator's role and, hopefully, at least some of its far-reaching consequences. The translator's unsettling visibility is also a central theme in Cortázar's "Letter to a Young Woman in Paris" (Cortázar 1985, trans. Blackburn), originally published in Argentina in 1951, which offers readers a stirring representation of the translator's ambivalent relationship with his own irrepressible creativity, ingeniously conveyed by the little rabbits that at times must come out of his mouth. The translator's bunnies, for which he secretly cares like beloved children, are also powerful agents of change as they alter and ultimately destroy the composition of the borrowed textual space that the translator is temporarily allowed to occupy, the same space that he has pledged to protect and defend mostly from himself.

While Borges's hilarious, cerebral plot can be read as a merciless deconstruction of the most recurrent clichés associated with translation and its relationship with the writing of "originals," Cortázar's whimsical, poignant story invites readers to reflect on issues directly associated with prevailing conceptions and how they have taught translators to view and, most significantly, to feel about their own agency and the role it plays, or should play, in their work. When Cortázar's story is read against the background of Borges's and vice versa, each of these readings is likely to produce insights that enrich the other, providing multifaceted portrayals of the translator's transformative role and a unique opportunity to critically evaluate the usual platitudes that underestimate its scope and effects. Borges's and Cortázar's surreal storylines and characters are particularly efficient in sensitizing non-specialists to the productive nature of translation and in stimulating them to get acquainted with fundamental theoretical issues that have redefined the translator's task in the last few decades. As pedagogical tools, these stories are notably suitable for the introduction of scholarship on translation to undergraduate or beginning graduate students following academic programs in translation studies, comparative and world literature, classical and modern languages and literatures, philosophy, linguistics, or any other field directly or indirectly dealing with questions of language. The two stories are also appropriate for the introduction of theoretical issues to translators in training or practicing translators interested in reflecting more broadly on their work and, perhaps, in becoming acquainted with the concerns of formal theories as well.

Learning from Pierre Menard

As a quintessential fictional text about translation, "Pierre Menard, Author of the *Quixote*" can be uniquely helpful in raising questions and stimulating productive discussions on some of the most obvious commonplaces associated with originals and their reproductions (cf., for example, Arrojo 1986: 11–21; Waisman 2005: 93–109; and Kristal 2002: 29–31). It is a perplexing story in the format of a short review essay that is also an alleged tribute to the recently deceased Pierre Menard, an obscure French Symbolist writer who lived in Nîmes at the beginning of the twentieth century. Borges's third-person narrator is an established critic who claims to have been a "true friend" of the deceased and catalogued all his "visible" nineteen pieces – monographs, translations, scholarly essays, drafts, sonnets – whose brief descriptions, instead of elevating the seemingly ambitious Menard, actually suggest the profile of a minor, somewhat ridiculous intellectual and writer. It is, however, Pierre Menard's "invisible," "subterranean," and, yet, unfinished work, that is the focal point of the story, and which exposes the French writer's peculiar ambition: the "composition" of "the ninth and thirty-eighth chapters of Part I of *Don Quixote* and a fragment of Chapter XXII" (Borges 1998: 90). Even though the word "translation" is never used to describe Menard's invisible work, which was "perhaps the most significant writing" of his time, we are told that the project was indeed the repetition "in a foreign tongue of a book that already existed" (ibid.: 95). Ultimately, it is this very project that allows Pierre Menard to see himself as a "novelist," a definition that appears to echo his own conviction as well as the narrator's suggestion that the work of the translator, far from being secondary, may actually be even more complex than the author's.

As Menard plausibly explains, he "assumed the mysterious obligation to reconstruct, word for word, the novel that for [Cervantes] was spontaneous" (ibid.: 92). His "problem," "without the shadow of a doubt," was much more difficult than Cervantes's: the Spanish author "did not spurn the collaboration of chance; his method of composition for the immortal book was a bit *à la diable*, and he was often swept along by the inertia of the language and the imagination" (ibid.: 93). According to Borges's narrator, Menard "did not want to compose another *Quixote*, which surely is easy enough – he wanted to compose *the Quixote*." However, he "had no intention of *copying* it. His admirable ambition was to produce a number of pages which coincided – word for word and line for line – with those of Miguel de Cervantes" (ibid.: 91). In order to achieve his goal, Menard devised a method that was "relatively simple": "Learn Spanish, return to Catholicism, fight against the Moor or Turk, forget the history of Europe from 1602 to 1918 – *be* Miguel de Cervantes" (ibid.). After "weigh[ing] that course," and after "pretty thoroughly master[ing] seventeenth-century Castilian," he "discarded it as too easy" (ibid.). As he reasoned, "[b]eing, somehow, Cervantes, and arriving thereby at the *Quixote* – that looked to Menard less challenging (and therefore less interesting) than continuing to be Pierre Menard and come to the Quixote *through the experiences of Pierre Menard*" (ibid.). As we learn, Menard died with the conviction that he had indeed achieved his "astonishing" goal, that is, his translation of a few fragments from the *Quixote* seemed so perfectly faithful that they literally reproduced the original in its original language. It is, however, the narrator's comparison of Menard's *Quixote* to Cervantes's, both verbally identical, that brings out a host of differences between the two, a comparison that also suggests that, while Menard had not composed *the* one and only *Quixote*, paradoxically neither had Cervantes.

Of the multiple interpretive paths that can be pursued in any close reading of "Pierre Menard," I have chosen to concentrate on a few interrelated topics directly associated with the sharp contrast generally drawn between the creative role translators actually play and the role they are typically expected to play as they practice their profession. My goal, as mentioned, is to show how Borges's text may help instructors guide students through an initial exploration of key notions associated with the translator's visibility, which emerged as a central topic for theorization about thirty years ago, mostly under the sway of post-Nietzschean conceptions of language and text (for early discussions on this, see, for example, Graham 1985; Arrojo 1986 and 1993; Venuti 1992). As a starting point, instructors might invite students to express their own views on what translations and the translator's role entail. Those new to the field, like most non-specialists, will quite probably abide by notions of translation that take for granted the stability of the original and, consequently, the possibility of faithfully reproducing it in different linguistic, cultural, and historical contexts. Hence, they are likely to believe that sameness could in fact be repeated and that translators and interpreters in general could choose whether to be neutral or partial when translating or interpreting texts. Students motivated to search for more formal statements on translation, whether associated with lay, institutional, or scholarly perspectives, will probably encounter conceptions that will not be very different from their own. Let us examine, for example, the following statement from the American Translators Association, according to which their members "accept as [their] ethical and professional duty to convey meaning between people and cultures *faithfully, accurately, and impartially*" (American Translators Association, "Code of Ethics and Professional Practice," emphasis added). For them, a "faithful, accurate and impartial translation or interpretation conveys the message as the author or speaker intended with the same emotional impact on the audience," a seemingly sensible comment according to which, in order to achieve their goals, translators or interpreters are required "to adopt a mantle of neutrality" as they make it possible for texts to be available in different languages and cultural and historical contexts (ibid.).

Students could also be encouraged to compare Menard's approach to repeat Cervantes's text to more formal statements on translation ethics from different times and traditions. In Alexander Fraser Tytler's comments on "the proper task of a translator," presented in his *Essay on the Principles of Translation*, of 1791, for example, students will likely identify notions that resemble Menard's methods. Consider, for instance, Tytler's "laws of translation"

> I. That the translation should give a complete transcript of the ideas of the original work. II. That the style and manner of writing should be of the same character with that of the original. III. That the translation should have all the ease of original composition.
>
> (Tytler 1978: 16)

In the following quotation students will also find appropriate material to relate to Borges's story:

> The translator [...] uses not the same colours with the original, but is required to give his picture the same force and effect. He is not allowed to copy the touches of his own, to produce a perfect resemblance. The more he studies a scrupulous imitation, the less his copy will reflect the ease and spirit of the original. How then shall a translator accomplish this difficult union of ease with fidelity? To use a bold expression, *he must adopt the very soul of his author, which must speak through his own organs.*
>
> (Ibid.: 211–212; emphasis added)

In order to probe these issues and what they could imply, instructors may want to encourage students to reevaluate them in the light of the "method" devised by Menard to reach Cervantes's original, namely his plan, mentioned above, to learn Spanish, "forget the history of Europe from 1602 to 1918 – [and] *be* Miguel de Cervantes" (Borges 1998: 91). Such a description could be read as a refined mockery of the usual, apparently reasonable recommendation that translators should hide under "a mantle of neutrality" in order to "adopt the very soul" of their authors and produce translations that faithfully reproduce the same meanings as their originals. Therefore, strictly speaking, in order to erase the differences involved and to be truly faithful to Cervantes's original, Menard would have to stop being himself, turn into the Spanish author, and forget or erase the long history that separated them. As students are invited to examine Borges's amusing treatment of the recurrent commonplaces involving the translator's role and its suggestion that what mainstream conceptions prescribe, far from being reasonable, is not only impossible, but utterly nonsensical, they may be inclined to entertain a more critical perspective on the complexities of translation.

An attentive examination of Menard's further elaboration of his method will show students that Borges's convincing satire can be even more corrosive. As mentioned, after the French translator practically mastered seventeenth-century Castillian, he gave up on his initial plan to become Cervantes and decided to continue being Pierre Menard and come to the *Quixote* through his own experiences (ibid.). Hence, we may conclude, the translator's pursuit of invisibility and sameness seems to be even more absurd than his initial plan to forget centuries of history and literally become the author of the text he plans to reproduce. And yet, if we rephrase Borges's description of Menard's method with the kind of seemingly reasonable language used, for instance, by the American Translators Association, that is, if we take note that his goal is to reach the exact same text produced by Cervantes and repeat it verbatim elsewhere, in completely different circumstances, we may find in Menard a model translator who, in his own peculiar way, appears to be trying to follow most of the ethical guidelines commonly prescribed by mainstream notions and institutions. I say "most" because, apparently, Menard did not intend his *Quixote* to produce "the same emotional impact on [his] audience" as the original had. As Menard himself recognized, what Cervantes's book may have represented for his contemporaries in the seventeenth century was quite different from what it actually became a few centuries later: the *Quixote* "was first and foremost a pleasant book; it is now an occasion for patriotic toasts, grammatical arrogance, obscene *de luxe* editions" (Borges 1998: 94).

Students will find an unforgettable lesson on the relationship that readers can establish with texts in the story's climactic point, which is quite probably one of the most enthralling moments of twentieth-century fiction: the narrator's comparison of two verbally identical fragments from *Don Quixote*, one by Cervantes, the other by Menard. "It is a revelation," we are told,

> "to compare the *Don Quixote* of Pierre Menard with that of Miguel de Cervantes. Cervantes, for example, wrote the following (Part I, Chapter IX):
>
> '... truth, whose mother is history, rival of time, depository of deeds, witness of the past, exemplar and adviser to the present, and the future's counselor'"
>
> (ibid.).

For the narrator, "this catalog of attributes, written in the seventeenth century, and written by the 'ingenious layman' Miguel de Cervantes, is mere rhetorical praise of history". (Ibid.) Menard, "on the other hand, writes: '... truth, whose mother is history, rival of time, depository of deeds, witness of the past, exemplar and adviser to the present, and the future's counselor'" (ibid.). According to Borges's narrator, "Menard, a contemporary of William James, defines history not as *a delving* into reality but as the very *fount* of reality. [...] Historical truth, for Menard, is not 'what happened'; it is what we believe happened" (ibid.). Furthermore, the narrator points out that:

> the contrast in styles is equally striking. The archaic style of Menard – who is, in addition, not a native speaker of the language in which he writes – is somehow affected. Not so the style of his precursor, who employs the Spanish of his time with complete naturalness.
>
> (Ibid.)

As a reader of both excerpts, the narrator does not "forget history," so to speak, and sees Menard as the actual writer of the fragment that supposedly coincides with Cervantes's. For the narrator, because they were composed at different times, in different contexts and circumstances, motivated by quite different goals and, most importantly, produced by different individuals, those two apparently identical fragments could not possibly mean the same thing. There is hardly a more eloquent example, in fiction or otherwise, that could stimulate reflection on issues pertaining to the relationship between words and meaning and the nature of language, as well as the roles played by readers and authors in the composition and interpretation of texts, issues that are directly associated with the main tenets of post-Nietzschean thought and its impact on the ways in which originals and translations are viewed (for texts that address these issues in ways that are generally accessible to most students, see, for instance, Arrojo 2010 and Van Wyke 2010. See, also, Chapters Three, Four, and Five in this book).

Instructors and students working with the story could begin their examination of such issues by probing Menard's alleged definition of history as "the very *fount* of reality" (Borges 1998: 94). If, like Borges's narrator, we see in Menard's fragment the basis of a non-essentialist conception of the relationship between truth and history, according to which it is history that produces truth and not the other way around, we will have to consider the possibility that no text could ever remain the same and be repeated as such, beyond or above history. Following this rationale, it would be impossible for Menard, even if he had indeed managed to become Cervantes, to ever reach the *Quixote* as an original that could have remained immune to the differences brought about by the constant, inexorable flow of history. Therefore, we may argue, from such a perspective, it would be impossible for translators to ever be invisible or neutral as they are always and inescapably reconstructing meaning within the undefinable limits of a certain historical context that anchors their interpretations and shapes their work. At the same time, the narrator's own reading could also be used as an illustration of this line of argument. As an obviously visible reader of Menard's and Cervantes's fragments, the narrator is explicitly interpreting them from a certain point of view that is intimately connected to his historical context, a context that also informs and is informed by what he has learned about both Miguel de Cervantes and Pierre Menard. (In order to expand their students' notions of authorship and reading, instructors might want to introduce them to Michel Foucault's take on the topic [see, e.g., Foucault 1979]. For a commentary on authorship that is indebted to both Borges and Foucault, see Van Wyke 2012.)

The translator's unsettling visibility

There is at least one fundamental issue that deserves to be explored in greater depth in relation to the reading of "Pierre Menard" sketched above: Menard's own description of his translation as his "subterranean" project, to which he "dedicated his scruples and his nights," but of which he left no traces (Borges 1998: 95). This issue, together with the apparent contradiction between the translator's awareness of his visibility and his determination to repeat verbatim a few fragments from Cervantes's masterpiece, can be associated with the overall difficulty Menard seems to share with most readers, translators, and writers in truly accepting the fact that translations cannot leave originals untouched just as translators are necessarily visible and, consequently, unable to stop being themselves when they make such originals available in other languages and cultural contexts. This difficulty and some of its implications can be further investigated through a reading of Cortázar's "Letter to a Young Lady in Paris" (Cortázar 1985), a story that, like "Pierre Menard," can be read as a perceptive examination of the often perverse ambiguities associated with the translator's invisibility as the necessary foundation for translation ethics. In addition, since Cortázar's piece, unlike "Pierre Menard," provides us with the translator's own voice on the matter, it constitutes an appropriate complement to Borges's story, giving us the opportunity to compose a more thorough portrait of the translator's often repressed or veiled agency. (As a side note, I must confess that I would like to consider the fact that in "Letter to a Young Lady in Paris," the two friends who apparently understand the plight of the translator protagonist are Borges's namesakes – "Jorge" and "Luis" – as a kind of channeling of Borges by Cortázar himself.) Its use for pedagogical purposes can help instructors and students reevaluate the impossible position constructed for the translator by traditional, mainstream narratives and deepen their understanding of some of the most recurrent prejudices and misconceptions regularly associated with translation and its relationship with the writing of originals (for another reading of Cortázar's story as a text about translation, see Guzmán 2006).

Cortázar's story is actually the letter mentioned in the title, a letter that, in the end, turns into the suicide note that its unnamed male protagonist is writing to Andrea, the "young lady" in whose impeccably organized Buenos Aires apartment he is temporarily living. (About the story's title, instructors familiar with the original Spanish – "Carta a una señorita en Paris" [Cortázar 2006] – might want to call their students' attention to the differences between "señorita" and "young lady," and reflect on how such differences might impact the ways in which they view Andrea.) The initial purpose of the letter is to inform Andrea about the bunnies as well as the discomfort he feels as an intruder in her home. While he tries to explain himself, Cortázar's protagonist lets us know that he has agreed to live in Andrea's apartment for a few months until she comes back from Paris. He leaves for work every morning and spends time in an office where he begins to write the letter we are reading. Even though the nature of his office work is not revealed, we do know that he also translates – he mentions he is behind in his translation of Gide, the French author and winner of the 1947 Nobel Prize in Literature whose novel *The Immoralist* (Gide 2008) Cortázar translated into Spanish (cf. Guzmán 2010: 66). (Also, attentive readers of the story will likely note that Gide's first name, "André," is clearly echoed in "Andrea" and, more obviously, in "Andrée," as "the young lady" is called in Cortázar's original.)

If we take into account that the translator does not feel at home, so to speak, in Andrea's apartment, this space that does not belong to him, and which allegedly encapsulates the style and the very soul of its owner, could be interpreted as a felicitous metaphor for the original as an idealized artifact that has been carefully composed by an author, in this case a "young lady," who would like it to remain unchanged even when she is not present. As a representation of the author's textual space, Andrea's apartment has to be kept intact during the four months – "perhaps with luck three" (Cortázar 1985: 43) – in which it will be inhabited by the translator, a period that could be associated with the time it usually takes him to finish a translation project before he has to move on and get acquainted with another textual space. Irremediably divided between the urge to express himself and the duty to fully accept and submit to the author's feminine universe, a universe that, to him, is fundamentally foreign, Cortázar's translator protagonist tries to explain his ambiguous position: "Ah, dear Andrea, how difficult it is to stand counter to, yet to accept with perfect submission of one's whole being, the elaborate order that a woman establishes in her own gracious flat" (ibid.: 40). The translator's position is further complicated by his awareness of the fact that, no matter how hard he tries, it is impossible for him to adequately protect the author's space from his own interventions. It is significant to point out that the first visible change the translator brings to Andrea's apartment is represented by the moving of a small metal tray to "the far end of the table" at which he plans to work so that he can place his English dictionaries "within easy reach of the hand" (ibid.). Hence, it is not merely his presence, but his presence as someone who uses dictionaries on a regular basis that begins to alter the singular composition defining Andrea's apartment as her home. As the translator writes to her, he is painfully aware of the impact of his presence upon the foreign space in which he finds himself and which he must, nonetheless, domesticate and adapt to his own needs so that he can live in it, even if temporarily:

> To move that tray is the equivalent of an unexpected horrible crimson in the middle of one of Ozenfant's painterly cadences, as if suddenly the strings of all the double basses snapped at the same time with the same dreadful whiplash at the most hushed instant in a Mozart symphony. Moving that tray alters the play of relationships in the whole house, of each object with another, of each moment of their soul with the soul of the house and its absent inhabitant.
>
> (Ibid.)

If the apartment in question can be interpreted as the representation of someone else's textual space that is temporarily occupied and altered by a translator and his dictionaries, in what terms can Andrea be viewed as an author figure in the story? One could speculate, for instance, that, like the author figure widely idealized by stereotypical, "commonsense" notions, Andrea enjoys special rights over a certain space that is not only viewed as her property, but, also, as "a visible affirmation of her soul" (Cortázar

1985: 39). Hence, her apartment as text is supposed to contain, protect, and mirror her feelings and thoughts, as well as whatever is significant and aesthetically pleasing to her. This brief characterization of the relationship between the author and her text could be associated, for example, with what Lawrence Venuti has called "the individualistic conception of authorship," that is, the prevalent notion that "the author freely expresses his thoughts and feelings in writing, which is thus viewed as an original and transparent self-representation, unmediated by transindividual determinants (linguistic, cultural, social) that might complicate authorial originality" (Venuti 2008: 6). In other words, the underlying foundation of the conception of authorship that seems to be represented in the story is the belief that the author's meanings, as well as her feelings and thoughts, could actually remain stable and protected, in the text, from the passing of time and the interventions of readers. Andrea's characterization as an author figure gives instructors and students a unique opportunity to rethink the role the author is usually expected to play in the scene of translation. A productive discussion on the topic could explore, for example, the fact that, in Cortázar's story, the author figure is a woman or, more specifically, as the Spanish title suggests, an unmarried woman who is supposedly used to living alone, and who could be quite particular about the ways in which her apartment is arranged and should be maintained. In addition, readers could examine what kind of relationship the translator seems to have established with this female figure that he affectionately addresses by her first name and for whom he apparently harbors feelings of admiration, but also a certain rivalry. As he confesses, he cannot touch anything in Andrea's apartment "without feeling a rivalry and offense swinging before [his] eyes like a flock of sparrows" (Cortázar 1985: 45). Those who have also worked with Borges's "Pierre Menard" may be interested in comparing the ambivalent feelings that Cortázar's translator protagonist seems to harbor towards Andrea to Pierre Menard's ambivalent statements about Cervantes and his *Quixote*. Note, for example, that, as Borges's narrator suggests, even though the *Quixote* was the impossible target of Menard's secret efforts, the French Symbolist viewed Cervantes's masterpiece as simply "contingent" and unnecessary (Borges 1998: 92), something that we may have to take with a grain of salt since Menard had the "resigned or ironic habit of putting forth ideas that were the exact opposite of those he actually held" (ibid.: 93) (see Chapters Four and Eight for a more in-depth reflection on Menard's relationship with Cervantes).

As someone who feels uncomfortable in a space that does not belong to him, Cortázar's conflicted protagonist invites us to rethink the impossible position of translators in a culture that idealizes originals as unmediated expressions of their authors' thoughts while it expects translators to be neutral and invisible in their work. At the same time, the conscious efforts of Cortázar's protagonist to protect the author's interests as well as the composition of her textual space are radically challenged by his irrepressible urge to express himself, an urge that is splendidly represented by the little rabbits that at times forcefully push their way up his throat and come out of his mouth. The peculiar circumstances of their "birth" and the amusing (and, at the same time, distressing) details of their characterization are likely to trigger myriad associations, providing readers with a privileged look into the translator's psychology and the ambiguity of his role as an invisible partner to (or a temporary replacement of) the author whose text he has (reluctantly) accepted to temporarily call home. Hence, the translator who feels uncomfortable in a space that belongs to someone else must also feel uncomfortable about his visibility and the expression of his agency. In broad terms, the metaphor of the bunnies offers a moving, multifaceted representation of the translator's own humanity, a humanity that cannot be made invisible or altogether silenced while he is a guest in the author's text. For pedagogical purposes, this metaphor is especially efficient in getting students interested in examining the plight of the translator as someone who is expected to give up or repress his need to express himself in the name of a translation ethics that both rejects and underestimates his creativity.

Students engaging with the story might start exploring the multiple implications and nuances this metaphor suggests by considering that the little rabbits can be, in more than one way, associated with some form of linguistic expression. Their basic, obvious connection with language is first of all related to the fact that they come out of the translator's mouth in a manner that evokes what is commonly viewed as the inappropriate visibility of translators in the process of translation: the bunnies actually force Cortázar's translator protagonist to open his mouth when it is normally expected to be shut. While the bunnies represent the translator's subterranean voice that at times needs to come out, they can also be more specifically associated with creative writing. For instance, the translator compares a newborn bunny to "a poem in its first minutes" (Cortázar 1985: 43), a poem that is, then, soon after birth, very much a recognizable product of its creator. At the same time, though, the translator also knows that a bunny, like a poem, cannot be immobilized in time and space as it grows and changes: "A month puts a lot of things at a distance; a month is size, long fur, long leaps, ferocious eyes, an absolute difference, Andrea, a month is a rabbit, it really makes a real rabbit" (ibid.). Finally, and precisely because the translator's bunnies do grow and cannot be fully controlled, not even by the translator himself, they can take over and potentially destroy the author's textual composition, the same composition that the translator has pledged to protect from change and from himself. From this perspective, it is significant to note that Andrea's books, that is, the textual material she collects in her authorial space, and which the translator finds organized in a rigorous order when he first moves in, are the first targets of the little creatures when they are big enough to "nibble away" at those arranged on the lowest shelf (Cortázar 1985: 46).

Instructors and their students can further elaborate on Cortázar's rich metaphor of the bunnies by examining the translator's ambivalent feelings towards them, feelings that range from the tenderness with which he welcomes and cares for his rabbits to the discomfort and embarrassment involved in vomiting them up and hiding them from others. As the translator first tells Andrea about their birth: "Always I have managed to be alone when it happens, guarding the fact much as we guard so many of our privy acts, evidences of our physical selves which happen to us in total privacy" (ibid.: 41). Even though the translator's voice, as a concrete, physical expression of his humanity and creativity, is viewed as improper and unwelcome in the author's space, it cannot be completely silenced and is in fact secretly cultivated. Like the Borgesian Pierre Menard, who devotes his nights to the project of composing – not copying, not simply repeating – fragments from the *Quixote*, the translator in Cortázar's story spends his nights furtively tending to the bunnies he releases from the wardrobe where they are left asleep and locked during the day. Just as Menard surreptitiously takes the author's place and does not see himself as a mere translator, Cortázar's protagonist can somehow take over the author's home at night, as soon as Sara, Andrea's live-in housekeeper, retires to her room and he can finally free his bunnies and allow them to play around. Moreover, it is particularly revealing that it is, first and foremost, from Sara that the translator has to hide his bunnies during the day. After all, it is precisely her job to make sure that the apartment stays as impeccable as its owner left it. It is also mostly for the housekeeper that, after spending his nights caring for the bunnies, the translator puts them back in the wardrobe and cleans up their mess in an attempt to restore the original order: "That way Sara always finds everything in order, although at times I've noticed a restrained astonishment, a stopping to look at some object, a slight discoloration in the carpet, and again the desire to ask me about something" (ibid.: 47). As someone who should be able to notice any unusual interference in the organization of Andrea's apartment, Sara could very well represent a reader figure, maybe even a critic or a strict editor, who knows the original extremely well and appreciates it exactly the way it is, and is then faced with its translation, a reader whose allegiance belongs to the author of the original, not the translator. Like Borges's narrator in "Pierre Menard," who is in a position to compare Menard's writing to Cervantes's, Andrea's housekeeper could potentially detect at least some of the changes that the translator's bunnies bring to the author's space.

Attentive readers examining the relationship that Cortázar's translator protagonist establishes with his bunnies may notice that it is while staying at Andrea's that, for the first time, he becomes aware of his desire to actually keep and cultivate the little rabbits that more and more frequently must come out of his mouth. As he explains, in the past he would vomit a bunny every four or five weeks, "maybe six with a little luck," and he would put the newborn rabbit in the same flowerpot that he kept on the balcony of his "other house," where he also grew the clover he needed to feed the little animals (ibid.: 42). Then, when he felt that another bunny was about to come out, he would give the grown rabbit away and have another flowerpot on the balcony ready with the necessary tender clover for the next newborn. Thus, "vomiting bunnies wasn't so terrible once one had gotten into the unvarying cycle, into the method" (ibid.). This "method," which made it possible for the translator to spare his bunnies and keep at least one around for a while, could be interpreted as a touching representation of the limitations imposed by the dominant tradition on the work of translators, a tradition that establishes that they cannot really own or get attached to the products of their somewhat controlled creativity. If we take into account that he abandoned his usual method of dealing with bunnies soon after moving to Andrea's, we may argue that what Cortázar's translator protagonist needs to hide from Sara, or from Andrea, up to the last moment, is not only the changes that his rabbits bring to the apartment, but, also, his authorial desire, that is, his desire to legitimately occupy the author's space and, consequently, to be entitled to having an appropriate environment where he could enjoy the comfort and the pleasures involved in cultivating and keeping his bunnies around.

In addition, while describing his interactions with the little creatures, Cortázar's protagonist reveals how this authorial desire is also associated with a longing to be all-powerful, like a god who could fully control his rabbits and, implicitly, the ways in which his creative endeavors would be received. As he confides to Andrea, "I'd like to see [the rabbits] quiet, see them at my feet and being quiet – somewhat the dream of any god, Andrea, a dream the gods never see fulfilled" (Cortázar 1985: 45). Those working with the story might also investigate possible connections between the translator's idealized conceptions of authorship as mastery and the original as a stable object and the notion of translation as a form of destructive invasion, a notion to which, on some level, the translator also seems to subscribe: not only does he see his creative visibility as potentially destructive, but he must be constantly trying to repair the "damages" it brings to the author's original. An early example in the storyline involves a broken porcelain lamp that the translator manages to fix with a "special" English "cement" that is particularly efficient for the job (ibid.: 47), and which could perhaps be interpreted as a reference to English as a language that adapts well to translation. However, regardless of the appropriateness of English as a language for translation, the end result of the translator's efforts will inevitably show that the translated text is basically flawed as it has to be "fixed" and patched up and, therefore, will always be an inadequate replacement for the allegedly perfect, flawless original.

Instructors and students also working with "Pierre Menard" may note that what is secretive about the invisible work developed by the French translator, described as a "novelist," can also be related to his authorial desire or, more specifically, to his desire to actually occupy the same position enjoyed by the great Cervantes, a position that would distance Menard from his mediocre visible accomplishments. Just as the latter's invisible work is only publically revealed after his death, Cortázar's protagonist can only confess the existence of his little rabbits in the letter that turns into a suicide note when he fully realizes, after the birth of the eleventh bunny, that he is unable to control their proliferation and how they may impact Andrea's authorial space and the textual material it contains. As he explains, "going from ten to eleven is like an unbridgeable chasm." Ten seemed manageable: "with a wardrobe, clover and hope, so many things could happen for the better. But not with eleven, because to say eleven is already to say twelve for sure, and Andrea, twelve would be thirteen" (ibid.: 49). At the same time, though, the translator's decision to jump off the balcony together with the bunnies also suggests that he could not simply give up on his own creativity and pursue a life without it. Thus, it seems that the impossibility of reconciling his desire to express himself and his duty to preserve the author's composition is what constitutes the translator's tragedy, a tragedy whose impact is made quite clear even as he prepares for his last act. In the very end, when he is about to jump, the translator is concerned about his posthumous visibility. As he ponders, while the eleven rabbits splattered on the pavement may not attract too much attention, it would be "more proper" for his own body to be removed as quickly as possible so that it would not be visible to the students who pass by on their way to school early in the morning (ibid.: 50).

The translator's unfortunate legacy

The embarrassment that Cortázar's protagonist seems to feel in relation to his own visibility could be interpreted as a symptom directly associated with the formidable weight of conventional thinking on the translator's role, the same thinking that determines that there is, or there should be, an indisputable, clear-cut opposition between the allegedly original writing produced by authors and the ideally invisible, protective service that translators are supposed to provide. While authors are expected to fully exercise their creativity, whose expression is believed to be preserved and readily accessible in their originals, translators must pretend not to be agents while making such originals available in other languages and cultural contexts. In their secret efforts to undermine the asymmetry of this overwhelming hierarchical opposition, Cortázar's protagonist and Pierre Menard have tried and failed to achieve the impossible: to keep the author's original intact without giving up on being themselves. In Borges's story, Menard's acknowledgment of his visibility as a translator inspires the narrator to view his apparently perfect translation of the *Quixote* as a text that is altogether different from Cervantes's. Similarly, in Cortázar's story, the translator dares not to repress his creativity while inhabiting Andrea's authorial space and ends up destroying her carefully arranged composition. In the end, in spite of their deconstructive thrust, the two stories seem to mirror the traditional narratives about the relationship between original writing and translating, narratives that routinely protect and side with authors and do not have much sympathy for the translator who dares to challenge the established hierarchy.

Considering that both Borges's and Cortázar's stories revolve around the death (or imminent death) of their fictional translators, instructors and students could pursue the associations these stories seem to suggest between their characters' deaths and the legacy they leave behind. In Borges's "Pierre Menard," the significance of his protagonist's death could be contrasted, for example, with that of Cervantes: while the Spanish author, who has been dead for more than four centuries, lives on in countless translations of *Don Quixote* and also inspires the translator Menard, the latter's death, just like his life-long dedication to Cervantes's work, has had no real impact on the *Quixote*, apart from the brief, arguably sarcastic reading proposed by Borges's narrator. More importantly, Pierre Menard leaves hardly anything behind, with the exception of his unimpressive visible texts and projects. While Cervantes still excites readers and is highly visible as an author known worldwide thanks, mostly, to the work of his many, mostly invisible translators, Menard "allowed no one to see [his endless drafts of the *Quixote*] and took care that they not survive him" (Borges 1998: 95). As for Cortázar's protagonist, as far as we know, he will only leave behind the destroyed original, that is, the same textual space he had promised to cherish and protect, and where he felt like an intruder. While in Borges's story, Menard's death could be interpreted as a telling representation of the invisibility most institutions typically demand from translators as well as the disregard these same institutions have shown for their work and dedication, in Cortázar's, the protagonist's imminent suicide could be directly related not only to the translator's angst from having failed to keep intact the conventional distinctions between translator and author, translation and original, but, also, to the sentiments of loss and destruction that, in the story, are clearly associated with the translator's work.

Finally, and on a more subtle level, instructors and students working with these stories could further reflect on the legacy of the fictional translators they portray by examining the kind of treatment these translators seem to receive from their creators. In Borges's story, readers might note the puzzling contrast between the narrator's apparently enthusiastic determination to celebrate Menard's work and the generally ironical tone of the story as well as its ambiguous, mostly unflattering portrayal of the dead translator, and ponder how such a contrast could be related to the ways in which traditional conceptions regularly favor originals and their authors over translations and translators. After all, as shown, in spite of all the praise supposedly given to the translator, in the end it is the celebrated Cervantes who undoubtedly lives on while the dead Menard is a pathetic figure that, instead of being comparable to Cervantes, is, rather, reminiscent of the Quixote, the great master's unfortunate character whose madness is also imagining that he could emulate his favorite authors and repeat their texts (for detailed commentaries on the treatment given to Menard in the story, see Arrojo 2014 and, also, Chapters Four and Eight). In Cortázar's story, it is worth noting the obvious contrast the translator protagonist establishes between his melancholy, conflicted struggle to come to terms with his own creativity and Andrea's luminous, well-organized textual environment. As suggested, Cortázar's translator figure and Pierre Menard cannot help but idealize the original even though they are also aware of the inevitability of change and the impossibility of being invisible. In spite of their incisive questioning of the typical dichotomies that have divided originals from translations and authors from translators, the two stories, in the end, seem to affirm the power and the privileges of authorship or, at least, the authority that our culture, in its broadest sense, usually attributes to writers of originals and denies to those who make them available in other languages and contexts.

Bibliography

American Translators Association (ATA) "Code of Ethics and Professional Practice." Available at: www.atanet.org/governance/code_of_ethics_commentary.pdf (accessed May 29, 2014).

Arrojo, R. (1986) *Oficina de Tradução – A Teoria na Prática*, São Paulo: Ática.

—— (1993) *Tradução, Desconstrução e Psicanálise*, Rio de Janeiro: Imago.

—— (2010) "Philosophy and Translation," in Y. Gambier and L. van Doorslaer (eds.) *Handbook of Translation Studies*, Volume 1, Amsterdam: John Benjamins, 247–251.

—— (2014) "The Power of Fiction as Theory: Some Exemplary Lessons on Translation from Borges's Stories," in Klaus Kaindl and Karleinz Spitzl (eds.) *Transfiction – Research into the Realities of Translation Fiction*, Amsterdam: John Benjamins, 37–49.

Borges, J. L. (1980) "Pierre Menard, autor del *Quijote*," in *Prosa Completa*, vol. 1, Barcelona: Editorial Bruguera, 425–434.

—— (1998) "Pierre Menard, Author of the *Quixote*," A. Hurley (trans.) *Collected Fictions*, New York: Penguin, 88–95.

Cortázar, J. (1985) "Letter to a Young Lady in Paris," P. Blackburn (trans.) *Blow-Up and Other Stories*, New York: Pantheon, 39–50.

—— (2006) "Carta a una señorita en Paris," in *Bestiario*, Madrid: Santillana, 19–30.

Foucault, M. (1979) "What Is an Author?" in J. V. Harari (ed./trans.) *Textual Strategies: Perspectives in Post-Structuralist Criticism*, Ithaca, NY: Cornell University Press, 141–160.

Gide, A. (2008) *The Immoralist*, D. Watson (trans.), London: Penguin Books.

Graham, J. (ed.) (1985) *Difference in Translation*, Ithaca, NY: Cornell University Press.

Guzmán, M. C. (2006) "The Spectrum of Translation in Cortázar's 'Letter to a Young Lady in Paris'," *Íkala, revista de lenguaje y cultura* 11(17): 75–86.

—— (2010) *Gregory Rabassa's Latin American Literature – A Translator's Visible Legacy*, Lewisburg, PA: Bucknell University Press.

Kristal, E. (2002) *Invisible Work—Borges and Translation*, Nashville, TN: Vanderbilt University Press.

Tytler, A. F. (1978) *Essay on the Principles of Translation*, Amsterdam: John Benjamins.

Van Wyke, B. (2010) "Imitating Bodies and Their Clothes: Refashioning the Western Conception of Translation," in J. S. Andre (ed.) *Thinking Translation through Metaphor*, Manchester: St. Jerome, 17–46.

—— (2012) "Borges and Us – Exploring the Author–Translator Dynamic in Translation Workshops," *The Translator* 18(1): 77–100.

Venuti, L. (ed.) (1992) *Rethinking Translation – Discourse, Subjectivity, Ideology.* London: Routledge.

—— (2008) *The Translator's Invisibility – A History of Translation*, 2nd edition, London: Routledge.

Waisman, S. (2005) *Borges and Translation – The Irreverence of the Periphery*, Lewisburg, PA: Bucknell University Press.

2 Fiction as theory and activism
Rodolfo Walsh's "Footnote"

> I find increasingly that it is fiction and, at times, autobiography, rather than translation theory *per se* that probes the wondering as well as the wandering of translation.
>
> Carol Maier, "The Translator as *Theôros* – Thoughts on Cogitation, Figuration and Current Creative Writing"

The reading of fiction on the theme of translation, rather than merely confirming or echoing the arguments and conclusions of philosophers and translation studies scholars, can illuminate certain issues that are rarely explored in more conventional scholarship. It can bring fresh insights, for instance, into the psychology involved in the power relationships that are usually at work in the composition and the publication of translations and the cultural and historical contexts in which such practices take place. By making such relationships visible on several levels, stories about translators and their work tend to reveal conflicting points that are typically represented by the different voices that usually frame fictional plots and, as a consequence, offer a privileged perspective into the ways in which translators and their translations have been treated throughout history. In this chapter, I will focus on a poignant short story by the Argentine Rodolfo Walsh entitled "Nota al pie" ("Footnote"), which was first published in Buenos Aires in 1967 (Walsh 2008, hereafter quoted from my unpublished translation from the Spanish). Of all the fictional pieces on the topic that I have encountered and written about over the years, Walsh's has been by far the most emotionally charged as it seems to echo not only its author's own experience as a translator, but also his courageous opposition to the authoritarian Argentine regime of the 1960s, an opposition that ultimately led to his assassination a decade after the publication of the story. In its moving combination of fiction, autobiography, and reflection, "Footnote" brings us a translator character – a *theôros*, in the terms described by Carol Maier – that offers an optimum illustration of "translation as a contemplative and possibly transformative activity that has not been factored into the theory of many translation theorists" (Maier 2006: 171).

The story is particularly efficient in echoing the clear divide separating those in charge of processes of cultural production from those who, like most translators, are seen as invisible marginal players. Walsh's characterization of the translator as an oppressed laborer freelancing for a publishing house in Buenos Aires – presumably from the mid-1950s to the mid-1960s – will allow me to reflect on issues of visibility and power and how they can be associated with the fundamental question as to what and whom translations and translators ultimately serve. Walsh's inventive narrative shows that he definitely takes sides in the conflict between the establishment and the timid dissidence represented by his protagonist, the dead translator, and that he is, indeed, a fierce advocate of the translator's right to be visible and recognized. In the following pages, "Footnote" will be read as a powerful example of fiction not only as a privileged form of theory, but, also, as a persuasive form of activism, an activism that reflects Rodolfo Walsh's own passionate defense of free speech and the rights of the working class in a dark period of his country's recent history.

Walsh's split narrative

In "Footnote," we are introduced to León de Sanctis, a lonely and unhappy translator who has just killed himself in the cheap boarding house where he lived. Ironically, as the story opens, we are told that the self-effacing translator, who spent most of his life perfecting the art of being invisible, "undoubtedly wanted" Otero, his boss and editor at La Casa, the publishing house for which he worked, "to come and see him, naked and dead [...] and that is why he wrote [Otero's] name on the envelope containing the letter that might explain everything" (Walsh 2008: 69). In spite of feeling "betrayed" by the translator (ibid.), Otero has come to the boarding house to identify his body at the request of the police and is guided by the elderly housekeeper to the shabby bedroom where the dead León lies naked and covered by a sheet. She hands him León's letter, a letter that Otero does not open "because he wants to imagine the dead man's version," and, as we are informed in the very last line of the first page, Otero does imagine "its general tone of lugubrious apology, his first sentence of farewell and regret" (ibid.). At this point a footnote is inserted, dividing the text into two narratives: while in the main body of the text, the omniscient third-person narrator allows us to learn about Otero's take on León and what has happened, at the bottom of the page, in the first-person narrative that constitutes the footnote – which occupies more and more space on each page up to the last one when it actually takes over and replaces the main narrative – we are given access to the translator's suicide letter and his own version of the facts.

The story's split narrative provides an eloquent illustration of the hierarchical dichotomies that oppose the establishment to the margins, the "they" to the "I," the main body of the text to the footnote, as well as the employer and editor, represented by Otero, who holds the almost exclusive power to establish what can be read and how it should be translated, to the subservient translator, who is expected to be invisible and blindly serve the publisher's interests. In addition, as Walsh's story suggests a clear connection between La Casa – literally "The House" or "The Home" – and the country itself, this is a dichotomy that also reflects some key aspects of the complex relationship that opposes the elite to the working class, with whom Walsh's narrator clearly identifies or, even, the authoritarian state to the Argentine people who, like León, are also expected to be subservient and conveniently quiet. Appropriately, these two opposing worlds find their representation in the language and the style that give us access to Otero's thoughts in the main narrative and to León's letter at the bottom of the page. While Otero's perspective is presented in an elegant, controlled prose that can be associated with the conventions of highbrow literature, rich in insightful descriptions and subtle associations, León's letter is simple, emotional, and often touchingly naïve.

In the main body of the text, we are told that, for Otero, being invisible, "erasing" one's personality is in fact the "hardest of all the secrets" a translator needs to learn: "to go unnoticed, to write like another and not let anybody know that" (Walsh 2008: 75). While the translator must accept a passive role in the production of translations, it is the publishing house's "mission" to "nourish the dreams of the people and build a culture for them, even against themselves" (ibid.: 76). According to Otero, in the beginning, as a struggling translator, León was "innately loyal" and seemed to understand the heroic "sacrifice" that was part and parcel of La Casa's mission (ibid.). However, just like the housekeeper, Otero does not seem to know much about the man who managed to go unnoticed for so long. Together with Otero we learn from the housekeeper – a simple, older woman also hardened by relentless work and loneliness – that León was poor but paid his rent on time. He never disturbed anybody even though at night one could many a time hear the noise made by his typewriter in the room he shared with another boarder. In the last few months he got sick and seemed sadder and more reserved and did not want to leave the bedroom. "Then he just went mad" (Walsh 2008: 72) and ended up killing himself. (The translator's decision to use poison for his suicide seems a fitting choice, one might add, considering that his goal was to end a life that had been for so long figuratively poisoned by poverty, loneliness, and disappointment.) The housekeeper's reminiscences of León bring to Otero's mind some of the translator's "eccentricities" such as his insistence on delivering a handwritten assignment just a couple of months before, alleging some vague problem with his typewriter (ibid.). We also find out that in the last few months León was no longer welcome in the editor's office as the translator would generally bring annoying questions and complaints, often expressing a surprising "aversion" towards "certain types of books" – the same kind he used to enjoy at the beginning – as well as a "secret (and laughable) desire" to influence La Casa's editorial policies. At other times he would mention his desire to maybe start writing his own stories, or his wish to work on "the greatest classics," a promotion that Otero thought to be "undoubtedly risky" considering León's modest background (Walsh 2008: 82).

As he reminisces about his working relationship with León, and even though he has been forced to come to the boarding house so that he can identify the translator's body and, hence, metaphorically speaking, also acknowledge the latter's unpleasant presence and visibility, Otero reveals himself to be incapable of actually seeing León and comprehending his context, let alone empathizing with the translator and his plight. Indeed, the central issue that informs the development of the main narrative is the process through which Otero comes to terms with his potential role in León's death, a process that begins with his awareness that he has come to the boarding house most of all "to be at peace with his own conscience" (ibid.: 70). For Otero, since "nobody can live with the dead," we must "kill them inside ourselves and reduce them to an innocuous image that will forever be safe in our memory" (ibid.: 71). In the end, after he formally identifies the body, Otero concludes that he can now see things clearly: everything that happened was undoubtedly León's own fault. After all, it was the translator who actually chose to live the way he did, surrounded by so much "ugliness," an ugliness that he probably could not see (ibid.: 74). Therefore, the translator's suicide was actually a solution to which only a mediocre man might resort, a man whose tendency to be melancholy and always question the status quo also reflected the chaos of their times as well as "the metaphysical malady that was destroying the country" (ibid.: 84). (The background against which Otero makes his comments about León and the country's "malady" reflects the Argentine context of the early to mid-1960s: oppressive labor policies, social unrest, and the growing authoritarianism of the government that resulted in the "Argentine Revolution," the misnomer given by the military to the establishment of a dictatorship in 1966. For a helpful contextualization of the country's history between the mid-1950s and the mid-1980s, see Foster 1995.) As far as Otero is concerned, if he had to be blamed for anything, it would be for, as usual, being too good and too soft, and not forcing León to change his ways and return to the right path.

At the bottom of the page, León apologizes for not having finished the last translation assignment he received from La Casa and explains why he was unable to type his manuscript in recent months: after spending the last of his money to treat a serious sinus infection, he was forced to pawn his typewriter, which he never managed to reclaim. At the same time, he tries to make arrangements to pay for his rent and burial expenses counting on the money he should be paid for the one hundred and thirty pages of the unfinished, handwritten translation he left on his desk and with whatever could be obtained from the sale of his pawned typewriter. He also apologizes for the "abuse" of asking Otero to help him with such arrangements and expresses his gratitude and his affection by leaving his old dictionary, his only personal possession, to the editor (Walsh 2008: 77–78). Furthermore, León's letter briefly describes his difficult childhood as a destitute orphan, then his job as a manual laborer at a tire shop and his efforts to improve his lot. After several years studying English at night, he managed to find employment as a freelance translator of detective fiction at La Casa. Soon, though, León realized that he worked more hours and made less money than he did fixing tires and, after a few years, as science fiction began to replace detective stories in the publishing house's catalogue, he became increasingly aware of his painful role as a servant to the "imbecile" authors he was assigned to translate (ibid.: 94). In the end, alone and physically and emotionally drained after years of continuous hardship and total dedication to an activity of which he could no longer be proud, León decides to end his life. He blames only himself for his decision and has no complaints about La Casa.

A subversive footnote

A footnote could arguably be introduced as an appropriate metaphor for the marginal, ambivalent position generally occupied by translators divided between the demands of invisibility prescribed by tradition and their need to be heard and participate in the virtual dialogue with readers. To the extent that it betrays the presence of the translator as an active participant in the writing and/or reading of someone else's text, even if it is at the bottom of the page, the translator's footnote breaks the illusion of the transparency of translation and of the translator's invisibility and, consequently, also the fantasy of the author's original as a closed, stable object, identifiable as some sort of reliable presence. At the same time that it is expected to separate and protect what belongs to the author and the original from the translator's commentary or supplement, the translator's footnote is also a reminder of the incompleteness and the instability of any text, always open to uninvited or unexpected interventions (for my comments on another story about translation that relies on the use of footnotes as a narrative device, see Chapter Seven).

In "Footnote," Walsh potentializes the basically subversive character of the footnote by employing it as an efficient device first to challenge and, then, slowly but surely invade and take over the main text. Readers familiar with the work of Jacques Derrida will probably associate Walsh's footnote to one of the French philosopher's first texts ever published in English, "Living On. Borderlines" (Derrida 1979, trans. Hulbert), which appeared more than ten years after the publication of "Footnote." In his essay, Derrida uses the footnote as a text in its own right, which he turns into a space devoted to an ongoing reflection on the visibility of translation and on its inextricable relationship with the "main" text, and which also allows him to establish a dialogue with his potential translators. As the central focus of the storyline, Walsh's footnote is fundamental not merely for what it actually says but, more importantly, for what it does. Since it makes the translator visible to us, readers, and brings us the narrator's take on what is being narrated, the footnote allows León's letter to challenge what is being narrated in the main body of the text. Although León's letter tells Otero that he had no complaints about La Casa, when this letter is intercepted by the narrator and inserted as a footnote into the very line in which we are told that Otero will not read the translator's message, it functions as part of the narrator's strategy to empower the dead translator, turning his suicide letter into a compelling amendment to Otero's perspective in the main narrative – a perspective that is, for the editor, the definite, established version of the facts. Hence, as León's letter becomes the narrator's footnote, or his "message" to his readers, it ends up telling a different story, suggesting that León's tragedy could also be associated with the general, heavily hierarchical regime of La Casa, characterized by authoritarian editorial policies and adverse working conditions, under which there was hardly any room for the translator to grow and thrive.

The narrator's use of the translator's unopened letter as an invasive footnote is particularly meaningful when we consider that footnotes were unacceptable in the translations produced for La Casa, as León painfully learned after receiving Otero's feedback on his very first assignment, a lesson that made the translator decide to forever give up his visibility on the pages of his translations and stay away from that "abominable device" (Walsh 2008: 88). Just as Otero's visit to the boarding house at the request of the police forces him to at least acknowledge the presence of the translator's body lying in his shabby room and the dreary working-class environment in which he lived and did his translations, León's letter is made visible despite Otero's refusal to open it, allowing the subaltern translator to speak – at least to us – and present his side of the story. Ironically, as the dead translator becomes visible, he is finally given the opportunity to reveal the misery of his life and the behind-the-scenes of the kind of translation activity that sustained La Casa. As a vehicle that restores and brings forth León's repressed voice and little by little takes over the whole page, the narrator's footnote is especially efficient in destabilizing the asymmetries that generally define the dynamics between the main text and its margins or between the editor and the translator – and, one may arguably infer, also the Argentine elite and the working class – at the same time that it offers a somewhat hopeful sign of resistance promising the empowerment and the rise of the oppressed.

The translator as laborer

As we learn from the last few lines of his suicide letter, after twelve years devoted to the publishing house, León found himself in a more dire situation than when he had begun. He was alone, exhausted, and felt that his efforts only served the useless authors he was assigned to translate. After having translated one hundred and thirty books, eighty thousand words each, six letters per word, that is, after sixty million strokes on the typewriter keys, all he had was two outfits (one for summer, the other for winter), one pair of shoes, an old dictionary, and no accomplishment of which he could be proud. His tragic end provides a moving contrast with the sheer joy with which he started his career, when translation represented the promise of a better life away from poverty and the rigors of manual labor. As he came to understand later on, his initial enthusiasm for his work as a translator was not merely associated with the opportunity to replace English originals with Spanish versions, but with the enticing possibility that he could actually "translate" himself into someone different (ibid.: 86). While León's trajectory – from the tire shop and a less than adequate formal education to his first translation assignment – may seem unrealistic, at least in some contexts, it does reflect some fundamental aspects of a profession that is still largely underestimated worldwide and whose protocols are generally defined by those who commission rather than those who actually produce translations. It is in this context that, for León, becoming a translator also involved the development of basic skills that had to be learned on the job and under the guidance of the editor.

When he received his first translation assignments – of detective fiction by minor authors – León could barely contain his enthusiasm, bordering on "fanaticism," with which he went about doing his work (ibid.: 84). For him then, translation was a labor of love: since no word was "definitive," he used to prepare several drafts and write countless notes in the margins, reading and rereading his originals as if they were great literature, always in search of new nuances and subtleties (ibid.). (Readers familiar with Borges's views of translation as a legitimate form of creative writing might recognize some echoes of his vision in León's initial approach to translation. Consider, for example, Borges's take on the concept of the "definitive text," which, as he suggests, "corresponds only to religion or exhaustion" [Borges 1999: 69, trans. Weinberger].) León also became a ferocious reader of contemporary detective fiction, recommended by Otero, and, later on, of major literary figures such as Coleridge, Keats, and Shakespeare, even if he could not fully understand them, so as better to prepare himself to do his work. The translator's attitude and work habits obviously clashed with the publisher's more pragmatic views and from the start Otero urged León to work harder and produce more. While for León translation represented a combination of intellectual endeavor and creative writing, for Otero it was just one of the stages in the process of mass producing cheap books that were compatible with the publishing house's agenda. Under Otero's guidance León applied himself to curbing his authorial impulse – and all the care and dedication as well as the pleasure and pride that it involved – and finally managed to translate a three-hundred page long novel in fifteen days and, after a while, five pages in one hour.

As León attempted to depersonalize his work he also began to question where his own transformation had actually taken him. Although his external transformation was clearly visible – he was now frailer, his hands were softer, and he needed prescription glasses – León's greatest transformation was internal: he felt more and more apathetic and exhausted. His disenchantment seemed to come from the realization that even though he had somehow managed to translate himself into an intellectual and appeared to have an easier life than his fellow boarders – all of them manual laborers – he was at least as alienated from the product of his labor as they were from theirs, with the painful difference that the translator's work involved a type of investment in and a relationship with what he produced that was much more personal. As León explained in his letter, even though his fellow boarders seemed to think that he was privileged and maybe even envied him, they certainly could not know what it meant "to feel inhabited by another, who [was] often an imbecile: to lend your head to a stranger and only recover it when it [was] worn out, empty, devoid of ideas, useless for the rest of the day" (Walsh 2008: 94). While manual laborers were required to "rent their hands," the translator had to "rent [his] soul" and was, therefore, a truly "used man," an expression that, according to León, translates the word "Yung-jen," "servant" in Chinese (ibid.).

While León's own experience taught him that the translator had to lend his head and his soul – his mind and his individuality – to the authors and texts he translated, La Casa generally treated translation as a mere replacement of words. It was basically the obvious gap between these different conceptions of translation that gradually undermined León's enthusiasm, as well as his work ethic, to the point that one day "he began not to pay attention, to get distracted, to skip words, and then sentences" (ibid.: 96), and to simply omit any particularly difficult fragment, focusing instead on counting the words of his translations, as he probably counted tires in his previous job, in order to calculate the meager remuneration he was entitled to receiving. In the end it was León's inability to reconcile the complex nature of the translator's work – which "nobody around him could truly understand" (ibid.: 94) – with the limited role it seemed to play in the general economy of La Casa that made it difficult for him to continue to live. Caught up in a system where there was no room for self-expression, León was not only invisible and impotent as a translator and as an intellectual, but socially isolated as well. Working as a freelancer, he had no peers, no colleagues, no one with whom he could discuss his work or exchange ideas, with perhaps the exception of his old dictionary, which he fondly called Mr. Appleton in the "conversations" they used to have while he tackled his assignments (ibid.: 79). In the highly stratified social structure that serves as the story's backdrop, the translator felt he did not have much in common with the "rough and small-minded" laborers among whom he lived in the boarding house (ibid.: 73), just as the editor kept distant from the translator whose background and education seemed to qualify him to take on only minor genres, such as detective stories and science fiction. Finally, in Walsh's representation of the translator as a social and professional pariah, the translator's invisibility can also be related to the paternalistic structure defining labor relations in the context portrayed in the story, a structure that, among other things, prevented León – who saw Otero as a father figure, a benefactor – from recognizing the role played by the editor and the publishing house in the mechanisms that made the system work for the elite, and from acknowledging his own role as an important component of such mechanisms. Consequently, as his enforced invisibility also seemed to blur his vision of his own context, what León failed to see, as a translator working for La Casa, was that he was actually much more of a servant to them than to the authors he had learned to despise.

"The Dead Man Who Speaks"

Rodolfo Walsh's representation of the translator as a subservient laborer is further enriched when we take into account his own commitment to the struggle of the oppressed in Argentina in the 1960s and 1970s. Born in the province of Rio Negro in 1927, Walsh was a prolific translator, a prominent journalist and author, as well as a passionate political activist when the state "unofficially" ambushed and executed him in Buenos Aires in 1977, one day after he began the clandestine distribution of his "Carta Abierta a la Junta Militar" ["Open Letter to the Military Junta"] that marked the first anniversary of the military *coup d'état* which had overthrown the elected President Isabel Perón in March of 1976. In The "Letter," Walsh denounces the horrendous crimes perpetrated by the military, giving special emphasis to their economic policies, in the name of whose enforcement they justified their heinous treatment of the working class, and which constituted an "even greater form of atrocity that punishe[d] millions of human beings with planned destitution" (Walsh 2007: 22). As we read Walsh's "Letter" against the background of León's in "Footnote," it is chilling to realize how the representation of the oppressed translator who could no longer remain invisible is not only reflected but deeply inscribed in the courageous "Letter" that somehow also announced its author's own death.

In "El muerto que habla" ["The Dead Man Who Speaks"], published on the thirtieth anniversary of Walsh's assassination, Alan Pauls describes him as "someone possessed by a compulsive need to speak" and who cherished the power of language as a form of "testimony and testament" that could change the status quo (Pauls 2007, my translation from the Spanish). And this is a compulsion that, as Pauls argues, was directly related to death and mortality: Walsh would not stop speaking or, rather, writing because he knew his time was limited and the enemy was always nearby. In an interview given to Ricardo Piglia in January of 1973, Walsh elaborated on his faith in the power of language and redefined the typewriter as a highly effective weapon – "with paper and a typewriter you can move people to an incalculable degree" (Piglia 2001, my translation from the Spanish) – a weapon that for him had a precise target: to give voice to the voiceless living under the repressive regime in Argentina. In the same interview, Walsh also mentioned his disillusionment with traditional fiction – which no longer played the subversive role it once did – and his decision, in the late 1960s, to abandon bourgeois literature and explore other forms of writing that would speak more directly to and for the people (ibid.).

Walsh's best-known book, *Operation Massacre* (Walsh 2013), first published in 1957, exemplifies the kind of writing he was interested in pursuing in the early 1970s. Anticipating by almost a decade the narrative strategies of Truman Capote's *In Cold Blood* (1993), which came out in 1965, Walsh's non-fiction novel has been recognized as the inaugural text of a new genre that combines investigative journalism and the techniques of fiction writing (Foster 1984: 42), a genre that he masterfully crafted in order to bring to light the story of a horrific massacre that officially had never happened. The clandestine event took place in 1956 as a group of innocent citizens were summarily executed by the police in the outskirts of Buenos Aires because they were allegedly plotting to overthrow the government. Six months later, after learning that some of the victims had actually survived the massacre and were in hiding, Walsh set out to investigate and then write their stories. Considered to be "perhaps the most sophisticated example of Latin American documentary narrative in the service of sociopolitical awareness," Walsh's text utilizes the techniques of fiction to "enhance the texture of truth and the density of human experience" and "demands to be read as a socio-historical document" (ibid.: 44).

As one of the last stories Walsh ever wrote, "Footnote," published ten years after *Operation Massacre*, seems to have helped him realize that he should devote his life and his writing to the oppressed, reconnecting him with his literary activism. In fact, in León's characterization and trajectory, readers can recognize echoes of Walsh's own biography. For example, in the early 1940s, a teenage Walsh moved to a boarding house for laborers in Buenos Aires and found work, among other things, as a dish washer and a window cleaner until 1944 when he was hired as a proofreader and then as a translator of detective fiction by Hachette, the well-known publishing house. From 1946 to 1953, he translated about twenty books of detective fiction by popular authors such as Ellery Queen, one of the authors León regularly read in his journey to improve his skills as a translator. Obviously, though, unlike his character, Walsh did fulfill his dream of becoming an author and in 1953 published his first book, *Variaciones en Rojo* ("Variations in Red") (Walsh 2002), a collection of three detective novellas whose protagonist and main crime solver, Daniel Hernández, is also a proofreader. In the end, unlike León, Walsh managed to turn his typewriter into a powerful weapon and make a difference with his writing, a difference that is clearly illustrated in the visibility he brings to his translator protagonist in "Footnote."

Fiction as activism

Rodolfo Walsh's "Footnote" is a superb illustration of the power of fiction as a privileged locus for reflection and, hence, for theory and theorizing, particularly in a context of oppression and inequality. In its felicitous combination of autobiography, philosophical insight, and enthusiastic activism, and in line with Walsh's most important work, the story constitutes a memorable space for the exploration of the hierarchical opposition between the elite and the subaltern as it is transformed into an inspiring plot, in which the silenced translator, in spite of his tragic end, is finally heard at the same time that his voice becomes an optimistic reminder of the possibility of resistance and empowerment for and in the margins. Besides offering us a moving glimpse into the life and death of an oppressed worker and aspiring intellectual in the difficult years of the Argentine history of the 1960s, "Footnote" provides us with a sensitive portrait of the translator that transcends the more specific context in which it is presented.

Even though "Footnote" invites us to imagine what it might have been like being a translator caught up in the limiting mechanisms of a cultural industry that was fully committed to the interests of an authoritarian state, Walsh's stirring characterization of the translator as a subservient laborer, forced to be alienated from the product of his work and to repress his creativity, brings to mind what is typically ignored about translators and their activity, regardless of their context and circumstances, that is, the fact that translators are, inescapably, the writers and the authors of their translations and, as a consequence, directly and intimately invested in how originals are rewritten in other languages. As Walsh's story exposes the contrast between the powerful editor's views and the humble translator's, as well as the conditions in which their work is developed, it provides readers with invaluable material for a reflection on the precarious organization of the profession, about which, as León appropriately remarks, nobody seems to know much. And it is precisely because translation is still largely misunderstood and underestimated as an innocuous replacement of words that it can generally (and unapologetically) be used to serve interests that are not necessarily the translator's or even the original author's. From this point of view, one can argue that the story potentially underscores asymmetrical relations of power even in contexts that are allegedly more democratic than the Argentine background that ultimately produced and killed Walsh's translator protagonist and, sadly, Walsh himself as well.

"Footnote" is not merely telling a story: it constitutes a space for reflection on the practice of translation and on the translator's (in)visibility, a reflection that is also an eloquent form of activism. As Walsh's narrator openly takes a stand and actually forces the translator to be visible right before our eyes and take over the main narrative, he seems to be playing a role that is quite similar to that of contemporary translation studies scholars who are committed to a form of theory that is also inseparable from activism.

Lawrence Venuti, for example, whose name is widely associated with what could be considered as the central focus of contemporary translation studies – the recognition and exploration of the translator's visibility and its consequences – sees the "motive" of his well-known book, *The Translator's Invisibility – A History of Translation*, as making "the translator more visible so as to resist and change the conditions under which translation is theorized, studied, and practiced today" (Venuti 2008: 13). More specifically, as he declares in the opening page of another book, his project is precisely "to expose" the "scandals of translation" that are "cultural, economic, and political" and basically refer to the marginal status of the translator's activity, which "is stigmatized as a form of writing, discouraged by copyright law, depreciated by the academy, exploited by publishers and corporations, governments and religions institutions" (Venuti 1998: 1). For Venuti, perhaps "the greatest scandal of translation" is that "asymmetries, inequities, relations of domination and dependence exist in every act of translating, of putting the translated in the service of the translating culture" (ibid.: 4).

Although both fiction, as represented here by Walsh's story, and scholarly texts on translation, such as Venuti's, may in fact be addressing similar issues and even lead to similar conclusions, we cannot simply collapse the usual distinctions between literature and theory. They are after all different genres, shaped by different goals and conventions, and are usually addressed to different readers with different motivations and in different contexts. However, in spite of such differences, the reading of stories about translation can certainly enrich our reading of scholarly texts on the topic just as the reading of such texts can make readers interested in translation more attuned to the ways in which translators are actually represented in fiction. An intertextual dialogue between Venuti's comments briefly mentioned above, for example, and Walsh's story might help readers of "Footnote" to better contextualize and deepen their understanding of the implications and consequences of León's precarious status as a professional and the absurd demands imposed on the translator by the publishing house and the power relations they represent.

At the same time, however, it seems fair to conclude that perhaps because of the ways in which we are generally expected to treat fiction – as a multilayered network of texts and textual relations that may include the author's biography, context, influences, and overall work – a story like "Footnote" can offer us a portrait of the translator that is also multilayered and, hence, potentially more nuanced than the kind of investigation on the translator's role that we usually find in scholarly texts. Moreover, because the construction of fictional characters tends to rely on psychological and emotional elements and to elaborate on how such characters might feel or react, whether consciously or unconsciously, the reading of fiction is likely to promote a closer, more personal relationship between readers and texts. Therefore, as readers, we are likely to get more involved with characters like León and Otero and, arguably, be more personally touched or impacted by them and what they represent than by the sound, rational arguments of our most lucid theorists on, say, the translator's invisibility or the power relations that constitute translation. After all, it is fair to assume that it might be quite difficult for us to find a more unforgettable or more poignant representation of the translator's (in)visibility than Walsh's image of León's covered dead body, whose disturbing presence must be acknowledged by the editor and is, consequently, also made concretely visible to us, readers, by the rising, invading footnote that takes over the page, overwhelms the original, and literally blurs the limits between the author's and the translator's voices.

Bibliography

Borges, J. L. (1999) "The Homeric Versions," in E. Weinberger (trans. and ed.) *Selected Non-Fictions*, New York: Penguin Books, 69–74.

Capote, T. (1993) *In Cold Blood – a True Account of a Multiple Murder and its Consequences*, New York: Vintage.

Derrida, J. (1979) "Living On. Borderlines," J. Hulbert (trans.), in H. Bloom, P. de Man, J. Derrida, G. Hartman, and J. H. Miller (eds.) *Deconstruction & Criticism*, New York: The Seabury Press, 75–176.

Foster, D. W. (1984) "Latin American Documentary Narrative," *PMLA* 99(1) (January): 41–55.

—— (1995) *Violence in Argentine Literature: Cultural Responses to Tyranny*, Columbia: University of Missouri Press.

Maier, C. (2006) "The Translator as *Theôros* – Thoughts on Cogitation, Figuration and Current Creative Writing," in T. Hermans (ed.) *Translating Others*, vol. 1, Manchester: St. Jerome, 163–180.

Pauls, A. (2007) "El muerto que habla," *Suplemento Especial, Radar*, "30 años sin Walsh," March 25, 12. Available at: www.elortiba.org/walsh3.html#El_muerto_que_habla_ (accessed May 28, 2016).

Piglia, R. (2001) "Rodolfo Walsh," in S. Saitta and L. A. Romero (eds.) *Grandes Entrevistas de la Historia Argentina (1879–1988)*, Buenos Aires: Punto de Leitura. Available at: www.elortiba.org/walsh.html#Walsh_entrevistado_por_Ricardo_Piglia (accessed May 28, 2016).

Venuti, L. (1998) *The Scandals of Translation – Towards an Ethics of Difference*, London: Routledge.

—— (2008) *The Translator's Invisibility – A History of Translation*, 2nd edition, London: Routledge.

Walsh, R. (2002) *Variaciones en rojo*, Madrid: Espasa.

—— (2007) "Carta Abierta a la Junta Militar," in E. Vannucchi (ed.) *Recordar y entender: a 30 años de la "Carta Abierta a la Junta Militar*," Buenos Aires: Ministerio de Educación – Gobierno de la Ciudad de Buenos Aires, 145–158.

—— (2008) "Nota al pie," in *Un Kilo de Oro*, Buenos Aires: Ediciones de la Flor, 69–96.

—— (2013) *Operation Massacre*, D. Gitlin (trans.), New York: Seven Stories Press.

3 The illusive presence of originals

Oscar Wilde's *The Picture of Dorian Gray* and Edgar Allan Poe's "The Oval Portrait"

> There is something fatal about a portrait. It has a life of its own.
> Oscar Wilde, *The Picture of Dorian Gray*

> "Egli è vivo e parlerebbe se non osservasse la rigola del silentio."
> Inscription beneath an Italian Picture of St. Bruno
> Edgar Allan Poe's epigraph, "The Oval Portrait"

The complex relationship that both separates and brings together the work of translators and the writing of originals, particularly when these are viewed as valuable literary pieces, has been compared to the one often imagined between portrait painters and their live models, or the one between such models and the paintings that are meant to reproduce them. These comparisons usually point not only to the typical status of translators when viewed as mere copyists in their effort at being invisible and respectfully faithful to their objects, but also to the ways in which their work is generally perceived as a clumsy attempt at reproducing an allegedly present, unchangeable original in another context, language, or medium. In the blatant contrast between the model and its portrait, in which the supposed shortcomings of translation are associated with a form of death, or loss of spirit or soul, the translator tends to be the one to blame for whatever happens to go wrong or get lost in the process. An early example can be found in Joachim du Bellay's "Defense and Illustration of the French Language," written in 1549 (Du Bellay 2002, trans. Smith and Parks). Addressing the claim that translations of the classics might enrich the target language and culture, Du Bellay defends the superiority of literature originally written in the vernacular by claiming that all

> the energy and incomparable spirit which [is in the works of the ancients and] that the Latins call genius [...] can hardly be expressed in translation, any more than a painter can represent the soul with the body of the person whom he attempts to represent from nature.
> (Ibid.: 104; see also Hermans 1985: 104)

As Du Bellay recommends, those "who wish to do work worthy of a place in their own language" should leave the "labor of translation, especially of poets, to those who inevitably distill more boredom than glory from a thing that is laborious and without profit. I dare say useless, nay even pernicious, for the enrichment of their language" (Du Bellay 2002: 104).

As I will be arguing, an in-depth critical look into the metaphor of translation as painting can produce an insightful illustration of the basic hierarchical oppositions that conventionally define the relationships routinely imagined between originals and translations, authors and translators, calling attention to the recurrent stereotypes that dominate the discourse on the translator's activity. These stereotypes are generally associated with the assumption that while meaning is alive and readily accessible in the original, it is either partially lost or dead in the translation. More importantly, a closer look at the metaphor of translation as portrait painting can also show that the basis for such stereotypes is not grounded on intrinsic or "natural" truths, but engendered by conceptions of meaning and authorship that cannot resist a more incisive probe. The intricacies involved in comparisons of allegedly dead translations to their "vibrant" originals and the associations they tend to trigger can be productively reflected upon with the help of two remarkable fictional pieces: Oscar Wilde's *The Picture of Dorian Gray*, the novel that first appeared in 1890 (Wilde 2014a), and Edgar Allan Poe's "The Oval Portrait," the short story originally published in 1842 as "Life in Death" (Poe 1983a). Those age-old metaphors that ultimately associate the translator's craft with death and loss may be especially compelling if we approach them with an interest in the broad ideological ground that has shaped the general mainstream conception of translation as a derivative, secondary form of writing practice that is usually taken for granted by the reading public, as well as professionals and even specialists who share the typically essentialist belief in the possibility of reproducible meanings that are expected to stay the same, regardless of contexts or circumstances.

Even though my exploration of the rich material provided by Poe's and Wilde's plots is nurtured in postmodern conceptions of language and text, it is my belief that it will be generally accessible also to those who are not necessarily familiar with this kind of thought and it may serve as an introduction to the implications of post-Nietzschean thinking for a reflection on originals and their translations. From this perspective, the readings proposed in the next pages constitute a fitting example of how fiction can be approached as a more accessible form of theory, or, even, as an enticing strategy that can stimulate those who may not be interested in tackling theoretical texts to critically reflect on the main assumptions that have defined translations and their relationship with originals and, hence, forged the prevailing narratives about the role of translators and how they should relate to authors and/or readers.

Plato and the dichotomies traditionally associated with translation

The dichotomies that place originals above their representations and the creator of originals above those who attempt to represent them, as well as the myriad consequences they imply, are inseparable from the ideological bedrock that has sustained Western thought for millennia and are famously addressed, for example, in Plato's philosophy. As is taken for granted in "Book X" of his *Republic*, written around 360 BC (Plato 1991, trans. Jowett), and featuring a conversation between Socrates and Glaucon, the production of true originals, so to speak, is a divine attribute. It is, thus, only a superior, non-human entity "who is able to make not only vessels of every kind, but plants and animals, himself and all other things – the earth and heaven, and the things which are in heaven or under the earth" (ibid.: 362). Humans, on the other hand, try to imitate such an omnipotent God, but can only produce appearances. In the well-known example involving beds and tables, Plato lets Socrates and Glaucon explain that while God is "the natural author or maker of the bed" and, hence, the creator of the idea or the "essence" of a bed, which is "essentially and by nature one only" (ibid.: 364), the carpenter who makes a particular bed is twice removed from the true bed because he can only imitate God's idea, producing nothing more than "a semblance of existence" (ibid.: 363). Following this rationale, the painter, who may be able to paint any bed but, unlike the carpenter, cannot construct one, is "the imitator of that which the others make" and, therefore, finds himself only "in third in the descent from nature" (ibid.: 364). Since the painter is "a long way off the truth and can do all things because he lightly touches on a small part of them, that part an image," his "ruinous" imitations can mislead and confuse those who do not know better. For example,

> "a painter will paint a cobbler, carpenter, or any other artist, though he knows nothing of their arts; and, if he is a good artist, he may deceive children or simple persons, when he shows them his picture of a carpenter from a distance, and they will fancy that they are looking at a real carpenter".
>
> (Ibid.: 365)

In this category Plato includes "the tragic poet" who, like all imitators, is "thrice removed from the king and from the truth" (ibid.: 364). Refuting those who seem to think that imitators such as Homer and the tragedy writers did "know all the arts and all things human, virtue, as well as vice, and divine things too," Socrates argues that even though they might have written about medicine, for example, they did not cure patients. As for Homer, he may have written about "military tactics, politics, [and] education," but he never governed any state (ibid.: 367), that is, he was never a true "maker." As a clear example of imitative art, poetry is "an inferior who marries an inferior, and has inferior offspring" (ibid.: 373). If given a choice between producing an original or a mere representation of the original, anyone would choose the former:

> Now do you suppose that if a person were able to make the original as well as the image, he would seriously devote himself to the image-making branch? Would he allow imitation to be the ruling principle of his life, as if he had nothing higher in him?
>
> (Ibid.: 366)

Furthermore, the "real" artist, the one "who knew what he was imitating, would be interested in realities and not in imitations [...] and, instead of being the author of encomiums, he would prefer to be the theme of them" (ibid.). Consequently, unless they produce "hymns to the gods and praises of famous men," poets should have no place in Plato's utopian State.

The kind of poetry written by Homer, for example, is not only useless as it can only offer "an inferior degree of truth," but also harmful because it is "concerned with an inferior part of the soul" (Plato 1991: 375) and, as a consequence, "awakens and nourishes and strengthens the feelings and impairs the reason" (ibid.: 376). While the inferior part of the soul is "deemed to be the part of the woman," Socrates and Glaucon pride themselves "on the opposite quality," that is, "the manly part" (ibid.), a conclusion that obviously echoes another fundamental binary opposition. Predictably, Plato's worldview, which relies on hierarchically organized oppositions such as human/divine, the maker/the imitator, truth/imitation, reason/emotion, man/woman, philosophy/poetry, original/representation, does not recognize as legitimate any difference brought about by perspective: "you may look at a bed from different points of view, obliquely or directly or from any other point of view, and the bed will appear different, but there is no difference in reality. And the same of all things" (Plato 1991: 365). Since, for Plato, everything is simply what it is or should be, his is a worldview that depends on a belief in the possibility of meaning as presence, that is, as something that exists and is to be irrefutably recognizable, regardless of perspective, context, or interpretation, and that could forever stay the same as an unchangeable core or essence. Plato's belief in the possibility of essences and eternal sameness is exemplarily reflected in his conception of the soul as that which "must exist forever, and, if existing forever, must be immortal" (ibid.: 384). Therefore, it "must always be the same" (ibid.) and will remain so because even though the body will perish, the soul will survive and continue to live on in other bodies as it is "able to endure every sort of good and every sort of evil" (Plato 1991: 397).

Although Plato never refers to actual translations or translators, it is reasonable to speculate that at least within the context of the Dialogue commented on above, the translator's work would likely be seen at best as a form of imitation and it would not be difficult to imagine the implications of Socrates's and Glaucon's arguments for the fundamental issues that are at stake in the process of translation. As Ben Van Wyke explains, in spite of the many changes involving general conceptions of text and authorship in the last two millennia, what we call today an "original" is usually a text believed to represent the "essence" of its author's thinking that demands "to be treated with a reverence similar to that which Socrates shows towards forms" (Van Wyke 2010: 32). Since the essence of a text is supposed to directly reflect the author's thoughts, "which are comparable to the first remove," the so-called original could represent the second remove and, as such, it constitutes the basis for the translation as "third remove imitation" (ibid.: 32–33). Consequently, any translation will be "but an image of the original because it is created without a direct link to truth" (ibid.: 33). Along the same lines, one might say that "a translator is, as Glaucon says of the painter, an imitator of what others make" (ibid.), a conception that is compatible with the reverence customarily paid to the author of originals, frequently treated almost as a divine figure. From this Platonic stance translation would be considered as potentially misleading because it may fool those who do not know the language of the original into believing that they can have access to it when in reality they only have a devalued, "third-remove" representation of the author's actual text.

"Is it the real Dorian?" cried the original of the portrait [...] "Am I really like that?"

Oscar Wilde's *The Picture of Dorian Gray* can be read as an unsettling deconstruction of the fundamental opposition that has generally defined translation and its relationship with the original, separating the latter as an idealized object that could be forever the same from its interpretations or translations, routinely viewed as inadequate representations of whatever the original is believed to contain, carry, or convey. The novel is precisely about the impossibility of keeping such a binary as a clear-cut opposition and provides a convincing illustration of the fact that the relationship between originals and their representations is far more complicated than essentialist thinking would have it. Wilde's well-known storyline takes place in Victorian London and features the handsome Dorian Gray as the subject of a portrait painted by Basil Hallward who manages to (almost literally) capture the young man's beauty. When the picture is finished, Gray is so impressed by the result that he wishes he would never age so that he could always look exactly the way he does in the portrait. He receives the painting as a gift from the painter and displays it in his mansion. Through Hallward Gray meets Lord Henry Wotton, whose main goal in life is to live exclusively for the senses, ignoring any moral principle that may hinder his obsessive pursuit of pleasure. Under Lord Henry's influence, Dorian Gray descends into a life of unbridled hedonism. After the suicide of Sybil Vane, the humble, innocent girl whom he seduces and abandons after promising her marriage, Gray happens to glance at his portrait and realizes that while he still looks as handsome as he did when he first posed for it, the painting has miraculously changed, betraying subtle signs of his now corrupted life. He immediately locks the portrait in a room that is never used. Time passes and even after almost two decades of unrestrained self-indulgence he still keeps his youthful looks while his portrait reflects his physical and moral decadence. One day, after showing the horrendous picture to Hallward, whom he blames for his fate, Gray kills the painter. Soon he regrets it, but realizes that it may be too late for him to make amends and find a better path. In a desperate attempt to undo his past Dorian Gray stabs the painting with the same knife he used to kill Hallward. The next day his servants find the body of a withered, old man with a knife stuck in his heart lying near the infamous portrait. They can identify the body as their master's because of the rings he was wearing. In the picture, on the other hand, Dorian Gray looks as young and handsome as he did when it was first painted.

Wilde's storyline explores the rarely recognized fact that any representation, regardless of its quality, cannot perfectly repeat what it supposedly represents, not simply because the process may be inadequate, but because the original, or the model, can never remain exactly the same. Even before Dorian Gray's portrait seems to acquire magic powers, Wilde's plot shows us that because the original as a live model does not stop changing, its representation or translation can at best portray a certain moment in its trajectory and, inevitably, always within a certain context and from a certain perspective. As Gray sadly posits soon after his picture is finished, while he "shall grow old, and horrible, and dreadful," the painting "will remain always young. It will never be older than this particular day of June" (Wilde 2014a: 19), a statement that will have to be reevaluated later on, but that even in this preliminary version so to speak already constitutes a reversal of the expected binary found, for instance, in Plato, as briefly shown above. Therefore, in Wilde's plot, it is the original model that will be further and further removed from its translation as painting, not the other way around. As the central focus of the narrative, the painting that supposedly acquires the original's "soul" or "essence" clearly subverts the kind of opposition that regularly distinguishes the original from its reproduction and, also, what is allegedly alive and, hence, always different from itself, from that which is not expected to change or have a life of its own. It is, in fact, this startling subversion that produces the effect of horror for which the story is most well known and remembered. Contrary to the typical notion according to which representations are undoubtedly inferior to their originals because they fail to capture the latter's essence, soul, or spirit, in Wilde's novel it is in the picture, and not in the original, that Dorian Gray's supposedly true self is made visible in different stages of his life. As we are told, at the beginning of the narrative, when the picture is completed, it is in the portrait that the "real" Dorian is to be found, and it is thanks to the portrait that he is able to fully acknowledge his own physical beauty for the first time (ibid.:

21). Moreover, as "the most magical of mirrors," the portrait will soon reveal to him "his own soul" (ibid.: 68).

While the picture is constantly changing, Dorian Gray's own body functions as a simulacrum that, for most of his adult life, will not reflect the passing of time and the ravages brought about by his destructive behavior. According to Wilde's narrator, Gray decided to hide the portrait because it

> had a corruption of its own, worse than the corruption of death itself – something that would breed horrors and yet would never die. What the worm was to the corpse, his sins would be to the painted image on the canvas. They would mar its beauty and eat away its grace. [...] And yet the thing would still live on. It would be always alive.
>
> (Ibid.: 76)

In this case, once again, it is the original that will be unfaithful to its representation and fail to accurately reflect what goes on in Dorian Gray's life, not its translation into painting. Even in the end, when the exceptional power of the painting is gone and the stabbing of the portrait turns out to be a suicide, the gap between the representation and the original being represented still persists, albeit in a different way. Still, the original model, now dead, and its translation into painting, now apparently restored to its original splendor, are not equivalents. At the same time, though, it will be in the picture that the original Dorian Gray or, rather, a certain dated version of him, will somehow live on, and as such, that is, as a representation of Dorian Gray that lives on through time and difference, the painting will impact new audiences in ways that cannot really be commensurable or equivalent, for instance, to the way in which Gray himself first reacted to it when Hallward finished the project.

Besides subverting the hierarchies that shape the familiar relationship conceived between originals and their representations, and besides redefining what might be supposedly lost or dead in translation, Wilde's plot destabilizes the very essentialist notion of the soul, or any immutable core, that could determine once and for all what constitutes an object or a subject, that is, the same *thing* to which one should be indisputably faithful when translating or representing it. Even though the subversion of such a notion in Wilde's text suggests that Dorian Gray's soul actually resides in the portrait, rather than in his body, as Gray himself, Hallward, and Lord Henry imagine, the development of the storyline indicates that wherever his soul is to be found, it never remains identical to itself. Before Dorian Gray embarked on a life of unrestricted hedonism, he was, according to the painter, "simple, natural, and affectionate [, ...] the most unspoiled creature in the whole world" (ibid.: 69), qualities that Hallward was apparently able to capture in his painting. Years later, when the painter was confronted with the picture, he was shocked to see that it depicted the "face of a satyr," the same face that, as Gray remarked, was the face of his soul (ibid.: 99). While Hallward attributed the transformation of Dorian Gray's character (or soul?) to Lord Henry's influence, Gray reminded the painter that it was in fact the latter's work that first changed him as it taught him how to be proud of his own appearance (ibid.: 69). More specifically, the changes that Dorian Gray goes through, and which become imprinted in his portrait, are directly associated with his interaction with the other characters and are, thus, clearly related to influence, a conclusion that also implies that all the characters involved seem to lack a true, stable core that could remain forever the same.

Influence is, actually, a recurrent topic in the novel and provides another convincing illustration of the impossibility of eternal stability for meanings, feelings, "souls," and everything else that shapes the narratives that have defined humans. At the beginning of the novel, we learn, for example, that Hallward is trying to resist being influenced by Dorian Gray's "fascinating" personality, something that could "absorb [his] whole nature, [his] whole soul, [his] very art itself" (ibid.: 7). As he declares, "I have always been my own master; had at least always been so, till I met Dorian Gray" (ibid.). Even the cynical Lord Henry finds himself "strangely stirred" by the young man's personality (ibid.), but it is Gray who completely succumbs to Lord Henry's influence. According to the narrator, Lord Henry was

> brilliant, fantastic, irresponsible. He charmed his listeners out of themselves, and they followed his pipe, laughing. Dorian Gray never took his gaze off him, but sat like one under a spell, smiles chasing each other over his lips and wonder growing grave in his darkening eyes.
>
> (Wilde 2014a: 29)

An even stronger source of influence affecting Gray proves to be a "poisonous book," which, like the portrait, functions as a mirror for the young man, a book that readers of Wilde have associated with *À rebours* (*Against Nature*), the French novel written by Joris-Karl Huysmans (Huysmans 2009) in 1884 (for example, Ellmann 1988: 316). Presented as "a psychological study of a certain young Parisian who spent his life trying to realize in the nineteenth century all the passions and modes of thought that belonged to every century except his own" (Wilde 2014a: 80), the book became to Dorian Gray "a kind of prefiguring type of himself. And, indeed, the whole book seemed to him to contain the story of his own life, written before he had lived it" (ibid.), and in an intoxicating style that "produced in the mind of the lad [...] a form of reverie, a malady of dreaming, that made him unconscious of the falling day and creeping shadows" (ibid.). Dorian Gray himself became an important influence for many of his contemporaries, especially "the very young men," who saw,

> or fancied that they saw, in Dorian Gray the true realization of a type of which they had often dreamed in Eton or Oxford days, a type that was

to combine something of the real culture of the scholar with all the grace and distinction and perfect manner of a citizen of the world.

(Wilde 2014a: 82)

Moreover, Gray's "mode of dressing" and the styles that from time to time "he affected" influenced "the young exquisites of the Mayfair balls and Pall Mall club windows, who copied him in everything that he did, and tried to reproduce the accidental charm of his graceful, though to him only half-serious, fopperies" (ibid.). As an important agent of change, influence precludes the possibility of stability for any human project, and, hence, also the possibility of establishing any kind of clear-cut distinction between what is viewed as an original and what could constitute its supposed derivations.

"The Oval Portrait" and the scandal of translation

Poe's unnamed narrator in "The Oval Portrait" finds himself wounded and feverish in an abandoned chateau in the Apennines while he tells us about his "reverent awe" towards the "lifelikeliness of expression" in the portrait he sees hanging from one of the walls (Poe 1983a: 737). The narrative's central focus involves the story of the portrait, its painter, and the latter's beautiful model and bride, a story that the narrator finds in a book at his bedside and that has moved him deeply. She was "a maiden of rarest beauty, and not more lovely than full of glee," who loved and married the painter and "cherish[ed] all things: hating only [her husband's] Art which was her rival: dreading only the pallet and brushes and other untoward instruments which deprived her of the countenance of her lover" (ibid.). On his part, the "wild and moody" painter, who was "passionate, studious, austere, and having already a bride in his Art," worked so obsessively that he would not see that his young wife was getting weaker and "more dispirited" every day (ibid.). When the picture was almost completed, he was so absorbed with his work that he failed to see that "the tints which he spread upon the canvass were drawn from the cheeks of her who sate beside him" (Poe 1983a: 738). After the final brush stroke was applied and the painter looked closely at what he had accomplished, "he grew tremulous and very pallid, and aghast, and crying with a loud voice, 'This is indeed Life itself!' Turned himself suddenly round to his beloved who was dead. The painter then added: 'But is this indeed Death?'" (ibid.).

Apart from the relationship between the painter and his bride, other relationships in the story have been associated with translation: "the woman and her painted likeness, [... the] portrait and the wounded narrator, and [...] the quaint anecdote in the art book and the narrator's truncated story" (Kennedy 1987: 60). According to J. Gerald Kennedy, each of those pairings "figures an opposition between life and art, between one who gazes and one who is gazed at; more revealingly, each implies a relationship between translator and text or between text and translation" (ibid.: 61). In addition, Kennedy associates the death of the model to the perils of translation:

> The painter translates his wife in a double sense – into a visual icon and into a lifeless model. Like all translation, this process entails duplication and effacement, a retracing which both mirrors the original and abolishes it in the sense that every translation sacrifices the letter of the original text to reconstitute its spirit in another language. The young bride and the portrait manifest the fatality of translation, inasmuch as the picture lives by virtue of the wife's death; yet the wife paradoxically "lives on" in the painting and her essence in effect sustains the life of the translation. [...] The narrator, for his part, translates the painting into writing, into a text which is twice removed from the original.
>
> (Kennedy 1987: 61)

The contrast that Kennedy establishes between the live model who has to be "sacrificed" in order for the painting to live on and, also, between the painting and the text that tells its story, the latter being "twice removed from the original," might serve as an illustration of the typical idealization of the original as the encapsulation of its "essence" as well as the widespread devaluation of the process of translation and underlying suspicion regarding its product. This view is compatible with the usual notion that the alleged violence of translation is somehow the translator's fault and, thus, something that might be avoided, or controlled, as Kennedy's synthesis of Poe's tale suggests:

> the volume of art criticism [which happens to describe the paintings in the bedroom] provides a brief account [of a] painter who worked so obsessively to idealize his young bride through portraiture that he did not notice her failing health and so completed his masterpiece only to discover that he had killed the beloved subject.
>
> (Ibid.: 60)

In his commentary, Kennedy seems to bypass the fact that "The Oval Portrait" reverses the customary equation of life and death associated with the relationship that takes place between originals and their representations. While in the usual comparison the original allegedly remains forever alive and energized and the translation somehow carries the sign of death, in Poe's story it is the model that slowly dies as her life seems to be miraculously transferred from her beautiful face to its representation. While the young woman is long gone and transformed into a corpse, it is her portrait as translation that lives on and impresses Poe's narrator who initially "mistakes the head [in the painting] for that of a living person" and then remains, "for some hours perhaps, half sitting, half reclining, with [his] vision riveted upon the portrait" (Poe 1983a: 737). In contrast with the commonplace notion according to which what a translated text lacks is somehow the life, or the spirit, or even the soul or the essence of the original, in Poe's main plot, as in the subplot that involves the portrait and the narrator, there is actually no loss associated with the process of translation. Rather than the alleged killing of the original, it could be argued that what Poe's scene of translation seems to inadvertently expose are some of the limitations related to traditional conceptions of fidelity as the link that should bind the model to its representation. As mentioned, even though the picture managed to register a specific moment in the life of the original, it was only provisionally faithful, and, as far as we know, only from the painter's point of view.

According to Kennedy, the fact that in Poe's story, both for the painter and for the narrator, the portrait, or the translation, seems to take on "an independent life more real [...] than that of its original" could be viewed as "the scandal of translation":

> in its preternatural vividness, the portrait has become a frightening double of the young bride. Its "lifelikeliness" simultaneously signifies an immortality and a fatality: while the beauty of the portrait will endure, its living counterpart will not; the woman will resemble the sign of herself less and less until she is at last translated into a corpse.
>
> (Kennedy 1987: 63)

However, if we consider that Poe's narrator appreciates the portrait as a work of art and can do without the original and, also, that the painter sacrifices his model's well-being for her translation into painting, even if inadvertently, what might be "scandalous" in the frame of reference constructed by Poe's plot is not so much the fact that the translation becomes independent from the original, as Kennedy suggests, but that both Poe's narrator and his painter character are clearly more interested in the portrait than in the model and have practically ignored the hierarchical binary that is expected to separate them. Following this rationale, we should focus more attentively on the painter's behavior and how he related to his work in order to further understand why he seemed to be punished with the death of his beloved wife at the very moment that he finished the painting that absorbed him so thoroughly. Even though he apparently fulfilled the ethical expectations that usually regulate the relationship between originals and their reproductions and produced a picture that at least for a brief moment seemed to be miraculously faithful to his original, he broke one of the fundamental principles generally established by such ethics, that is, in spite of his effort at producing a perfect representation of his model, he was oblivious to the hierarchy that traditionally underscores the opposition between original and reproduction, and between author and translator. Instead of protecting the original above all other interests and, thus, instead of repressing his authorial will to power, which also implies being invisible and self-effacing in order to respectfully honor someone else's right to be creative, Poe's translator/painter dared to behave like an artist, or an author, and subverted the fundamental hierarchy that places creation above reproduction, original above translation. Considering that the painter loses his bride after having failed to treat his work as a mere copying exercise, and, perhaps more significantly, because of his unsuspected capacity to seemingly recreate life itself, what appears to be ultimately defended as proper in Poe's tale is the Creator's exclusive right to produce or destroy life.

Following the logic that generally supports most thinking about the relationship that relates originals to their reproductions, the activity of translation as portraiture poses a dangerous threat to the original as it may improperly replace it with a deceiving simulacrum. Thus, in order for it to be safe, the translator's craft must keep intact the conventional hierarchy that separates the model from its reproduction so that the translation never speaks to its readers as if it were the original. From this perspective, Poe's epigraph to the story becomes especially relevant: "Egli è vivo e parlerebbe se non osservasse la rigola del silentio" ("He is alive and would speak if he did not observe the rule of silence"), which is, as we are told, "an inscription beneath an Italian Picture of St. Bruno" (Poe 1983a: 734). If we relate Poe's epigraph to his actual storyline, we could argue that the oval portrait, like the picture of St. Bruno, should have "observed the rule of silence" and, consequently, should *not* have spoken in the place of the original. Hence, if the translator/painter overstepped his boundaries, so to speak, and got punished for that, it seems that it is only the Author as Creator who can legitimately decide what his creation is supposed to say to others. However, if this is so, what still needs to be accounted for in my reading of Poe's tale is precisely the painter/translator's seemingly miraculous success. If the power to control meaning is to be the exclusive attribute of those who create originals, how could Poe's character actually succeed in producing such a perfect copy and, furthermore, how does he succeed in making his translation speak so forcefully to the impressed narrator?

The answer may be found precisely in the characterization of Poe's narrator who also happens to be the privileged viewer of his painter character's work. Recall, for example, that, as the story opens, the first thing we learn about the narrator is his peculiar state: he was seriously wounded, had lost a lot of blood and his fever was "excessive and of long duration" (ibid.). After resorting, without success, to all the remedies available, he reached for a little package of opium. (In the past, as we are told, the narrator used to smoke a mixture of opium and tobacco and, at times, as a consequence, would experience "symptoms of mental derangement" [ibid.].) In utter desperation, he did swallow some of the opium without knowing how much to take or what kind of reaction it might produce (ibid.). Therefore, from the start, Poe's narrator was not only seriously wounded and feverish, but, also, heavily drugged, and it was his "incipient delirium" that might have "caused [him] to take deep interest" in the paintings hanging from the walls of his dark chamber (ibid.). Moreover, gazing at the paintings and looking through the book that discussed them became an alternative to sleep, an escape from his desperate condition. While he perused the book and gazed at the pictures, the narrator felt "the voluptuous narcotic stealing its way to [his] brain" and recognized that "in its magical influence lay much of the gorgeous richness and variety of the frames – much of the ethereal hue that gleamed from the canvas – and much of the wild interest of the book [he was looking through]" (ibid.).

If we acknowledge the fact that the narrator is not by any means a reliable source, what Poe's intricate storyline seems to convey is that the painter/translator's alleged capacity to recreate life is, quite probably, only a product of the narrator's feverish delirium. In his altered state, as he approached his own death, the possibility of a painting that supposedly managed to keep intact the beauty and the life of a woman long dead was certainly a welcome, soothing illusion. Thus, the possibility of a translation or painting that would rob the original of its life and beauty and even "speak" in its place could only be conceivable from the narrator's obviously unreliable point of view. Since the translator/painter's alleged ability to recreate beauty might be just an illusion produced by an inadequate reader's altered perception, the real notion of translation with which Poe's story ends up leaving us is, after all, permeated by the widely repeated belief that translation is indeed unable to preserve the "spirit" or the "energy" of the original. In fact, this is precisely the notion of translation we find in Kennedy's conclusion to his interpretation of the story as he claims that the narrator "fails" to successfully translate the painting for us. According to Kennedy, while the narrator tries to translate the painting, "he can tell us about 'the true secret' of the painting's effect, its astonishing 'lifelikeliness', but the verbal account does not leave us 'confounded, subdued, and appalled'," as it does the narrator. "What has been lost is precisely the life of the twice-translated text; what has been gained is access to the idea of the painting" (Kennedy 1987: 61–62).

Contrasts and consequences: reading Poe and Wilde against each other

In spite of sharing some similarities in their treatment of the metaphor of painting as translation, Poe's and Wilde's pieces can be associated with contrasting views on how the relationship between originals and their representations should be articulated as well as the kind of role painters or translators are supposed to play in the process of representing an object in a different medium or environment. I will start with Poe's tale and focus on his painter character who does not seem to have any control over his work, and the narrator, who, as it turns out, is in no physical or mental condition to critically evaluate the portrait that has impressed him so deeply. In order to further scrutinize the composition of both characters, I will compare them to the idealized author and reader figures that Poe discusses in "The Philosophy of Composition," the essay first published in 1846 (Poe 1983b).

Its declared goal is to offer the reading public "a peep behind the scenes, at the elaborate and vacillating crudities of thought [... ,] in a word, at the wheels and pinions [...], which, in ninety-nine cases out of the hundred, constitute the properties of the literary *histrio*" (ibid.: 1080). Above all, Poe seems to be interested in discrediting the notion, often associated with Romanticism, that it is the intuition of authors that guides them in the creation of their work. As he carefully argues, their ultimate goal should be to obtain full control over what they create and, more importantly, over how their writing is viewed and understood. In order to make sure that such control is properly exerted, creative writers should strive to turn their writing process into a purely rational endeavor:

> nothing is more clear than that every plot, worth the name, must be elaborated to its *dénouement* constantly in view that we can give a plot its indispensable air of consequence, or causation, by making the incident, and especially the tone at all points, tend to the development of the intention.
>
> (Ibid.: 1079)

As an illustration of his point that every detail of the text must be subject to calculation, Poe offers a description of "the *modus operandi* by which some one of [his] own works was put together" (ibid.: 1081). The piece chosen is "The Raven," the widely known poem whose central motif is, according to Poe, the premature death of a beautiful young woman, a topic that is, "unquestionably, the most poetical topic in the world" (ibid.: 1084), and, of course, also explored in "The Oval Portrait." (My reader will probably agree that Poe's affirmation about "the most poetical topic in the world" flagrantly undermines his determination to be absolutely rational and objective.)

As he discusses his strategy regarding the creation of the poem, Poe explains that his "design" is "to render it manifest that no one point in its composition is referrible either to accident or intuition – [and] that the work proceeded, step by step, to its completion with the precision and rigid consequence of a mathematical problem" (ibid.: 1081). The ultimate goal of these strict calculations is to render "the work universally appreciable" (ibid.: 1082) and to make sure that what readers get from the text is exactly that which the author intends them to get. For Poe, writing, and particularly the literary *histrio*'s writing, also entails having total control over a reader, whose role is then reduced to that of a predictable, passive receptor and decoder of the author's conscious intentions. As Poe explains the "progressive steps" of his composition of "The Raven," he points out, for example, that "the initial consideration was that of extent" (ibid.: 1081). Therefore,

> if any literary work is too long to be read at one sitting, we must be content to dispense with the immensely important effect derivable from

unity or impression – for, if two sittings be required, the affairs of the world interfere, and every thing like totality is at once destroyed.

(Ibid.)

Similarly, if the writer should consider "to dispense with any thing that may advance his design, it but remains to be seen whether there is, in extent, any advantage to counterbalance the loss of unity which attends it" (ibid.).

From this rather limiting viewpoint, according to which a literary text is ultimately nothing but a faithful representation of its author's consciously intended meanings, authorship is, once again, implicitly associated with the divine, that is, with the power to decide what words should mean and to make them immune to change and the passing of time. Since reading is conceived as an idealized form of decoding only that which the author has deliberately intended to say, it is understandable why translation as portraiture should be viewed as a somewhat suspicious or illegitimate activity that is likely to endanger the life of the original it attempts to reproduce. Consider, for instance, the flagrant contrast between the scene of translation in "The Oval Portrait" and the idealization of original writing that takes place in "The Philosophy of Composition." While in the latter there can be no surprises and the roles of the author and the reader are unequivocally distinguishable, leaving nothing to chance, in the first both the painter and the narrator could not in any sense be viewed as rational or even aware of what actually surrounds them. From the perspective of the kind of rationale that shapes Poe's essay, it could be argued that the painter/translator character in "The Oval Portrait" lacks the stability and the rationality that might qualify him to produce a reliable representation of his beloved wife. Consequently, the "moody" painter, who is oblivious to his model's condition and cannot control the impact produced by his work, should not be treated as an artist, or an author, and only appears to be one from the perspective of a heavily drugged viewer who is definitely unable to distinguish life from death, or an original from its reproduction. In harmony with key arguments exposed in "The Philosophy of Composition," "The Oval Portrait" implicitly defends a conception of authorship that is comparable to a divine attribute and, thus, must discredit the legitimacy of translation or painting as a creative practice just as it downplays the value of reading when it is not closely attuned to whatever the author or the artist intended to convey.

Let us direct our attention now to Basil Hallward, the painter character in Oscar Wilde's novel who is killed by his model and friend Dorian Gray. As noted, it is from the portrait created by Hallward, that is, from the revealing mirror of the painter's representation or translation of Gray that the latter begins to learn about himself. Hence, the model, who has not been exactly present even to himself, only comes into contact with some understanding of his own evolving character after having it masterfully re-presented by the talented painter. It is, thus, precisely his extraordinary depiction of Dorian Gray that in the end proves to be deadly for the painter who, like Poe's character, could not foresee the bizarre power his work could exercise and how it might affect his viewers. As we are informed, Gray kills "the friend who had painted the fatal portrait to which all his misery had been due" (Wilde 2014a: 100) and, later on, also tries to "kill the painter's work, and all that that meant," hoping that he would then be free from the influence of Hallward's creation (ibid.: 139). If we compare the painter character's fate in Poe's story to Hallward's, it is worth noting that even though Wilde's character is somehow also "punished" for his incapacity to control the outcome and the impact of his work, the rationale that seems to justify such a punishment is not relatable to any authorial figure's desire to assert his supposedly exclusive right to be creative, as my reading of "The Oval Portrait" has concluded. Rather, Hallward's death, which has no impact on the power that his painting exercises over Dorian Gray's life, could be interpreted as a subtle commentary by Wilde on what Gray and his expectations may represent. More specifically, even though what Gray expects from Hallward is compatible with Poe's conception of the artist as someone who is supposed to control what his work could do or accomplish, this is a conception that Wilde's text disavows, a disavowal that can also be associated with Gray's death and the restoration of his portrait to its original beauty at the end of the novel.

Just as I have attempted to establish a meaningful link involving Poe's views on the creation and the reception of literature between "The Oval Portrait" and "The Philosophy of Composition," I can identify in Oscar Wilde's brief preface to *The Picture of Dorian Gray* a pertinent articulation of the author's conception of the artist's role that is also recognizably interwoven in the plot of his novel. According to Wilde, even though "[t]he artist is the creator of beautiful things," such a role does not imply any form of authorial control over what is produced as art. Rather, for Wilde, the artist's goal should be to "reveal art and conceal the artist" (Wilde 2014b: 3). Since it is "the spectator, and not life, that art really mirrors" (ibid.) and, therefore, since art is not meant to reveal anything about the artist or life in general, the impact of any artistic object is necessarily unpredictable. Consequently, the vitality of a work of art does not depend on any form of carefully planned synchronization between the artist's intentions and the reception of his work, as Poe's texts suggest. For Wilde, "[d]iversity of opinion about a work of art shows that the work is new, complex, and vital. When critics disagree, the artist is in accord with himself" (ibid.). Some echoes of this line of reasoning can be identified in Wilde's storyline as well. A suitable example is provided by Hallward's comment on the relationship he develops with the magnificent picture he has painted:

> "I cannot help feeling that it is a mistake to think that the passion one feels in creation is ever really shown in the work one creates. [...] It often seems to me that art conceals the artist far more completely than it ever reveals him".
>
> (Wilde 2014a: 73)

Moved by the concern that he has probably, albeit unintentionally, revealed too much of himself in his painting, Hallward decides not to exhibit the picture and gives it as a gift to Gray, a gesture that can be interpreted figuratively as well: since whatever the artist intends to convey is not exactly present in the object created and since it functions like a mirror that will give potential viewers or readers an opportunity to see and reflect about themselves, any work of art could be viewed as a gift to anybody who may take an interest in it, a gift that is not intrinsically good or uplifting, as Dorian Gray eventually finds out.

Within the ideological framework that sustains Oscar Wilde's plot there appears to be no room for the kind of idealization of originals and authorship that plays such a defining role in Edgar Allan Poe's story. For Wilde, at least in the fictional space created by *The Picture of Dorian Gray*, the dichotomy that traditionally places the creation of originals above translations is not only meaningless, but irrelevant as well. For a more specific illustration, let us recall, for example, another gift that, as mentioned above, also plays a fundamental role in the novel – the "poisonous book" about "a certain young Parisian" that Dorian Gray receives from Lord Henry (ibid.: 80). Like the portrait, this French book, which Gray may have read in translation, functions like a reflecting mirror for the young man and has a major impact on the shaping of his life, an impact that is not in any way dependent on, or even related to whatever the author of the original might have intended to say or accomplish. Following this rationale, it could be argued that what makes an artistic object – whether an original or a translation – present or alive is determined by its receptor's disposition or inclination to relate to it and learn from the reflection it may provide. Therefore, if we compare Wilde's perspective in *The Picture of Dorian Gray* to Poe's texts analyzed above, it is fair to conclude that Wilde does not expect readers or viewers to be faithful to whatever the artist might have tried to convey. Hence, it is not surprising, for instance, that Wilde's Lord Henry brings up the issue of fidelity at least twice in the novel's plot. The first time it comes up is in a remark he makes soon after Hallward finishes the portrait and Gray wonders which one is "the real Dorian," the original or its representation: "What a fuss people make about fidelity! [...] Why, even in love it is purely a question for physiology. It has nothing to do with our own will" (ibid.: 21). Lord Henry's comment as well as Dorian Gray's apparent doubt on how he should view his representation in painting not only undermine the usual hierarchies defining the limits between originals and translations, but also the notion that what is created in the name of art could be indisputably tied to the artist's goals or desires. A few pages down, even though this time he refers to the role fidelity plays, or should play, in romantic or sexual liaisons, Lord Henry seems to get to the heart of the matter when he directly relates the conception of "faithfulness" to a "passion for property" (ibid.: 33). Or, if we translate Lord Henry's observation into terms that are closer to the actual reality of textual practices: the demand for fidelity that is "naturally" imposed upon translators and/or readers by a tradition that idealizes authors and their originals could very well be associated with these authors' (and/or their surrogates') fear of losing that which, perhaps naively, they believe they own and control.

Bibliography

Du Bellay, J. (2002) "Of Bad Translators and of Not Translating the Poets," *The Defense and Illustration of the French Language*, J. H. Smith and E. W. Parks (trans.), in D. Robinson (ed.) *Western Translation Theory – from Herodotus to Nietzsche*, Manchester: St. Jerome.

Ellmann, R. (1988) *Oscar Wilde*, New York: Vintage.

Hermans, T. (1985) "Images of Translation – Metaphor and Imagery in the Renaissance Discourse on Translation," in T. Hermans (ed.) *The Manipulation of Literature: Studies in Literary Translation*, London: Croom Helm, 103–136.

Huysmans, J. K. (2009) *Against Nature*, M. Mauldon (trans.), Oxford: Oxford University Press.

Kennedy, J. G. (1987) *Poe, Death, and the Life of Writing*, New Haven, CT: Yale University Press.

Plato (1991) "Book X," *The Republic*, B. Jowett (trans.), New York: Vintage, 360–397.

Poe, E. A. (1983a) "Life in Death [The Oval Portrait]," in *The Unabridged Edgar Allan Poe*, Philadelphia, PA: Running Press Book Publishers, 734–738.

—— (1983b) "The Philosophy of Composition," in *The Unabridged Edgar Allan Poe*, Philadelphia, PA: Running Press Book Publishers, 1079–1089.

Van Wyke, B. (2010) "Imitating Bodies and Clothes: Refashioning the Western Conception of Translation," in J. St. André (ed.) *Thinking Translation through Metaphor*, Manchester: St. Jerome, 17–46.

Wilde, O. (2014a) *The Picture of Dorian Gray*, Brooklyn, NY: Millennium Publications.

—— (2014b) "The Preface," *The Picture of Dorian Gray*, Brooklyn, NY: Millennium Publications.

4   The translation of philosophy into fiction

Borges's "Funes, His Memory" and "Pierre Menard, Author of the *Quixote*"

Pedro Leandro Ipuche has written that Funes was a precursor of the race of supermen – "a maverick and vernacular Zarathustra" – and I will not argue the point[.]

Jorge L. Borges, "Funes, His Memory," trans. Andrew Hurley

It is a matter of common knowledge that [in Chapter XXXVIII, Part I] don Quixote comes down against letters and in favor of arms. Cervantes was an old soldier; from him, the verdict is understandable. But that *Pierre Menard*'s don Quixote [...] should repeat those cloudy sophistries! Mme. Bachelier sees in them an admirable (typical) subordination of the author to the psychology of the hero; others (lacking all perspicacity) see them as a *transcription* of the Quixote [sic]; the baroness de Bacourt, as influenced by Nietzsche. To that third interpretation (which I consider irrefutable), I am not certain I dare to add a fourth[.]

Jorge L. Borges, "Pierre Menard, Author of the *Quixote*,"
trans. Andrew Hurley

In two of Borges's earliest and best-known stories, "Funes, His Memory" (Borges 1998a, trans. Hurley), which first appeared in Spanish in 1944, and "Pierre Menard, Author of the *Quixote*" (Borges 1998b, trans. Hurley), originally published in 1939, his narrators express an understated compatibility with Nietzsche's thought, as suggested by the two fragments quoted above. That Borges had read Nietzsche is undeniable, as is documented, for instance, in two newspaper pieces he published in *La Nación* in the 1940s, still unavailable in English: "Algunos pareceres de Nietzsche" ("Some of Nietzsche's Views") (Borges 2001a) and "Nietzsche: el propósito de 'Zarathustra'" ("Nietzsche: The Purpose of Zarathustra") (Borges 2001b), which suggest that the Argentinian author was not only familiar with the German philosopher's work, but also well-informed about its reception in Europe. The main goal of this chapter is to explore some key associations between Nietzsche's thought and the lessons on language, translation, and interpretation to be learned from both "Funes" and "Pierre Menard."

Even though Borges's views on issues of language and translation are explicitly exposed in his essays from the 1930s, "The Homeric Versions" (Borges 1999a, trans. Weinberger) and "The Translators of *The One Thousand and One Nights*" (Borges 1999b, trans. Allen), it is in his short stories that his views on the topic can be explored in greater depth, an exploration that also serves as a fitting illustration of the ways in which fiction can function as a privileged form of theory. As I will be arguing, "Funes" can be read as a sophisticated meditation on issues of language and translation that finds a compatible reflection in the German philosopher's thought. At the same time, my reading of "Funes" will shine a light on the peculiar relationship that Borges's narrator seems to establish with Pierre Menard in the homonymous story. Even though it is not my goal to examine the overall relationship that Borges might have established with Nietzsche's philosophy, and particularly whether this relationship could be described in terms of influence, it is my claim that Nietzsche's conception of language could very well be the link connecting Borges's views to those entertained, for example, by contemporary thinkers usually associated with poststructuralism (see, for example, Waisman 2005 and Kristal 2002, for discussions on Borges's views of translation).

Echoes of Nietzsche in Borges's views on language and translation

It is mostly on the basis of a conception of language as something that produces rather than merely represents meaning that Borges elaborates his views on translation. In "The Homeric Versions" and "The Translators of *The One Thousand and One Nights*," he questions the common clichés that typically define translation such as the hierarchical opposition between the so-called original and its translations, at the same time that he explores the complex issue of the translator's agency and the role it plays in the shaping of world literature. The main focus of this section will be the theoretical basis underscoring Borges's non-essentialist conceptions of language and translation that share a great deal with Nietzsche's radical critique of Platonic notions of truth and representation and, implicitly, the possibility of translation as a faithful rendering or reproduction of the original as a stable, unchanging entity.

In Nietzsche's "On Truth and Lies in a Nonmoral Sense," an essay presumably written in the early 1870s and left unfinished, we find an overall exploration of the workings of language that sets up a scenario in which arbitrariness, conventionality, and the multiplicity of languages are indissolubly connected: "The various languages, placed side by side, show that with words it is never a question of truth, never a question of adequate expression; otherwise, there would not be so many languages" (Nietzsche 1999: 82, trans. Breazeale). As Nietzsche argues, language is basically metaphorical since "every concept arises from the equation of unequal things": a word can only become a concept "precisely insofar as it is not supposed to serve as a reminder of the unique and entirely individual original experience to which it owes its origin," and is, therefore, able to fit "countless more or less similar cases – which means purely and simply, cases which are never equal and thus altogether unequal" (ibid.: 83). It is this process involving "unconsciousness" and "forgetfulness" that makes it possible for humans to "universalize" their sensations and impressions into "less colorful, cooler concepts so that [they] can entrust the guidance of [their] life and conduct to them" (ibid.: 84). A good illustration of Nietzsche's vision of how meaning is crystallized into words and concepts can be provided by his example of the "leaf." As he argues, just "as it is certain that one leaf is never totally the same as another, so it is certain that the concept 'leaf' is formed by arbitrarily discarding these individual differences and by forgetting the distinguishing aspects," an argument that is in explicit opposition to the notion, obviously reminiscent of Plato and his theory of forms, according to which "in addition to the leaves, there exists in nature the 'leaf'," that is, the original model on the basis of which "all the leaves were perhaps woven, sketched, measured, colored, curled, and painted – but by incompetent hands, so that no specimen has turned out to be a correct, trustworthy, and faithful likeness of the original model" (ibid.: 83). Following Nietzsche's argument that there is no original leaf to which all other leaves should be compared, it could be argued that what we call an "original" text is always already between quotation marks and it does not, in any conceivable sense, represent a true origin that could remain the same forever and, hence, be clearly separated from its repetitions or from other similar texts, written either before or after it. Just as "the concept 'leaf' is formed by arbitrarily discarding [...] individual differences and by forgetting the distinguishing aspects" that are not relevant for its construction and use (ibid.), there is no text that could be truly and objectively original. As a consequence, if we consider the implications of Nietzsche's arguments for the usual opposition between originals and their reproductions, we may also argue that a text can only be thought of as an original if we either ignore or forget all the other texts that have made its writing possible and with which it is directly or indirectly related.

In "The Homeric Versions" one finds a superb exploration of these issues as Borges destabilizes the traditional dichotomy separating originals from translations and exposes its purely affective and conventional foundation. According to him, the "modest mystery" that seems to involve literary originals is a result of "forgetfulness," which is "induced by vanity" and "the fear of confessing mental processes that may be divined as dangerously commonplace," as well as "the endeavor to maintain, central and intact, an incalculable reserve of obscurity" (Borges 1999a: 69). Hence, whatever separates originals from translations is not "objective," or intrinsic to them, but determined, first and foremost, by an affective bond. Every original, like every text, is not a stable object that exists apart from the value that is attributed to it and which, ultimately, constitutes it as well. Originals, like translations, are basically "recombinations of elements" (ibid.). Consequently, the traditional hierarchy established between originals and their alleged reproductions is also destabilized:

> to assume that every recombination of elements is necessarily inferior to its original form is to assume that draft nine is necessarily inferior to draft H – for there can only be drafts. The concept of the 'definitive text' corresponds only to religion or exhaustion.
>
> (Ibid.)

Furthermore, given "the incalculable repercussions of words," "the superstition about the inferiority of translations – coined by the well-known Italian adage" – can only be "the result of absentmindedness" as there is "no good text that does not seem invariable and definitive if we have turned to it a sufficient number of times" (ibid.). What stabilizes and even sacralizes texts in certain contexts and at certain times is, therefore, not the result of "impartial divinity" (Borges 1999a: 70), but the affective connection that readers may develop with them, a connection that, as I will elaborate further in the next section, might very well be another name for what Nietzsche has called the "will to power." Rather than merely reproduce originals, what translations ultimately do is to reflect the different interpretations and changes imposed on them by powerful readers and/or translators whose readings and/or versions have been considered "definitive," or at least relevant in certain contexts and at certain times. As Borges's argument goes, translations "are a partial and precious documentation of the changes the text suffers" through time: "[a]re not the many versions of the *Iliad* – from Chapman to Magnien – merely different perspectives on a mutable fact, a long experimental game of chance played with omissions and emphases?" (ibid.: 69).

Borges's views on the relationship between Homer's poetry and its different translations seem to echo Nietzsche's genealogically based approach to history outlined in "'Guilt', 'Bad Conscience' and Related Matters," the second essay in *On the Genealogy of Morality* (Nietzsche 2007, trans. Diethe), originally published in 1887. Such an approach obviously denies the possibility of fully recovering the past and acknowledges the inevitability of change and its consequences. Even though Nietzsche's focus in the essay is to critique possible connections generally taken for granted between "the origin and purpose of punishment" and "the history of the emergence of law," his reasoning is quite relevant for any reflection on the mechanisms of interpretation:

> there is no more important proposition for every sort of history than that which we arrive at only with great effort but which we really *should* reach, – namely that the origin of the emergence of a thing and its ultimate usefulness, its practical application and incorporation into a

system of ends, are *toto coelo* separate; that anything in existence, having somehow come about, is continually interpreted anew, requisitioned anew, transformed and redirected to a new purpose by a power superior to it.

(Nietzsche 2007: 51)

According to Nietzsche, interpretation is practically a synonym for the will to power as the trigger behind any attempt to establish and control meaning, constituting a mechanism that echoes what occurs "in the organic world," where everything consists of "*overpowering, dominating*" (ibid.). At the same time, "overpowering and dominating consist of re-interpretation, adjustment, in the process of which their former 'meaning' [...] and 'purpose' must necessarily be obscured or completely obliterated" (ibid.). From this perspective, we can also argue that just as the original status of a text is arbitrarily and conventionally established, so is the potential equivalence between the original and its repetitions or the degree of faithfulness that these may seem to observe in relation to the original. As Borges asks, in regards to the several translations of Homer he mentions in the essay:

> Which of these many translations is faithful? My reader will want to know. I repeat: none or all of them. If fidelity refers to Homer's imaginations and the irrecoverable men and days that he portrayed, none of them are faithful for us, but all of them could be for a tenth-century Greek.

(Borges 1999a: 74)

In Nietzschean terms, we can say that from Borges's reflection emerges a conception of text that relies on the notion that any form of discourse is always in a state of becoming, a state that can only be provisionally stabilized by the will to power represented by an act of interpretation, a *sine qua non* for any process involving writing, reading, or translating.

These conceptions are further elaborated in Borges's "The Translators of *The One Thousand and One Nights*," in which he focuses on the highly visible role of translators in the process that transformed the *Nights* into one of the most widely appreciated texts of all time (Borges 1999b). As Borges notes, it was Antoine Galland's French translation of the *Nights* at the beginning of the eighteenth century that canonized it as a classic in world literature, celebrated by major poets and writers such as Coleridge, De Quincey, Stendhal, Tennyson, and Poe (ibid.: 92–93). Furthermore, even though "two hundred years and ten better translations have passed," when one thinks of *The One Thousand and One Nights* in the West it is this first translation that one has in mind. Such success is not attributable to anything that could be considered its inherent qualities as a translated text: of all the versions examined, Galland's was "the most poorly written [...], the least faithful, and the weakest" (ibid.: 93). Following Borges's rationale, the positive repercussion of Galland's version in eighteenth-century France was attributable to the fact that the translator not only "attenuate[d]" the "barbaric color" of the *Nights*, domesticating "his Arabs so they would not be irreparably out of place in Paris" (ibid.: 95), but that he also transformed the tales into a "repertory of marvels," as Enno Littmann, another translator of the *Nights*, has observed (ibid.: 96). As Borges adds, the "universal imposition of this assumption on every Western mind is Galland's work" (ibid.), a clear indication that, rather than acting like an invisible translator, Galland performed a role comparable to that of an author, a role that also involved the incorporation of stories "that time would render indispensable and that the translators to come – his enemies – would not dare omit" (Borges 1999b: 92). While Galland's version reveals his own beliefs and preferences and reflects a great deal of his own time and context, what we, "mere anachronistic readers of the twentieth century," see in the twelve volumes of his *Nights* is "the cloying flavor of the eighteenth century [...] and not the evaporated aroma of the Orient which two hundred years ago was their novelty and their glory" (ibid.: 93).

In his treatment of the several translators of *The One Thousand and One Nights* – Edward Lane, Richard Burton, Dr. Jean-Charles Mardrus, and Enno Littmann, in addition to Galland – Borges emphasizes the authorial will to power that inspired their work. Like ambitious authors, these translators can be shown to have had a discernible agenda that tended to prioritize their own interests over anything else. Burton, for example, had three main goals for his famous translation: "to justify and expand his reputation as an Arabist; to differ from Lane [the English translator who had completed a well-regarded English version of the text] as ostensibly as possible; and to interest nineteenth-century British gentlemen in the written version of thirteenth-century oral Muslim tales" (ibid.: 99). Like ambitious authors, those translators had to deal first and foremost with their anxiety of influence and were forced "to be different," a "rule" that, according to Borges, is "imposed" by the precursor, who is also the aspiring translator's "enemy" (ibid.: 95). As Borges elaborates:

> One of the secret aims of [Burton's] work was the annihilation of another gentleman [...] who was compiling a vast dictionary in England and who died long before he was annihilated by Burton. That gentleman was Edward Lane, the Orientalist, author of a highly scrupulous version of *The One Thousand and One Nights* that had supplanted a version by Galland. Lane translated against Galland, Burton against Lane; to understand Burton we must understand this hostile dynasty.
>
> (Ibid.: 92)

What interests Borges in the work of these translators is not their alleged fidelity, but their individual contribution to the shaping of the *Nights* or, in Nietzschean terms, the expression of their will to power in the writing of their interpretations of the text. For instance, even though Jean-Charles Mardrus, "Dr. Mardrus," author of an 1899 French translation of the *Nights*, has been hailed as "the most truthful translator" of the tales (ibid.: 102), for Borges, it is not his "fidelity" that we should celebrate but, rather, his "infidelity": "To celebrate Mardrus' fidelity is to leave out the soul of Mardrus, to ignore Mardrus entirely. It is his infidelity, his happy and creative infidelity that must matter to us" (ibid.: 106).

These translators' inescapable visibility is also constituted by the different cultural settings that have formed their tastes and nourished their work. As Borges argues, versions such as Burton's, Mardrus's, and Galland's "can only be conceived *in the wake of a literature*": "Whatever their blemishes or merits, [their "characteristic" translations] presuppose a rich (prior) process. In some way, the almost inexhaustible process of English is adumbrated in Burton," in whose *Arabian Nights* Borges finds echoes of "John Donne's hard obscenity, the gigantic vocabularies of Shakespeare and Cyril Tourneur, Swinburne's affinity for the archaic, the crass erudition of the authors of 17th-century chapbooks, the energy and imprecision, the love of tempests and magic" (ibid.: 108). Similarly, in Mardrus's version, Borges identifies echoes of *Salammbô* and La Fontaine. However, in Enno Littmann's early twentieth-century German version he finds "nothing but the probity of Germany," which is "so little, so very little," since, for Borges, "the commerce between Germany and the *Nights* should have produced something more" (ibid.). Considering that, "whether in philosophy or in the novel," what Germans have to offer is their "literature of the fantastic," Borges would like to see the "marvels" he enjoys in the *Nights* "rethought in German" (ibid.), a project that might have been masterfully pursued by someone like Kafka, who certainly had what it takes to rethink the fantastic in the *Nights* "in line with Germanic distortion, the *unheimlichkeit* of Germany" (Borges 1999b: 109). Borges's views on the task of the translator do not merely destabilize, but practically erase the typical hierarchy that tends to define the prescribed dynamic for the relationships that should take place between translations and originals and between translators and authors. As shown, he is not simply suggesting that readers become aware of the fact of translation and the translator's visibility, but explicitly claiming that what should be expected of translators of literary texts is nothing less than the inventiveness and the authorial skills commonly associated with creative writers who are also in tune with the literary tradition to which they belong. In a clear opposition to the usual discourse that tends to identify translation – and particularly the translation of literary texts – with loss and impoverishment, Borges focuses on the gain and the enrichment that translations can potentially bring not only to the original, but also to the cultural context of the translation.

In "The Argentine Writer and Tradition," originally presented as a lecture delivered in Buenos Aires in 1951 (Borges 1999c, trans. Allen), Borges proposes an approach to the relationship between Argentine literature and the Western tradition that unsettles the expected hierarchy separating the domestic from the foreign as well as dominating cultures from peripheral ones. Even though the piece is not directly about translation, it can be read as an appropriate supplement to Borges's views discussed above. As he writes, the peripheral position occupied by his country in the world of intellectual achievement involves an unsuspected advantage. Since the Argentines, like Latin Americans in general, are part of the European tradition but also find themselves outside its limits or, at most, in its remote periphery, their heritage is rightfully "the whole of Western culture" (ibid.: 426). This privileged position gives them a "right to this tradition, a greater right than that which the inhabitants of one Western nation or another may have," allowing them to take on all the European themes "without superstition and with an irreverence that can have, and already has had, fortunate consequences" (ibid.). Borges compares what he sees as the Argentines' privileged position to those occupied by the Jews in Western culture and the Irish in the context of English literature. Regarding the Jews, Borges refers to an argument defended by Thorstein Veblen, an American sociologist, according to which Jews "are prominent in Western culture because they act within that culture and at the same time do not feel bound to it by any special devotion" (ibid.). As a consequence, it will "be easier for a Jew than for a non-Jew to make innovations in Western culture" (ibid.). As for the Irish, for "illustrious" Irishmen such as Bernard Shaw, George Berkeley, and Jonathan Swift, "the fact of feeling themselves to be Irish, to be different, was enough to enable them to make innovations in English culture" (ibid.). Therefore, we may conclude, just as the "successful" translators of the *Nights* did not feel particularly bound to the original and seemed to be more motivated to be different and translate "against" their precursors, Argentine writers should not limit themselves to the local or the national and feel free to handle any topic or tradition "without superstition" (ibid.). In both cases, what seems to be at stake is precisely what Borges sees as the translator's or the writer's right to appropriate tradition and revitalize it, a conclusion that suggests a subversion not only of the hierarchy that routinely places the writing of originals above their translations, but, also, the one that tends to privilege the foreign over the domestic (for a thoughtful reflection on how writing and translation tend to overlap in Borges's conceptions and texts, see Waisman 2005: 84–123).

Translating European philosophy into Latin American fiction: "Funes, His Memory"

"Funes, His Memory" is presented as a testimonial by Borges's third-person narrator on Ireneo Funes, the bastard son of a local ironing woman and an English doctor. It is addressed to the editors of the special volume to be published about the young Uruguayan who became famous on account of his prodigious memory and was defined both as "a precursor of the race of the supermen – 'a maverick and vernacular Zarathustra' – [and …] also [as] a street tough from Fray Bentos, with certain incorrigible limitations" (Borges 1998a: 131). The narrator is pleased to write his testimonial even though he saw Funes "no more than three times, the last time in 1887" (ibid.). The first one was in 1884 when the narrator, then also quite young, while summering in Fray Bentos, learned that Funes could tell time "without consulting the sky, without a second's pause" (Borges 1998a: 132). In 1887 the narrator went back to Fray Bentos and found out that "chronometric Funes" had fallen off a half-broken horse and was hopelessly paralyzed. After hearing that the narrator had started studying Latin and brought a few books with him, Funes wrote him a note reminding him of their "'lamentably ephemeral' meeting 'on the seventh of February, 1884'," and begged to borrow one of the books, along with a dictionary, "for a full understanding of the text," since he "must plead ignorance of Latin" (ibid.: 133). The narrator sent him the dictionary, accompanied by a couple of books, among them, "an odd-numbered volume of Pliny's *Naturalis historia*," from the first century CE, a text which "exceeded (and still exceeds) [the narrator's] modest abilities as a Latinist" (ibid.). Not long after that, the narrator received the news that his father was not well. While packing his bag to return home, he realized he did not have some of his books and decided to walk over to Funes's to collect them. When he entered the young man's dark room, the narrator could hear Funes recite a memorized text in Latin, which, as he learned later, was the first paragraph of the twenty-fourth chapter of the seventh book of Pliny's *Naturalis historia*. Funes was then only nineteen and died two years later of a pulmonary congestion.

Borges's story can be read as a creative translation into fiction of some of Nietzsche's key concepts, particularly on language, as well as a perceptive, touching, and somewhat irreverent commentary on the philosopher's thought in the context of a small Uruguayan town in the beginning of the twentieth century (for other readings exploring possible connections between Nietzsche's thought and Borges's "Funes," see Kreimer 2000; Martin 2006; and Bell 2007). Just as Nietzsche's protagonist in *Thus Spoke Zarathustra* (Nietzsche 2006, trans. Del Caro), originally published between 1883 and 1891, is a translation of Zarathustra, the ancient Iranian prophet who may have lived around 600 BCE, Borges's Funes can be viewed as an appropriation of the German philosopher's character, the same character in which Nietzsche sees a reflection of himself and his dearest theses. In *Ecce Homo*, Nietzsche's last book, written in 1888, the philosopher elaborates on his personal investment in the construction of his character: since Zarathustra was the first "to see in the struggle of good and evil the true driving-wheel in the machinery of things," and since "the translation of morality into the metaphysical, as strength, cause, goal in itself, [was] *his* doing, [Zarathustra also had to be] the first to *acknowledge* the mistake" (Nietzsche 2009: 89, trans. Large). Nietzsche's Zarathustra represents, therefore, "the self-overcoming of morality out of truthfulness, the self-overcoming of the moralist into his opposite," that is, into Nietzsche himself, and this is exactly "what the name of Zarathustra means in [Nietzsche's] mouth" (ibid.: 90).

Motivated by Borges's reference to Funes as a Uruguyan Zarathustra, readers familiar with Nietzsche's text will likely find in the story echoes of the latter's character and, even, of the original prophet. For example, before his accident, as a remote, Latin American version of the original Zarathustra, whose name in old Avestan could probably have meant "he who can manage camels" (Pearson 2005: 86), Funes used to break horses or drive oxcarts for a living (Borges 1998a: 132). At the same time, as a passionate, nationalist version of Nietzsche's Zarathustra, Funes reflected and was completely focused on his immediate environment: with his "Indian features," his *mate* cup, his "baggy trousers [… and] straw-soled slippers" (ibid.: 131–132), he was appropriately immersed in a typically Uruguayan context that could also be associated with the Nietzschean prophet's ideal of a purely human world devoid of metaphysics. Like his German counterpart, Funes was known for "certain eccentricities, among them shying away from people" (ibid.: 132). In fact, the first time the narrator met Funes, the young Uruguayan was running along an elevated sidewalk that placed him on a higher plane, reminiscent of Zarathustra who, after living as a recluse for ten years, descends from the mountain, in the opening section of *Thus Spoke Zarathustra*, to bring the people the gift of his teachings about the "overman" (often also referred to in English as the "superman") (Nietzsche 2006: 3–4). Significantly, it was from this higher position, which could, of course, also be interpreted figuratively, that Funes talked to the narrator and his cousin, Bernardo, and showed them his gift: "Unexpectedly, Bernardo shouted out to him – '*What's the time, Ireneo?*' Without consulting the sky, without a second's pause, the boy replied: 'Four minutes till eight, young Bernardo Juan Francisco'" (Borges 1998a: 132). Thus, the bastard son of a poor ironing woman showed the two well-to-do cousins not only that he was acutely aware of the passing of time, but, also, that he was able to measure it relying solely on his own resources, without any help from what might be above or beyond him, and in a manner that was almost super human.

As a "precursor of the race of supermen" (ibid.: 131) and, hence, in harmony with Zarathustra's teachings, Funes was completely focused on earthly matters or, as Nietzsche's prophet might put it, truly "faithful to the earth" (Nietzsche 2006: 6), that is, immune to the allure of metaphysics and promises of transcendental objects and values. As Zarathustra teaches his disciples, the passing of time is an exemplary reminder of the inevitability of change and continuous flow of becoming that constitutes humans and everything else around them. However, as he recognizes, coming to terms with this constant movement of change and difference and what it implies is not easy to process. In Zarathustra's speech entitled "On the Blessed Isles," for example, "conjecturing" about God and the idea of eternal values and, consequently, on whether "all that is not everlasting" could be merely a lie, is something difficult for us to digest: "to think this causes whirling and dizziness to human bones and even vomiting to the stomach" (ibid.: 66). As Zarathustra points out, "all this teaching of the one and the plenum and the unmoved and the sated and the everlasting," which characterizes metaphysics and is often found in poetry, is "merely a parable" and, in order to counteract this, one should learn more about time through "the best parables," that is, through those that "speak about time and becoming" and praise and justify "all that is not everlasting" (ibid.). Returning to Funes, we may view his initial gift to Borges's narrator – and readers – as the opportunity to acknowledge and reflect on the workings of time and the provisional character of everything, an opportunity that also mirrors the main theme of the story, which could be described, among other things, as a parable about change and the irrevocable passing of time.

As Borges's story goes on, a few years later, when the narrator returned to Fray Bentos, he learned that Funes had been "bucked off a half-broken horse," "left hopelessly crippled," and confined to a dark room in his mother's modest house in the town's periphery (Borges 1998a: 132, 133). Again, readers of Nietzsche might recall the opening of Part II of *Thus Spoke Zarathustra* when the prophet returned to the mountain and to "the solitude of his cave and withdrew from mankind, waiting like a sower who has cast his seeds" (Nietzsche 2006: 63). At the same time, though, "his soul grew full of impatience and desire for those whom he loved, because he still had much to give them" (ibid.). Similarly, as the second stage of Funes's story begins, when "chronometric Funes" is transformed into "Funes, his memory," Borges's Zarathustra has also withdrawn from social life and "never stirred from his cot, his eyes fixed on the fig tree behind the house" (Borges 1998a: 132). However, just as Nietzsche's prophet desired to see his disciples, Funes longed to see the narrator and wrote him a "flowery, sententious letter" whose style and tone seem to mockingly echo Zarathustra's, to ask if he could borrow a couple of books and a dictionary so that he could teach himself Latin (ibid.: 133). In addition, one could associate the narrator's brief description of Funes's position – "his eyes fixed on the fig tree" – with the opening lines of Zarathustra's above-mentioned speech "On the Blessed Isles," which starts with a direct comparison of the prophet's teachings to the ripe "figs that fall from the trees," and whose flesh and juice he urges his disciples to consume (Nietzsche 2006: 65). The "teaching" emphasized here involves, once again, faithfulness to earthly matters, as Zarathustra preaches to his disciples that "everything be transformed into what is humanly thinkable, humanly visible, humanly feelable" (ibid.).

What made Funes's short life so extraordinary was the astounding capacity to remember that he developed immediately after his accident. In spite of his unusual perception of time, Funes considered that, before the accident, "he had been what every man is – blind, deaf, befuddled, and virtually devoid of memory. [...] He had lived, he said, for nineteen years as though in a dream: he looked without seeing, heard without listening" (Borges 1998a: 134). After the fall, when he recovered consciousness, "the present was so rich, so clear that it was almost unbearable, as were his oldest and even his most trivial memories" (ibid.: 135). Funes was so overwhelmed by the fact that "his perception and his memory were [then] perfect" that he "reasoned (or felt) that immobility was a small price to pay" (ibid.). And yet, what seemed to be an advantage or an extraordinary gift was also a source of distress and discomfort. As "the solitary, lucid spectator of a multiform, momentaneous, and almost unbearably precise world," Funes was unable to rest or sleep: "lying on his back on his cot, in the dimness of his room, [he] could picture every crack in the wall, every molding of the precise houses that surrounded him" (Borges 1998a: 136). Unable to adequately process his relentless, nightmarish perception of a reality practically unfiltered by interpretation, Funes was immobilized in the position of an obsessive spectator restricted to repeating – to and by himself – an endless, "pointless mental catalog of all the images of his memory" (ibid.: 135).

We may find a likely explanation for Funes's predicament in the first aphorism from "'Guilt', 'Bad Conscience' and Related Matters," in *On the Genealogy of Morality*, which begins by defining the human animal as the one "with the prerogative to promise," a prerogative that indicates that to be human is to be aware of the passing of time, to distinguish the present from the past and, consequently, "to be able to calculate, compute," skills that require that "man himself will really have to become *reliable, regular, necessary*, even in his own self-image, so that he, as someone making a promise is, is answerable for his own *future!*" (Nietzsche 2007: 36). Moreover, this human capacity to remember and to deal with time is directly dependent on its "opposing force, *forgetfulness*," which is not just a *vis inertiae*, but, rather, "an active ability to suppress," which Nietzsche compares to the process of digestion: it is to our ability to forget that "we owe the fact that what we simply live through, experience, take in, [...] enters our consciousness during digestion (one could call it spiritual ingestion) [much like] the thousand-fold process which takes place with our physical consumption of food, our so-called ingestion" (ibid.: 35). As the philosopher concludes, "there could be no happiness, cheerfulness, hope, pride, *immediacy*, without forgetfulness." In fact, the person "in whom this apparatus of suppression is damaged" can be compared "to a dyspeptic," that is, someone who, literally, suffers from dyspepsia ("difficulty in digesting food," "indigestion") or, figuratively, "ill humor," "disgruntle-ment" (*Merriam-Webster Dictionary*). Or, still, as Nietzsche sums it up, a dyspeptic is someone who "cannot cope with anything" (Nietzsche 2007: 35).

It was Funes's incapacity to digest reality that brought him an acute, disturbing awareness of the arbitrary nature of language and its inability to adequately represent what seems to be actually present. Such awareness prevented him from accepting the illusions that make it possible for words to appear meaningful and, consequently, for language to work. In this aspect, Borges's characterization of Funes seems to channel Nietzsche's conclusion in "On Truth and Lies in a Nonmoral Sense," according to which we "can only live with any repose, security, and consistency" provided that we manage to forget that "every concept arises from the equation of unequal things" (Nietzsche 1999: 83) and to deceive ourselves into believing that there are indeed stable objects to which we can refer as "*this* sun, *this* window, [or] *this* table" (ibid.: 85). As for Funes, he found it painfully difficult to deal with the limitations of a language that blatantly equates what is obviously unequal and owes its foundation to arbitrariness and conventionality. For instance, it was difficult for him to see that "the generic symbol 'dog' took in all the dissimilar individuals of all shapes and sizes" and it irritated him that "the 'dog' of three-fourteen in the afternoon, seen in profile, should be indicated by the same noun as the dog of three-fifteen, seen frontally" (Borges 1998a: 136). Borges's example of the "dog" could illustrate Nietzsche's basic argument about difference and the arbitrariness of language and remind readers of the philosopher's example of the "leaf" in "On Truth and Lies," commented on above. However, since it seems to bring a new twist to the philosopher's examples, Funes's irritation at a language that fails to be the faithful representation of an ever-changing reality does not simply mirror Nietzsche's reasoning. As Borges's text suggests, in order to trust and to be able to use language, we are not merely required to accept the illusion of stability brought about by the erasure of differences involving so many different "things" that we have accepted to call "dogs"; rather, we must also learn to ignore our personal memories associated with any particular "dog." Hence, in order for language to work, we need to ignore the diversity involved in the psychologically motivated elements associated with the ways in which we view and process concepts. As Borges's narrator explains, in a fragment that can be read almost as a supplement to Nietzsche's example of the "leaf" mentioned above, "[t]he truth was, Funes remembered not only every leaf of every tree in every patch of forest, *but every time he had perceived or imagined that leaf*" (Borges 1998a: 136; emphasis added). Similarly, just as it was impossible for Funes to forget anything and, thus, just as it was difficult for him to accept that the word "dog" could refer to so many different individuals, his "own face in the mirror, his own hands, surprised him every time he saw them" (ibid.), a statement that can also be related to another text by Nietzsche. In "The Uses and Disadvantages of History for Life," first published in 1874 and collected in *Untimely Meditations*, the philosopher argues that a man unable to forget would lose himself in "the stream of becoming: such a man would no longer believe in his own being, would no longer believe in himself, would see everything flowing asunder in moving points" (Nietzsche 1997: 62, trans. Hollingdale).

In order to placate his frustration, Funes contemplated the creation of a language that could be less ambiguous or less arbitrary, at least for himself, a project that Borges's narrator compares to that of John Locke, the English philosopher who, in the seventeenth century, "postulated (and condemned) an impossible language in which each individual thing – every stone, every bird, every branch – would have its own name" (Borges 1998a: 136). Funes, however, soon discarded the idea because it was "too general, too ambiguous" (ibid.). Another project discarded by Funes involved the invention of a new numeral system for which he would use apparently unconnected words instead of numbers as we know them. As the narrator suggests, Funes's project was originally motivated by "his irritation that the thirty-three Uruguayan patriots should require two figures and three words rather than a single figure, a single word," and it was this "mad principle" that he then applied to the other numbers: "Instead of seven thousand thirteen (7013), he would say, for instance, 'Máximo Pérez'; instead of seven thousand fourteen (7014), 'the railroad'; other numbers were 'Luis Melián Lafinur', 'Olimar', 'sulfur', 'clubs', 'the whale', 'gas', 'a stewpot', 'Napoleon', 'Agustín de Vedia'" (ibid.: 135–136). These projects seem to have brought Funes the fleeting illusion that by creating a new language and a new numeral system, that is, by creating and establishing new conventions, he would manage to elude arbitrariness. The thirty-three patriots that inspired his "mad principle" is a direct reference to the revolutionary group that was responsible for the foundation of Uruguay as a modern state in the 1820s, a reference that could also be related to Funes's inclusion of Napoleon, whose occupation of Spain at the beginning of the nineteenth century ultimately contributed to the independence of Uruguay. Similarly, all the other references could be associated with Funes's immediate surroundings such as the "railroad" or the "stewpot" and, also, "Olimar," which refers to both the river and the village located in Uruguay's department of Treinta y Tres, named in honor of the thirty-three patriots mentioned above. The other references not only give us a glimpse of Funes's strong nationalism and favorite heroes but also function as mirrors of himself as the author of failed projects: Máximo Pérez; Luis Melián Lafinur, who was Borges's uncle; and Agustín de Vedia, all of whom participated in unsuccessful attempts against the institutionalized power in Uruguay in the second half of the nineteenth century.

While we read "Funes" as a creative domestication of Nietzsche's philosophy we could also associate the Uruguayan's desire to shape conventions and his immediate reality with the philosopher's notion of the will to power, particularly as it is conceived as one of Zarathustra's most important lessons to those interested in the path leading to the overman. In the speech "On a Thousand and One Goals" Zarathustra asserts his argument that the creation of language and truths has been necessary for "human survival and preservation," elaborating on how it is inextricably connected with "esteeming," that is, with placing a value into one's creations: what one people esteems "hangs over" them as "a tablet of the good," and this "tablet of their overcomings [...] is the voice of their will to power," a voice that not only defines humans as such, but that also preserves their identity and marks their difference from one another (Nietzsche 2006: 42–43). In another speech, "On Self-Overcoming," Zarathustra explains that the very possibility of thinking involves the will to make all there is reflect the interests of the one who is doing the thinking, a claim that ultimately equates the will to power to the very will to live (ibid.: 89). Since the will to power, as "the essence of life," is the drive behind the construction and the imposition of what is regarded as true and valuable, and since truths and values are ultimately made up of language, the will to power can also be another name not just for writing, but, also, for interpretation, an activity that necessarily involves violence as it must always reshape what is being interpreted: "You do violence with your values and words of good and evil, you valuators; and this is your hidden love and the gleaming, trembling and flowing-over of your souls" (ibid.: 90).

In the end, one of the lessons that Borges's narrator learns from his Zarathustra can also be directly associated with Nietzsche's conclusions about memory, language, the inevitability of interpretation, and, thus, the impossibility of perfect repetitions. When the narrator visited Funes to pick up his books, and as he approached the latter's room, he heard his voice "speaking Latin" (Borges 1998a: 134). "With morbid pleasure," Funes's "mocking" voice was reciting what the narrator later learned to be "the first paragraph of the twenty-fourth chapter of the seventh book of Pliny's *Naturalis historia*, a chapter whose subject was memory, and which ended with the following words: '*Ut nihil non iisdem verbis redderetur auditum*'" (ibid.). Such a statement, which can be translated into English as "Nothing that has been heard can be retold in the same words," might very well synthesize one of the story's most fundamental lessons, a lesson that the paralyzed Funes could not really apprehend even though he had memorized Pliny's words and his voice was repeating them. On the other hand, as I will claim below, it is Borges's narrator who has surely learned this lesson as he has managed to transform the Uruguayan Zarathustra into a text. Furthermore, as Borges seems to appropriate Nietzsche's philosophy "without superstition," he expands and reframes it in another context, creating a story that is a superb lesson on the mechanisms of language as the material with which our will to power constructs and establishes meaning by provisionally domesticating difference. His paralyzed, dyspeptic Funes, who died prematurely of pulmonary congestion, shows us that without our ability to digest, transform, and to actively engage with what comes from outside, there is no production, no movement, or possibility of growth in any meaningful way. By creating a character that is both European and Latin American, both a hero and an anti-hero, as well as a text that is both – or between – fiction and philosophy, Borges irreverently undermines all these established hierarchies and, in the process, creates a remarkable story that, among other things, both translates and enriches key philosophical concepts also presented in Nietzsche's work.

The exemplarity of Borges's fiction as theory: "Funes" and "Pierre Menard"

As it scrutinizes lesser explored aspects directly associated with processes of meaning construction, Borges's fiction shows a unique capacity to translate philosophical questions into ingenious plots that serve as superb illustrations, many years later, of Jacques Derrida's defense of literature as a privileged site for the kind of thinking usually associated with philosophy. As Derrida's position has been summarized, "the thinking that takes place in philosophy" cannot be simply "confined to technical philosophy, or to the canonical history of philosophy, even if that is the place one starts" (Caputo 1997: 57–58). Rather, it can also be found "in many other places, in law, linguistics, and psychoanalysis. Above all, the thinking that occurs in philosophy communicates in a very special way for Derrida himself with literature" (ibid: 58). As "an institution which tends to overflow the institution," offering us the "unlimited right of writing and reading, the right to defy laws of prohibition, to engender fictions against the prevailing sense of reality" (ibid.), literature can be potentially richer and more daring than other discourses. Since it brings us plots with multiple voices representing multiple points of view, often in conflict or competition, literary fiction can take readers beyond the limits of what is conventionally called theory or philosophy and allows them to venture into less explored areas such as the more personal relationships involving the various agents engaged in the construction of meaning that produces writing, reading, interpreting, and translating.

While Borges's thought on language and translation is well represented in the essays discussed earlier, it is in his stories that we are likely to find an even more seasoned, more nuanced elaboration of his ideas as they are played out by his different characters and plots. If we probe, for example, the relationship that is established between Borges's narrator as an authorial figure and his protagonist in "Funes," we could get some insights into the subtle competitiveness that seems to underlie the relationships that produce texts and interpretation and that can also be associated with the will to power, arguably one of the key themes explored in the story. Even though Funes is described as a "precursor of the race of the supermen," it is in fact Borges's narrator who seems to be closer to the teachings of Nietzsche's Zarathustra, the prophet who defines himself as "a prelude to better players" (Nietzsche 2006: 168). In order to better understand the dynamics that underscore the narrator's relationship with Funes, I propose to examine it from the perspective of Zarathustra's "On the Three Metamorphoses," the first speech in Part I, in which Nietzsche's prophet elaborates on "how the spirit becomes a camel, and the camel a lion, and finally the lion a child," the child being the closest to the overman (ibid.: 16). In this light, chronometric Funes, that is, the apparently reverent young man we initially encounter in the story known for breaking horses and who can, thus, be reminiscent of Zoroaster ("he who can manage camels"), might very well be associated with the spirit as camel: "To the spirit there is much that is heavy; to the strong, carrying spirit imbued with reverence. Its strength demands what is heavy and heaviest. [...] It kneels down like a camel and wants to be well loaded" (ibid.). For Zarathustra, the heavy burdens endured by the spirit as camel seem to reveal an overall lack of wisdom or inability to effectively handle the challenges of life, an inability that is reflected, for instance, in our tendency to load our backs in order to "rejoice" in our strength and, also, to love "those who despise us, and [extend] a hand to the ghost when it wants to frighten us" (ibid.), traits that could be relatable to Borges's protagonist as well.

Funes's transformation after his accident, which significantly involved the young man's fall from a horse, could be associated with the camel's metamorphosis into a lion in Zarathustra's speech: when the spirit becomes lion "it wants to hunt down its freedom and be master in its own desert" (ibid.). In order to accomplish that, the lion "seeks its last master, and wants to fight him and its last god," that is, the "great dragon" that reflects and represents "the value of all created things," and whose name is "Thou shalt." However, in spite of its courage and strength, the spirit as lion is still incapable "of creating new values" (ibid.: 17). As mentioned, after his accident Funes became painfully aware of – and deeply irritated by – the arbitrariness of language and the conventions that ruled over and shaped his immediate context. However, like the lion in Zarathustra's speech, he was still unable to establish new conventions that would be reflective of his own interests and preferences. As Zarathustra explains, "[t]o create new values – not even the lion is capable of that: but to create freedom for itself for new creation – that is within the power of the lion. To create freedom for oneself and also a sacred No to duty: for that, my brothers, the lion is required" (ibid.). In Borges's story, to the spirit as lion in Zarathustra's speech we can relate, for example, the fact that, as soon as Funes acquired his prodigious memory, he could no longer be a subaltern handler of wild horses, and, also, his sudden interest in learning Latin – and, implicitly, in getting better acquainted with the general foundation that ultimately produced his language and "the values of all created things," the same values on which he would like to leave his mark. (Significantly, as mentioned above, the book that supposedly helped Funes learn Latin was the narrator's volume of Pliny's *Naturalis historia*, which is considered to be the most ambitious encyclopedia featuring the ancient world and the earliest to have survived [see Murphy 2004: 1–5].)

Besides his interest in encyclopedias and in learning Latin, Funes also seemed eager to outsmart the narrator who, like Bernardo, the narrator's cousin, represented a privileged social class and was, thus, ultimately related to the "great dragon," against whom the young Uruguayan needed to rebel. As Borges's narrator knows "with reasonable certainty," to Funes he represented a few "misfortunes" – "[*h*]*ighbrow, dandy, city slicker*" – even though the Uruguayan Zarathustra had never actually uttered "those insulting words" (Borges 1998a: 131). While Funes was unable to evolve past the lion, the narrator, on the other hand, could be related to the child, described in Zarathustra's speech as being capable of that which even the lion is not: "the child is innocence and forgetting, a new beginning, a game, a wheel rolling out of itself, a first movement, a sacred yes-saying" (Nietzsche 2006: 17). Unlike the lion, the child is able to forget the negative burden of human history and is free to be creative and exercise its will to power, revealing the strength of the human on the path to the overman. As Zarathustra says, "for the game of creation my brothers a sacred yes-saying is required. The spirit wants *its* will, the one lost to the world now wins *its own* world" (ibid.: 17). As a counterpoint to the dyspeptic Funes, Borges's narrator is capable of digesting the past and accepting the inevitability of change and knows that even though the Uruguayan has been dead for decades he can still live on, so to speak, as a product of both his memory and his absent-mindedness. Far from paralyzing him, this knowledge enables the narrator to write his own version of Funes, a version which, as he himself recognizes, is only one among many. However, even though the narrator "applaud[s] the idea" that all those "who had dealings with [Funes] should write something about him" and speculates that his own "testimony will perhaps be the briefest (and certainly the slightest) account in the volume" (Borges 1998a: 131), it is actually his version – the successful expression of his will to power – that makes it possible for Funes to live on for us, readers of Borges's story.

From the perspective opened up by my reading of "Funes" informed by Zarathustra's conception of the will to power, I propose to revisit "Pierre Menard, Author of the *Quixote*," Borges's quintessential story about translation and its most recurrent conundrums (Borges 1998b). (My comments on "Pierre Menard" have appeared in several texts: Arrojo 1986, 1993, and 2014, for example. In this book, the story also features in Chapters One and Eight.) As a story that pretends to be a scholarly piece or even an elaborate obituary, "Pierre Menard," like "Funes," destabilizes, first of all, the very distinction between commentary and fiction. As I have argued elsewhere, "Pierre Menard" practically questions every single cliché frequently associated with the translator's activity and can be read as a sophisticated, comical illustration of the perfect translator idealized by tradition who, in spite of being aware of the impossibility of his endeavor, imagines (or wishes) he could faithfully reproduce the totality of someone else's original in another language and in completely different circumstances (see Chapter One). Pierre Menard's "interminably heroic" project, which is also described as "invisible" and "subterranean" (Borges 1998b: 90), seemed to be the ultimate translation as he claimed he had miraculously repeated verbatim, in his French context of the early twentieth century, a few fragments from the original written by Cervantes at the beginning of the seventeenth. However, the cliché of the selfless translator working in the shadow with the sole purpose of reproducing someone else's text is called into question as the narrator's comparison of Menard's version to Cervantes's, both verbally identical, breaks the illusion of sameness and shows that the French translator could not have been invisible as the writer of his *Quixote* just as he could not have done away with his own place in time and context.

The similarities between Funes and Pierre Menard as characters are obvious: both are presented as extraordinary individuals who have been chosen by Borges's narrators as objects of commentaries that allegedly celebrate their exceptional skills and projects. Both are directly associated with translation and its multilayered implications: while Menard is a French translator and minor intellectual obsessed with Cervantes's *Quixote*, Funes is introduced as a Uruguayan translation of Nietzsche's Zarathustra. Both Funes and Menard are, to a certain extent, "heroes of the Same," to use the epithet with which Michel Foucault so appropriately refers to Cervantes's *Don Quixote*, whose journey was first and foremost also "a quest for similitudes" (Foucault 1973: 47, 46, trans. unnamed). Just as Funes was unable to handle the arbitrary process that matches a signifier to a signified and longed for an impossible stability of meaning, Pierre Menard hoped he could elude history and, literally, repeat Cervantes's text in twentieth-century France. Furthermore, the dead Menard, like the dead Funes, only lives on as a construction of Borges's narrator, a construction that also emphasizes the differences between the narrator and the object of his commentary. Like his counterpart in "Funes," Borges's narrator in "Pierre Menard" not only outlives his character, but also outsmarts him. In fact, the underlying competitiveness that colors the relationship between Borges's narrator in "Pierre Menard" and his protagonist seems even more obvious than the one suggested in "Funes." As mentioned, it is the narrator who, as a reader of Menard's *Quixote*, undermines the Frenchman's claim that he had indeed managed to compose a few fragments that were absolutely identical to Cervantes's original. (As I have argued in Chapter One, in addition to what it teaches us about translation and interpretation, "Pierre Menard" provides readers with an unforgettable lesson on the mechanisms of reading as an activity that clearly produces meaning: it is after all the narrator's reading of Menard's fragment that establishes its difference from Cervantes's, a reading that dares to see in the Symbolist's piece something he explicitly did not mean to write.)

With its generally mocking, pseudo-celebratory tone, instead of truly praising Menard's "achievement," as it unequivocally claims, Borges's story actually deconstructs it and ends up portraying the translator as a somewhat pathetic figure obsessed with the repetition of Cervantes's masterpiece. The kind of competitiveness that underlies the relationship between Borges's narrator and Pierre Menard is also mirrored in the relationship established between Menard, as the translator figure, and Cervantes, the exemplary author and master of fiction. From this perspective, it can be argued that even though the story apparently suggests that the translator and the author figures might be on par as both are presented as authors of the *Quixote*, actually they are not: in the end, while Menard is barely remembered as the minor French writer and translator who tried and failed to reproduce a few fragments from Cervantes's novel, Cervantes lives on as one of the greatest authors of all time thanks, at least in part, to all the Menards who have rewritten his text in many languages throughout the centuries. Assuming that one of the central themes explored in the story is the notion that translation and interpretation are activities that actually produce meaning and are, hence, not hierarchically inferior to the writing of originals, how can we account for the generally mocking treatment Menard and his subterranean project receive in Borges's plot? Should we conclude that Borges is perhaps siding with tradition by suggesting that even though the translator's invisibility is an absurd notion, the translator's contribution to the shaping of a text like *Don Quixote* could not be seriously comparable to the original author's? While it is clear that Cervantes's and Menard's legacies do not belong in the same category, we can find a more plausible explanation for the way in which the translator figure is treated in the story, an explanation that will reflect and expand some of the arguments Borges presented in his essays about translation discussed above, particularly in "The Translators of *The One Thousand and One Nights*" (Borges 1999b).

In order to begin unraveling what might define these complex relationships and how they could be related to representations of the ways in which authors and translators tend to be perceived, it will be productive to reflect on Menard's "method" to compose the *Quixote* in light of Zarathustra's "The Three Metamorphoses," the speech commented on above (Nietzsche 2006). According to Borges's narrator, Menard's initial method was meant to be "relatively simple: Learn Spanish, return to Catholicism, fight against the Moor or Turk, forget the history of Europe from 1602 to 1918 – *be Miguel de Cervantes*" (Borges 1998b: 91). Considering his reverence towards tradition, his willingness to ignore himself and his time and context, as well as his desire to fully embrace Cervantes's world, Menard, like "chronometric Funes," could be associated with the spirit as camel in Zarathustra's speech. Like Funes as "camel," Menard seemed to lack what it takes to function as an effective agent who is aware of and able to exercise his will to power and accepts being "well loaded" with values that are not necessarily his own (Nietzsche 2006: 16). As a revealing, albeit fantastic representation of a typically idealized translator, Menard considered the possibility of devoting a great deal of his time to the composition of someone else's text while remaining invisible in the process. Later on, as mentioned, he reconsidered his approach and decided to continue being Pierre Menard and come to the Quixote *through the experiences of Pierre Menard* (Borges 1998b: 91), a decision that could be related to the transformation of the camel into the lion in Zarathustra's speech. Like Funes as "lion," Menard managed to leave behind his "camel" phase and made an effort not to ignore himself. However, like Funes, Menard still believed in the possibility of exact repetitions and wished that words could actually capture and stabilize meaning, being unable to fully acknowledge his own hand in the *Quixote* fragment he allegedly produced and which the narrator compares to Cervantes's. In "Pierre Menard," as in "Funes," it is Borges's narrator who does not accept that the same can be repeated and teaches his readers about the power of interpretation to generate meaning.

On the basis of some key arguments from "The Translators of *The One Thousand and One Nights*" (Borges 1999b) highlighted above, we can further explain the apparent contradiction between what Borges's narrator seems to teach us about translation in "Pierre Menard" and his portrayal of the translator as a somewhat laughable Quixote. As Borges suggests in the essay, he does not expect to find in a translation an impossible repetition of the same, but a transformation of the original that reflects an optimum, creative expression of the "commerce" that should take place between the original (and what it represents) and the broad cultural matrix of the target language (ibid. 108). Thus, we might infer, translations should not be evaluated for their unavoidable failure to repeat the original or for what readers may allegedly lose when they do not have access to the original. Rather, what we should take into account in the evaluation of translations is precisely what they are able to bring to the original as it is reshaped in the target culture. From Borges's perspective, as translations are reconfigurations of texts in the light of another tradition and with the resources of another language, they could be potentially richer than originals. Borges's rationale is illustrated by his comment on Enno Littmann's "faithful" German version, in which he finds "nothing but the probity of Germany" and, hence, a limited, impoverished representation of what German culture could offer (ibid.). As noted, Borges follows his comment with an admission that there are "marvels in the *Nights* that [he] would like to see rethought in German" (ibid.) by a gifted writer of German – a Kafka, for example – that could handle the task of reconfiguring the *Nights* "in line" with Germanic tradition (Borges 1999b: 109).

As he reconceptualizes translation as a way of rethinking and recomposing the source text within the context of the target culture and language, Borges destabilizes the long-standing tradition that has relied on a limiting notion of fidelity as the yardstick for the evaluation of translations, triggering a complete revision of the relationships that have traditionally defined the translator's activity and separated translators from writers of originals. It is this revision that underscores the treatment given to the translators of the *Nights* in the essay as Borges praises the audacity of those who find ways to exercise their will to power in their work and are, at the same time, able to enrich and expand the original. The same break with tradition also nurtures Borges's plot in "Pierre Menard," which not only reflects but also refines some of the implications of the arguments presented in "The Translators of *The One Thousand and One Nights*." A good example of such a refinement can be found in the way "Pierre Menard" shines a light on the role of the reader and his or her will to power, something that is arguably only hinted at in the essay. While Borges's narrator in the story clearly shows that what he sees in Menard's Quixote is *not* what Menard intended him to see, in "The Translators of *The Thousand and One Nights*," the distinction between Borges, as the reader of the translations, and what the translators in question might have tried to achieve is at best blurred.

As pointed out, while the narrator in "Pierre Menard" presents Cervantes and Menard as equals, he also subtly suggests that their achievements make them anything but equals. From the perspective opened up by Borges's essay on the translators of the *Nights*, we could conclude that what Menard supposedly accomplished – that is, a few fragments from the *Quixote* that coincided with Cervantes's – was "so little, so very little," to repeat Borges's comment on Littmann's translation (Borges 1999b: 108). Arguably, in Borges's terms, if Menard's intention was to recompose Cervantes's masterpiece, we should expect from him a literary gift that would also be on par with Cervantes's, not simply a repetition of what had already been done. From this point of view, what Menard seemed to lack, as he needed to keep his project "subterranean," was perhaps the writing skills, the talent or the background, but, most importantly, the kind of audacity or boldness that Borges associates, for example, with some of the translators of the *Nights*. After all, Menard was only interested in repeating the very same text written by Cervantes and did not bring to his version anything of his own or his context, not even his language. Like the paralyzed Funes, Menard was still incapable of consciously appropriating the *Quixote* and making it his own. From this perspective, it is indeed comical that the timid translator could in any way compete with the great Cervantes. Finally, even though "Pierre Menard" reinforces Borges's views on the inescapable visibility of translations and translators, it also suggests that in order for translators to be revered or taken seriously as authors of their translations they should be able to exercise their will to power, own their authorship, and accept the responsibilities involved in their visibility.

Bibliography

Arrojo, R. (1986) *Oficina de Tradução – A Teoria na Prática*, São Paulo: Ática.
—— (1993) *Tradução, Desconstrução e Psicanálise*, Rio de Janeiro: Imago.
—— (2014) "The Power of Fiction as Theory: Some Exemplary Lessons on Translation from Borges's Stories," in K. Kaindl and K. Spitzl (eds.) *Transfiction – Research into the Realities of Translation Fiction*, Amsterdam: John Benjamins, 247–251.
Bell, M. (2007) "Nietzsche, Borges, García Marquez on the Art of Memory and Forgetting," *Romanic Review* 98(2/3): 123–134.
Borges, J. L. (1998a) "Funes, His Memory," A. Hurley (trans.) *Collected Fictions*, New York: Penguin, 131–137.

—— (1998b) "Pierre Menard, Author of the *Quixote*," A. Hurley (trans.) *Collected Fictions*, New York: Penguin, 88–95.

—— (1999a) "The Homeric Versions," E. Weinberger (ed. and trans.) *Selected Non-Fictions*, New York: Penguin, 69–74.

—— (1999b) "The Translators of *The One Thousand and One Nights*," E. Allen (trans.), E. Weinberger (ed.) *Selected Non-Fictions*, New York: Penguin, 92–109.

—— (1999c) "The Argentine Writer and Tradition," E. Allen (trans.), E. Weinberger (ed.) *Selected Non- Fictions*, New York: Penguin, 420–427.

—— (2001a) "Algunos pareceres de Nietzsche," *Textos Recobrados, 1931–1955*, vol. II, Buenos Aires: Emecé, 180–188.

—— (2001b) "Nietzsche: El propósito de Zarathustra", *Textos Recobrados, 1931–1955*. vol. II, Buenos Aires: Emecé, 211–216.

Caputo, J. D. (1997) *Deconstruction in a Nutshell – A Conversation with Jacques Derrida*, New York: Fordham University Press.

Foucault, M. (1973) *The Order of Things – An Archaeology of the Human Sciences*, trans. unnamed, New York: Vintage Books.

Kreimer, R. (2000) "Nietzsche, autor de "Funes, el memorioso," in W. Rowe, C. Canaparo, A. Louis (eds.) *Jorge Luis Borges – Intervenciones sobre pensamiento y literatura*, Buenos Aires: Paidos Iberica, 189–197.

Kristal, E. (2002) *Invisible Work – Borges and Translation*, Nashville, TN: Vanderbilt University Press.

Martin, C. (2006) "Borges Forgets Nietzsche," *Philosophy and Literature* 30: 265–276.

Merriam-Webster Dictionary. Available at: www.merriam-webster.com/dictionary/dyspepsia (accessed November 25, 2015).

Murphy, T. (2004) *Pliny the Elder's Natural History: The Empire in the Encyclopedia*, Oxford: Oxford University Press.

Nietzsche, F. (1997) *Untimely Meditations*, R. J. Hollingdale (trans.), D. Breazeale (ed.), Cambridge: Cambridge University Press.

—— (1999) "On Truth and Lies in a Nonmoral Sense," D. Breazeale (trans. and ed.) *Philosophy and Truth – Selections from Nietzsche's Notebooks of the Early 1870s*, New York: Humanity Books, 79–97.

—— (2006) *Thus Spoke Zarathustra – A Book for All and None*, A. Del Caro (trans.), A. Del Caro and R. Pippin (eds.), Cambridge: Cambridge University Press.

—— (2007) *On the Genealogy of Morality*, C. Diethe (trans.), K. Ansell-Pearson (ed.), Cambridge: Cambridge University Press.

—— (2009) *Ecce Homo – How to Become What You Are*, D. Large (trans. and ed.), Oxford: Oxford University Press.

Pearson, K. A. (2005) *How to Read Nietzsche*, New York: W. W. Norton & Company.

Waisman, S. (2005) *Borges and Translation – The Irreverence of the Periphery*. Lewisburg, PA: Bucknell.

5 Texts as private retreats

Franz Kafka's "The Burrow," Jorge Luis Borges's "Death and the Compass," and Deszö Kosztolányi's "Gallus"

"Will to truth" you call that which drives you and makes you lustful, you wisest ones?

Will to thinkability of all being, that's what *I* call your will!

You first want to make all being thinkable, because you doubt, with proper suspicion, whether it is even thinkable.

But for you it shall behave and bend! Thus your will wants it. It shall become smooth and subservient to the spirit, as its mirror and reflection.

That is your entire will, you wisest ones, as a will to power; and even when you speak of good and evil and of valuations.

You still want to create the world before which you could kneel: this is your ultimate hope and intoxication.

Friedrich Nietzsche, "On Self-Overcoming,"
Thus Spoke Zarathustra, trans. Adrian Del Caro

From the perspective of psychoanalysis, the writing of fiction and the desire to master reality are inextricably intertwined. According to Freud, as the creative writer "creates a world of fantasy which he takes very seriously – that is, which he invests with large amounts of emotion," his primary goal is "to rearrange the things of his world in a new way which pleases him" (Freud 1983: 25, trans. Strachey). This relationship that fiction writers establish with their work is comparable to the one that children establish with their play or games: like creative writers children at play create a world of their own, "rearrang[ing] the things of [their] world in a new way which pleases [them]" (ibid.). Similarly, creative writing and daydreaming have a lot in common: if "imaginative writers" are comparable to "dreamers in broad daylight," and if their creations are equated with daydreams over which they feel they can have complete control, what writers ultimately seek is a feeling of "invulnerability," which reveals "His Majesty the Ego, the hero alike of every daydream and of every story" (Freud 1983: 25–26).

In Nietzsche's philosophy the link between creation and the desire to master reality plays a much more encompassing role, reaching far beyond the limits of fiction writing with the concept of the "will to power," a general theory of human agency that names what we often identify as the will to truth or even the will to life (Nietzsche 2006: 90, trans. Del Caro). In fact, if we accept that language is fundamentally rhetorical and, as a consequence, unable to carry or reveal essences or intrinsic meanings, we will likely conclude that all the knowledge we produce is basically also a form of fiction writing. Since "between two absolutely different spheres, as between subject and object, there is no causality, no correctness, and no expression," but, at most, "an *aesthetic* relation," we are all "*artistically creating subjects*" (Nietzsche 1999: 86, trans. Breazeale). If there are no essences or forever stable truths to be discovered, our views about what we claim to know are not merely a reflection of our alleged discoveries, but constructions that we manage to impose on everything that constitutes our world, including our own identities. As the fragment from Nietzsche's *Thus Spoke Zarathustra*, reproduced above, suggests, the wish to make "all being thinkable," that is, the simple wish to actually understand or make sense of anything, which we would typically associate with the desire to find what is true and real, is in fact an expression of the will to power – the will to create that "before which [we] could kneel" and recognize as meaningful (Nietzsche 2006: 88).

The main focus of this chapter will be three pieces – Kafka's "The Burrow" (Kafka 1971, trans. Muir), a story first published posthumously in Germany in 1931; Borges's "Death and the Compass" (Borges 1998, trans. Hurley), originally published in Argentina in 1942; and the story of "Gallus," a translator character featured in Chapter XIV of Kosztolányi's *Kornél Esti* (Kosztolányi 2011, trans. Adams), which first appeared in Hungary in 1933. In light of Freud's views on creative writing, my readings of these texts will reflect on the affirmation of power represented by the unusual author and/ or narrator figures they bring us – a burrowing animal, an obstinate assassin, and a narrator that protects the interests of a second-rate English thriller writer – as well as the measures that such characters devise in order to neutralize the invasive, potentially destructive thrust of interpretation. When read together, these pieces illuminate and further enrich one another, offering readers a unique opportunity to reflect on the power struggles for the control to establish meaning taking place in the behind-the-scenes of textual practices such as reading, writing, and translating, struggles that will be directly associated with Nietzsche's concept of the will to power, particularly as it is implicated with a broad understanding of notions of textuality and interpretation.

The will to power as interpretation and construction

The conception of language sketched in Nietzsche's early essay "On Truth and Lies in a Nonmoral Sense" (Nietzsche 1999) could be summarized in the following terms: to the extent that language is arbitrary and conventional and, thus, a human creation, its role in the general economy of things is far more important than tradition would have it. Since there is no intrinsic, natural bond uniting words to things, language will never be a mere vehicle for the expression or representation of supposedly pre-existing meanings and truths that could be simply described, communicated, or circulated. Rather than offer us some form of access to the alleged "thing in itself," or that which could be "the pure truth," language actually works as an instrument with which humans try to establish what is accepted as true and real (Nietzsche 1999: 82). As Zarathustra declares in "On a Thousand and One Goals," "[i]ndeed, humans gave themselves all of their good and evil. Indeed, they did not take it, they did not find it, it did not fall to them as a voice from heaven" (Nietzsche 2006: 43). Furthermore, according to the philosopher, the creation of language is inextricably associated with our need "to exist socially and with the herd" (Nietzsche 1999: 81). This inclination towards gregariousness, which has had a direct impact on our survival as a species, makes possible a kind of "peace treaty" that temporarily curbs our tendency to "maintain [ourselves] against other individuals" and brings as a consequence the establishment of that "which shall count as 'truth', [that] is to say, a uniformly valid and binding designation is invented for things, and this legislation of language likewise establishes the first laws of truth" (ibid.: 80). These made-up "designations," whose ultimate origin were mere sensations, do not reveal or express anything essential or inherent about the objects to which they are supposed to refer, and are, rather, nothing but metaphors that can only register "the relations of things to men" (ibid.: 82). Instead of a stable, indisputable truth, or some form of literal meaning that could exist before or beyond language, what we find at the origin, or at the point where we imagine that a word could be allegedly united with a thing, is always already a metaphor, that is, something that may be taken to be the representation of an extralinguistic meaning or truth, but which is in fact, and from the very beginning, simply a fiction, an illusion. As Nietzsche's often quoted definition goes, "truth" is "a movable host of metaphors, metonymies, and anthropomorphisms: in short, a sum of human relations which have been poetically and rhetorically intensified, transferred, and embellished, and which, after long usage, seem to a people to be fixed, canonical, and binding" (ibid.: 84). Consequently, as "metaphors that have become worn out and have been drained of sensuous force," truths can be compared to coins that "have lost their embossing and are now considered as metal" (ibid.).

An important implication of Nietzsche's negation of any metaphysical status for truth is the belief that "the drive toward the formation of metaphors" – an early formulation for that which would later on be referred to as the will to power – not only defines us as humans, that is, as artistically minded beings who are the actual constructors of all we know and revere, but also gives us the organizing principles that make our lives and our survival possible. In order to nurture this essentially human, fundamental illusion that we can possess truth, or the "essence of things" (Nietzsche

1999: 82), we must forget that "the original perceptual metaphors are metaphors and [take] them to be things themselves":

> Only by forgetting this primitive world of metaphor can one live with any repose, security, and consistency: only by means of the petrification and coagulation of a mass of images which originally streamed from the primal faculty of human imagination like a fiery liquid, only in the invincible faith that *this* sun, *this* window, *this* table is a truth in itself, in short, only by forgetting that he himself is an *artistically creating* subject, does man live with any repose, security, and consistency.
>
> (Ibid.: 86)

Forgetfulness also plays a key role in the process of erasing differences that allows us to make language work, giving us the illusion that we are all talking about the same things when we refer "to *this* sun, *this* window, [or] *this* table." As Nietzsche argues, "every concept arises from the equation of unequal things": a word can only become a concept "precisely insofar as it is not supposed to serve as a reminder of the unique and entirely individual original experience to which it owes its origin," and is, therefore, able to fit "countless more or less similar cases – which means purely and simply, cases which are never equal and thus altogether unequal" (Nietzsche 1999: 83). It is only because we are generally unaware of this process that we manage to transform sensations and impressions into "less colorful, cooler concepts, so that [we] can entrust the guidance of [our] life and conduct to them" (ibid.: 84) (for a detailed commentary on Nietzsche's views on the role of forgetfulness in the workings of language, see Chapter Four).

Nietzsche's radical critique of the Platonic foundation of Western thought and its general conception of language as representation is intimately implicated with the kind of reflection that was developed almost a century later, and which has been associated with postmodernism and other trends in contemporary thought that basically share a non-essentialist perspective – poststructuralism, deconstruction, American neopragmatism, postcolonial studies, gender studies, among others. The common thread that brings such trends together is their exploration of the connection between language and the shaping of truths, an exploration that is deeply indebted to Nietzsche, widely recognized as one of the founding figures associated with the intellectual debate on issues of language and power that has ensued in the second half of the twentieth century and still informs contemporary thought and, therefore, important developments in translation studies as well. At least twenty years before Ferdinand de Saussure's conclusions on the arbitrary and conventional character of language, Nietzsche had not only theorized it but "had already taken the more radical step" of viewing everything that we seem to know, including ourselves, as a form of language, claiming that "nothing in the world has any intrinsic features of its own and that each thing is constituted solely through its interrelations with, and differences from, everything else" (Nehamas 1996: 82) (for a thorough reflection on the impact of Nietzsche's thought for poststructuralists such as Michel Foucault, Jacques Derrida, and Gilles Deleuze, see Schrift 1995: 77–119).

One of the most revealing paths to Nietzsche's groundbreaking reflection about the impact of language on the shaping of all that makes sense to us is the complex network of arguments he developed in association with his recurrent, and at times elusive, concept of the will to power, an incipient version of which, as mentioned, may already be found in "On Truth and Lies in a Nonmoral Sense" (Nietzsche 1999). If, as Nietzsche suggests, truths are necessarily and "thoroughly anthropomorphic," and do not contain any "single point which would be 'true in itself' or really and universally valid apart from man" (ibid.: 85), what the seeker of truth is actually "seeking [is] only the metamorphosis of the world into man," and, as he "strives to understand the world as something analogous to man, [what] at best he achieves by his struggles [is] the feeling of assimilation" (ibid.: 88). In Zarathustra's "On a Thousand and One Goals," Nietzsche reaffirms the argument that the creation of language and truths was necessary for human survival and preservation: humans "first placed values into things, in order to preserve themselves – they first created meaning for things, a human meaning!" (Nietzsche 2006: 43). As Zarathustra proclaims, "esteeming," or "placing values into things," which are synonymous with "creating," is what characterizes humans: "Esteeming is creating: hear me, you creators! Esteeming itself is the treasure and jewel of all esteemed things" (ibid.). What one people esteems "hangs over" them as "a tablet of the good," and this "tablet of their overcomings [...] is the voice of their will to power" (Nietzsche 2006: 42), giving them some sense of identity and distinguishing them from their neighbors. However, this constructed sense of identity also involves conflict and violence:

> Much that was called good by this people was called scorn and disgrace by another: thus I found. Much I found that was called evil here and decked in purple honors there. Never did one neighbor understand the other: always his soul was amazed at his neighbor's delusion and malice.
> (Ibid.)

At the same time, because our creations are forms of "esteeming" and do not carry intrinsic meanings that could be perfectly recoverable, any "change of creators," as Zarathustra states, involves a "change of values," and, therefore, "whoever must be a creator always annihilates" (ibid.).

The will to power has also been understood as the will to construct, an understanding that can be related to the fact that in Nietzsche's German the "will to power" is "der Wille zur Macht," in which "Macht" is related to "machen," "to make" (Strong 1975: 234). In fragment 521 collected in *The Will to Power* (Nietzsche 1968, trans. Kaufmann and Hollingdale),

Nietzsche writes about our "compulsion to construct the world of concepts, species, forms, purposes, [and] laws" that helps define us and organize our lives. It does not enable us "to fix the real world," but arranges "a world for ourselves in which our existence is made possible [, ...] a world which is calculable, simplified, comprehensible, etc.," a world that we can "esteem" and view as our own shelter from chaos and the unknown (Nietzsche 1968: 283). As Nietzsche synthesizes his argument, "the world seems logical to us because we have made it logical" (ibid.). Indeed, all human constructions are the necessary outcome of the will to power, a conclusion that is compatible with the general implications of Nietzsche's recurrent architectural metaphors – the beehive, the Tower of Babel, the medieval fortress, the Egyptian pyramid, the Roman columbarium, the spider's web, the dungeon, and the stronghold, among others (cf. Kofman 1993: 61–73). As they depict conceptual systems as types of construction, these metaphors are efficient in representing the will to power as the will to master and circumscribe reality while emphasizing both the fragility and the power struggles at stake behind the various models of knowledge that human beings have elaborated under the name of truth or science. Just as the production of meaning and knowledge can be conceived as a form of construction, architecture is, for Nietzsche, "the first art because it directly manifests the will to power" (Lahiji 2014: 4). As he elaborates, the will to power manifests itself in buildings, which represent "victory over gravity" (Nietzsche 2005: 197, trans. Norman). Following this rationale, architecture can be defined as "a way for power to achieve eloquence through form, sometimes persuading, even coaxing, at other times just commanding" (ibid.).

Considering that, for Nietzsche, language shapes meaning, there can be no clear-cut distinction between creation and interpretation. Just as the will to power constructs meaning, it is also that which interprets it, interpretation being understood here as "a means of becoming master of something": the "will to power interprets [... ;] it defines limits, determines degrees, variations of power" (Nietzsche 1968, fragment 643: 342). Hence, interpretation does not reproduce or explain meaning, but, rather, "introduces" it (ibid.: fragment 604: 327). Just as every creative endeavor is also a reinterpretation of previous material, every interpretation recreates the object that it proposes to interpret. As a consequence, both creation and interpretation are always forms of reinterpretation, which, as Alexander Nehamas puts it, is "anything but a compromise": "Since the institutions that guide our lives are the products of older interpretations, associated with different conditions and embodying other values, reinterpretation is the greatest means for change, for establishing new conditions and creating new values" (Nehamas 1996: 98). Thus, for Nietzsche, a "thing is not a subject that has effects but simply a collection of interrelated effects, selected from some particular point of view from within a much larger similar set" (ibid.: 92). A "thing" is, then, "a locus of the will to power, a focus of activity within a broader realm established through the very same activity on the part of some interpreter. It cannot remain unchanged as its effects multiply and enter into new interrelations or as other sets of effects undergo such changes".

(Ibid.)

The far-reaching consequences of this kind of reasoning for a general reflection on language and the subject have been often discussed, particularly in the last three or four decades, in connection with notions of textuality associated with post-Nietzschean thought. In fact, the significance of Nietzsche's philosophy for contemporary theory seems to be basically related to his textualization of all there is, a connection that implies a radical redefinition of our relationships with reality, with each other, and even with ourselves, to the point where nothing or nobody could claim to be outside the domain of interpretation. However, this vision of reality and even the subject as texts that can only be understood through a process of interpretation does not by any means entail the possibility of establishing fixed objects. Rather, it implies that, precisely as objects, they are the inevitable result of a comprehensive, incessant process of rewriting that is forever reconstructing them in difference. Therefore, Nietzsche's notion of textuality points to the conclusion that there is no text in itself apart from the activity of interpretation. Because we cannot separate the text from its reading, the latter is inextricably related to the will to power as that which takes over and cannot protect or merely reproduce someone else's meaning (see also Schrift 1990: 194–196).

Kafka's tormented architect of the labyrinth/text

Among the architectural metaphors to be found in Nietzsche's work, the one that relates the labyrinth to textuality and interpretation is notably effective in suggesting the perpetual proliferation of meaning that constitutes us and all that we claim to know in the world as text. As has been observed, the labyrinth is both "a basic Nietzschean image for the structure of the text" and "an allegory of his conception of textual interpretation" (Schrift 1990: 196), in which "text" and "textual interpretation" are identified with Nietzsche's basic notion of "becoming," or "the affirmation of becoming" (Deleuze 2006: 188, trans. Tomlinson), rather than the stability that could be associated with a permanent, pre-existing Ariadne's thread to which we could safely resort. In *Ecce Homo*, for example, Nietzsche refers to *Thus Spoke Zarathustra* as a "labyrinth of fearless knowledge," whose "perfect reader" should be "a monster of courage and curiosity, [...] cunning, cautious, a born adventurer and discoverer" (Nietzsche 2007: 40, trans. Large), that is, someone who is not passively looking for the text's or its author's hidden message, but ready to take on the challenge of exercising his or her own will to master the labyrinth. In order to further explore the metaphor of the labyrinth, especially in connection with the relationships that are usually established between writing and interpreting as expressions of the will to power, I invite the reader to join me on a visit to "The Burrow," a haunting, unfinished story by Kafka (Kafka 1971). Originally entitled "Der Bau" ("The Construction"), the story will be read as a poignant meditation on some of the consequences associated with conceptions of language and text that can be associated with Nietzsche's thought, with emphasis on the creator's desire to build an artifact that could be protected from difference as represented, for instance, by the potentially shattering interference of an intruder.

As the story opens, we learn from its narrator/builder, presumably an animal that lives underground, that he has "completed the construction of [his] burrow and it seems to be successful" (ibid.: 325). What follows, however, is a detailed, agonizing account of the builder's own recurring doubts regarding the actual completion of his work and his painful obsession to create a totally flawless structure, an object that could be absolutely protected from invasion and deconstruction. The basic paradox within which Kafka's narrator finds himself is thus presented from the outset: the allegedly finished construction that should shelter and protect its architect is also a hole, a burrow. Instead of success and joy, it brings failure and frustration; instead of a definite solution, it brings an indecipherable problem; instead of illumination, it brings darkness; instead of security, it brings fear and anxiety. In brief, "the construction is already a deconstruction to the same extent that it has been constructed" (Sussman 1979: 149). The burrow, like a text, has "passages" that have to be constantly reviewed because of the "manifold possibilities" of their uncontrollable "ramifications" (Kafka 1971: 329): "I begin with the second passage, but break off in the middle and turn into the third passage and let it take me back again to the Castle Keep, and now of course, I have to begin at the second passage once more" (ibid.: 342). The hard work involved in his unending task does not bother the builder who endows his construction with the utmost value even to the point that he can barely distinguish himself from what he is obsessively building: "It is for your sake, ye passages and rooms, and you, Castle Keep, above all, that I have come back, counting my own life as nothing in the balance. [...] What do I care for danger now that I am with you? You belong to me, I to you, we are united" (ibid.). Significantly, this textualized burrow is the "outcome rather of intense intellectual than of physical labor" (Kafka 1971: 327). Even the constructor's most important physical effort within the labyrinth, that is, the burrowing motion that constitutes his basic constructing strategy, is a form of compulsive "head work" since it is with his forehead, his "only tool," that the animal pounds the loose, sandy soil "thousands of times, for whole days and nights," feeling glad "when the blood comes" for that is "a proof that the walls [are] beginning to harden" (ibid.: 328).

Also like a text, the supposedly finished burrow adamantly resists completion as its builder does not seem to be able to devise a defensive strategy that would render it invulnerable to any other burrowing creature. Such a strategy would require not only the design of a perfectly disguised entrance but also the possibility of finding "a universal principle or an infallible method of descent" (ibid.: 336). Distressed at his own observations, which are "extremely heterogeneous, and both good and bad" (ibid.), Kafka's architect is painfully aware of the fact that the unequivocal mastery of his burrow is directly dependent on the definite establishment of his own conclusions: "now I am on fire to discover whether my conclusion is valid. And with good reason, for as long as that is not established I cannot feel safe, even if it were merely a matter of discovering where a grain of sand that had fallen from one of the walls had rolled to" (Kafka 1971: 344). If the construction of the unconditionally perfect burrow is intimately related to the discovery of unequivocal solutions, it also involves the pursuit of absolute silence because it is only in eternal stillness that the constructor could be completely assured of the invulnerability of his construction and, consequently, of his total control over it:

> "the most beautiful thing about my burrow is the stillness [...] For hours I can stroll through my passages and hear nothing except the rustling of some little creature, which I immediately reduce to silence between my jaws, or the pattering of soil, which draws my attention to the need for repair".

> (Ibid.: 327)

In the construction as text, the plenitude of stillness would guarantee not only the constructor's complete control over his passages, but also his indisputable mastery over time and chance. As a consequence, the noise that betrays the potentially uncontrollable dissemination of difference within the burrow, the sign of deconstructive danger, would also be forever kept at bay.

Because the dream of a blissful plenitude occurs when the idea of totality and absolute mastery – including total control over the proliferation of meaning and total neutralization of difference – seems conceivable within the labyrinth, it is expected that the constructing animal worries most of all about "the defect of the opening" that marks the end of his "domestic protection" (ibid.: 333). The opening is "that point in the dark moss" in which he is especially vulnerable and which prevents him from living "in peace, warm, well nourished, master, sole master of all [his] manifold passages and rooms" (ibid.). But who could be the potential intruder? Who might threaten the completion and the stillness of the labyrinth? First, as its architect imagines, the enemy, probably "a filthy scoundrel who wishes to be housed where he has not built" (Kafka 1971: 337), would obviously come from outside, through "that point in the dark moss" that makes the burrow potentially exposed. As the constructor himself recognizes, what makes his textual labyrinth particularly vulnerable and, also, what makes him enraged at the prospect of having to fight any possible invader, is his determination to be the sole master of his creation: "simply by virtue of being owner of this great vulnerable edifice I am obviously defenseless against any serious attack" (ibid.: 355). At the same time, though, as observed above, the burrowing creature comes to the unsettling conclusion that he and the burrow have somehow become one – "the joy of possessing it has spoiled me, the vulnerability of the burrow has made me vulnerable; any wound to it hurts me as if I myself were hit" (ibid.: 337) – and, also, and perhaps more importantly, that he cannot clearly separate himself from the deconstructive Other either.

As the borders between subject and object are seriously shaken, the architect finds it impossible to clearly distinguish the legitimate owner from the unlawful intruder, or the constructor from the deconstructor; he even considers the possibility that his worst enemy may not really be outside: "outside there nobody troubles about my burrow, everybody has his own affairs, which have no connection with me" (ibid.: 352). This awareness, however, is often conveniently forgotten:

> the danger is by no means a fanciful one, but very real. It need not be any particular enemy that is provoked to pursue me; it may very well be some chance innocent little beast which follows me out of curiosity, and thus, without knowing it, becomes the leader of all the world against me.
>
> (Ibid.: 337)

As the story develops, we are made to witness the builder's obsessive attempts to distinguish himself from the intruding Other whom he imagines as a faithful projection of himself, endowed, for instance, with "a furious lust for work" solely aimed at the definite conquest of the labyrinth (ibid.: 354). As this remarkably human animal cannot succeed in separating construction from deconstruction, even within the limits of his own text whose passages he cannot help changing with every revision and with each round, he seems to be ultimately driven by a will to power that is also an anxious attempt to defer the consciousness of mortality.

The total mastery over the construction that would provide its architect with absolute protection against difference, establishing a clear-cut opposition between inside and outside, proprietor and intruder, writing and interpreting, would also grant him full, undeniable control over that which could be an irrefutable origin or core: the burrow's "Castle Keep," "the inmost chamber of [the animal's] house," the ultimate protection and source of complete satisfaction, where he could finally "sleep the sweet sleep of tranquility, of satisfied desire" (ibid.: 326–327). Though this process of creation could be associated with the animal's will to power aiming at the exclusive possession of eternal truth and stability, the achievement of absolute completion and stillness seems to be conceivable only in death, as the constructor himself, while awake and still living, cannot help but undo and redo his own work. Since the construction of a text/labyrinth is related to revision and reinterpretation, forever resisting any possibility of completion or perfect closure, we find the creating animal painfully divided between his human condition, which binds him to the provisional and the finite, and his desire to be divine, that is, to be the totalitarian, sole master of truth and fate. As a dazzling illustration of such a division, Kafka's narrator reflects the pathos of all authors, interpreters, and translators, irremediably torn between their desire to control and forever stabilize meaning and the acknowledgment of their own human condition.

A reader/detective meets a deadly author figure in a Borgesian labyrinth

While Kafka's burrowing animal sheds some light on the impasse of a creator battling his own humanity, Borges's "Death and the Compass" (Borges 1998) allows us to examine certain aspects of the type of conflict and competition that Kafka's narrator seems to fear so intensely. In Borges's story we witness the complex encounter between a cultivated reader and a fierce author figure and labyrinth maker, both engaged in a power struggle that entails the virtual elimination of one of them. The reader in question is the detective Erik Lönnrot who, together with his colleague Treviranus, is investigating three alleged murders apparently committed by the same person in a town that resembles Borges's own Buenos Aires. Unlike Treviranus, however, Lönnrot is not interested in a plausible, simple solution to this criminal enigma. Instead, he proposes to find an answer in what he takes to be the murderer's written messages and in their connection with the books found in the first victim's hotel room. As an "objective," diligent reader/detective, Lönnrot is driven by the desire not to simply decipher the mind and the writings of the author/assassin but also to anticipate his moves, and, finally, to outwit and arrest him. Lönnrot's adversary and Borges's powerful author figure in the story is Red Scharlach, the cold, crafty criminal that had "sworn upon his honor to kill Lönnrot" (ibid.: 147). After learning of the first crime and of Lönnrot's investigation, Red Scharlach decides "to weave" a deadly, firm "labyrinth" around the man who once arrested his brother (ibid.: 155). He plans to construct his textual maze by plotting a second murder and by staging a third one in such a way as to make Lönnrot believe that the three supposed killings are the work of the same man and also connected with the written message found on a sheet of paper in the first victim's typewriter: *The first letter of the Name has been written* (ibid.: 149).

The text/labyrinth designed by Red Scharlach, whose first name can be read both as the English adjective "red" and the Spanish noun *"red,"* which means "net," is first and foremost a trap aimed at snaring and killing

Lönnrot. To the extent that the detective's obsessive reading is also aimed at entrapping the one who, according to him, is the author of the crimes, it seems that the goals and the will to power that trigger both Scharlach's and Lönnrot's textual enterprises are not very different. The assassin and the detective, the author and the reader, share similar motivations as they share a similar name: "Red," as a proper name in English, which also mirrors, as noted, the adjective "red," is echoed, in translation, in "rot" – "red" in German – in Lönnrot (for an enlightening discussion of possible meanings for the names used in the story, see Irwin 1994: 72–75). Furthermore, as Scharlach's name seems to echo Scheherazade's, particularly in its Spanish version, "Schaharazad," we can also relate Borges's peculiar author figure to the legendary narrator of *The One Thousand and One Nights*. Just as Scheherazade's life is saved by her ability to create a textual labyrinth in which she entraps the sultan whose immediate goal is to kill her, transforming her potential assassin into a loving husband, Scharlach's fate is reversed by his authorial strength as he manages to lure his intruding reader and worst enemy into a deadly, well-designed maze. Therefore, Scharlach's ability to weave the strong net of his textual trap not only misguides and imprisons Lönnrot, but also turns him, usually the tireless pursuer of Scharlach and his fellow gunmen, into the pursued, defenseless victim.

As the construction of a text that is both a protection and a trap, the labyrinth finds in Borges's story an exemplary representation in Triste-le-Roy, the abandoned villa whose name could be translated into English as "The Sad King," and which is, hence, appropriately occupied by the disgruntled Scharlach and, also, the site where the assassin finally catches Lönnrot. Significantly, the abandoned villa's architecture, with its "pointless symmetries and obsessive repetitions" (Borges 1998: 153), mirrors Scharlach's maze. Among such architectural devices and ornaments, a "two-faced Hermes" that "threw a monstrous shadow" (ibid.) reminds us of Scharlach and his double Lönnrot, both fittingly related to the Greek god, the interpreter and messenger among his fellow gods, also known for his rhetorical talent and his extraordinary skills as a trickster and an invisible thief (cf. Brown 1969: 4–14). Lönnrot's careful exploration of Triste-le-Roy's architecture may also be read as a reflection of his efforts to interpret Scharlach's misguiding clues. While attempting to undo that which he sees as the assassin's text, Lönnrot sets out to master his labyrinth:

> Lönnrot explored the house. Through foyers that opened onto dining rooms and on through galleries, he would emerge into identical courtyards – often the same courtyard. He climbed dusty stairs to circular antechambers; he would recede infinitely in the facing mirrored walls; he wearied of opening or half-opening windows that revealed to him, outside, the same desolate garden from differing heights and differing angles.
>
> (Borges 1998: 153–154)

The most representative of the repeated motifs that are found in both the assassin's alleged writings and Triste-le-Roy's design is the recurrent play on the numbers three and four, also mirrored in the references to rectangular and quadrangular shapes, pointing to the solution of the puzzle: the deciphering of the Tetragrammaton, or the four-letter name of God, spelled out by the murders staged by Scharlach. In the end, as the defeated Lönnrot is about to be shot dead inside Scharlach's retreat, his request that the next time he is trapped and killed it should take place in a "straight-line labyrinth" may also suggest that the kind of conflict the two represent is bound to be infinitely repeated in the vain search for that which could end all interpretation and all plotting: the final deciphering of nothing less than the name of God. From this viewpoint both Scharlach and Lönnrot share with Kafka's burrowing animal the same futile, human desire to achieve divine mastery over meaning, which is ultimately also the quest to control life and death. The intensity of this desire seems to allow Lönnrot to patiently accept his impending assassination and even reason with Scharlach about the way he would like to be killed in a future life. Paradoxically, the possibility of having an authorial participation in the planning of his next death is more attractive to Lönnrot than actually fighting for his life. Moreover, if the labyrinth, which for Scharlach reflects the world from which it is impossible to escape (ibid.: 154), could be a straight line and thus mirror any kind of relationship between subject and object (such as, for example, the one between a reader's gaze and the text being read), it also suggests that all acts of interpretation ultimately take place inside a text/labyrinth, which is the same as to say that there is no way out of it.

Finally, as Lönnrot tries to decipher Scharlach's text and as he ventures into the labyrinth in order to find his author's truth or, rather, the confirmation of his own truth regarding his author's writing, he also provides us with a reflection of ourselves, trained readers of literature. As such we cannot help but impose our own meanings on texts and, obviously, also on Borges's carefully designed structure in his detective story. Like Lönnrot and unlike Treviranus, we tend not to settle for simple, "uninteresting" interpretations and often run the risk of being caught by the narrator's misleading clues. Furthermore, if we identify with Lönnrot, Red Scharlach might very well be Borges himself, the real "Sad King" and labyrinth maker, partially disguised by his narrator, and who tries to dictate what must be true inside his construction and even makes a surprising, subtle appearance in the story in order to make it clear who actually "owns" "Death and the Compass." As his narrator informs us of Lönnrot's trip to Triste-le-Roy, we learn, for example, about the "sluggish stream of muddy water" that flows south of the city of *"my story"* (ibid.: 152, emphasis added). As the provisional designer and master of his plot, Borges turns Scharlach/Schaharazad into the eternal winner of the conflict that has brought a skillful author figure face-to-face with a cultivated reader in a storyline in which the latter is eternally doomed to be entrapped and eliminated by the former's forceful textual strategies. Yet, even if Borges expresses the strength of his authorial desire as he seems to side with Scharlach and the assassin's attempt to establish clear-cut limits between writing and reading, he cannot protect his story from the reading presented here, which, precisely because it is a reading, necessarily finds an opening in his text and interferes with it as it tries to produce a thread that will show a possible (and provisional) way out of the labyrinth.

The translator's compulsion to steal: Kosztolányi's Gallus

If the will to power is first and foremost an interpretation that necessarily constructs meaning, the implicit relationship that is usually established between authors and interpreters is not exactly inspired by cooperation or collaboration, as "commonsense" and the essentialist tradition would have it, but is, rather, constituted by an underlying competition for the power to establish that which will be accepted as true and definitive within a certain context and under certain circumstances. As my readings of Kafka's and Borges's stories suggest, in our textualized, human world, where immortal essences and absolute certainties are not to be found, the indisputable control over a text cannot be achieved even by its author. If one cannot clearly and forever separate the author from the interpreter, the text from its reading, or even one text from another, and if the will to power as the will to master meaning is what moves both writers and readers, is it ever possible for interpreters to be truly faithful to the authors or the texts they visit? It is not by chance that this has been the central issue and the main concern for those interested in the workings of translation, an activity that provides a paradigmatic scenario for the underlying struggle for the establishment of meaning that constitutes both writing and interpretation as it involves the actual production of another text: the writing of the translator's reading of someone else's text in another language, time, and cultural environment. As it constitutes material evidence of the translator's passage through the original, offering documented proof of the differences brought about by such passage, any translation is bound to be an exemplary site for the competitive nature of textual activity. In a tradition that generally imagines originals as the closed, fixed containers of their authors' consciously intentional meanings, the struggle for the power to determine the "truth" of a text is typically decided in favor of those who are considered as the rightful owners of their texts' meanings and who supposedly deserve unconditional respect from anyone who dares to enter their textual property.

A brief venture into Chapter XIV of Kosztolányi's *Kornél Esti* (Kosztolányi 2011) will allow us to reflect on the alleged inadequacies or shortcomings of translation and the widespread suspicion involving the translator's task cultivated by a tradition that tends to consider authorial power as the exclusive prerogative of those who write originals. If the author and the interpreter cannot enjoy a peaceful encounter inside the labyrinth as text, and if the author is usually viewed as the only legitimate producer of meaning to have property rights over this special retreat, it is not at all surprising that translators have often been associated with chronically improper behavior. In Kosztolányi's text we learn from the narrator, a respected writer, that Gallus, an old acquaintance of his, used to be a promising, well-educated young man of remarkable qualities: "a capable man, lively, spontaneous, and conscientious and cultured as well" (ibid.: 199). His language skills were more than exceptional: he "spoke English so well that it was said that even the Prince of Wales took lessons from him" (ibid.). His command of Hungarian was also "perfect" (Kosztolányi 2011: 201). And yet, all his accomplishments were unforgivably tarnished by "one fatal shortcoming," that is, a compulsion to steal, which defied all his serious efforts to change:

> "everything that came within reach he picked up. He thieved like a magpie. It didn't matter to him whether it was a pocket watch, a pair of slippers, or a great big stovepipe. [...] His enjoyment consisted simply in doing as he pleased – stealing".
>
> (Ibid.: 200)

The narrator and his friends urged Gallus to change, but "his nature was the stronger. He lapsed time and time again" (ibid.). At one point he was taken by the police after robbing a businessman on the Vienna express. Even though his friends tried to help him by arguing that "he was a kleptomaniac, not a thief, [he was] sentenced to two years in jail" (ibid.). When he came out, "hungry and in rags," he begged the narrator to help him find work. Since all Gallus could do was write, but could not do so under his own name, the narrator introduced him to a compassionate editor who needed someone to translate *The Mysterious Castle of Earl Vitsislav*, an English thriller described as the kind of trashy material that respectable writers would not even want to read or "soil [their] hands with" (ibid.). At most they would consider translating it, but only if they could "wear gloves" while tackling the unsavory project (ibid.). The desperate translator promptly accepted the task and devoted himself to the job so completely that long before the deadline he was able to deliver his neatly typed manuscript. Unfortunately, though, after a few days the editor concluded that Gallus's translation was "completely unusable" (Kosztolányi 2011: 201). Deeply shocked to hear the news, Kosztolányi's narrator decided to investigate the case. While reading the translation, he was filled with admiration for Galus's scrupulously meticulous work – "well-formed sentences, apt turns of phrase, clever linguistic devices, [...] more, perhaps, than that drivel deserved" (ibid.) – and could not understand why the project had been rejected. Urged by the editor, the narrator carefully compared the translator's manuscript to the original and the enigma was soon clarified. Even though there were no mistakes, no mistranslations, and the Hungarian version was "fluent, artistic, in places poetic" (ibid.), it became clear to the narrator that the translator had not managed to control himself and had simply stolen property from the author's settings and characters. Thus, for example, while in the original a female character was wearing precious jewelry, in the translation it was all gone. A similar fate was reserved for cash, rugs, safes, watches, suitcases, silverware, land, mansions, and even small objects of little value such as handkerchiefs, pocket pistols, and pendants (Kosztolányi 2011: 202–203).

In his hilarious comments on Gallus's "incurable disease," the narrator seems to ingeniously synthesize some of the most widespread notions about translation ingrained in essentialist conceptions of language and the subject. From the perspective of those who share a general belief in the possibility of stable meanings safely stored in texts, such meanings are not only considered to be objectively traceable to their authors' conscious intentions, but also viewed as their own property. Therefore, from such a stance, originals and translations, authors and translators do belong in radically different categories. As Kosztolányi's good-humored plot creatively portrays such conceptions, the inevitable differences produced by translation are traditionally viewed as losses and even the gains or the improvements brought about by the translator's intervention are associated with his incurable kleptomania. As the narrator concludes, Gallus stole from the English original precisely the objects or the usual traits that "are called upon to raise the tone in English literature" (ibid.: 201) and dared to transform what was viewed as a trashy piece of English fiction into an elegant Hungarian narrative. Coherently, while the translation is viewed as subservient to the original, regardless of the quality of the translator's writing, the translator is nothing but a mere copyist who is expected to be blindly faithful to the author's original and "simply" reproduce it without actually participating in the process. It is significant, for example, that, for Kosztolányi's narrator, as mentioned, respectable writers would not even want to read a piece of "rubbish" like *The Mysterious Castle of Earl Vitsislav*, even though they would consider translating it provided that they could wear gloves. In other words, for Kosztolányi's narrator, it is feasible for a translator to perform his task without touching the text in question, that is, while reading may involve some closer contact with the original, translating it could – and, apparently, also should – be accomplished without any direct intervention on the part of the translator.

Following tradition, the conception of translation ethics implicitly adopted by the narrator assumes that it is perfectly possible to translate without actually interpreting or rewriting the so-called original. Predictably, what needs to be repressed at all costs is the translator's authorial will to power, which, in Kosztolányi's storyline, is symptomatically rendered as a form of criminal behavior or, euphemistically, as an "incurable disease." The marginality and the oblivion to which the translator is condemned is explicitly presented as a form of punishment not only for his daring attempt to compete with his mediocre author and for having actually turned the latter's second-rate original into an artistic piece but, also, for having indulged in his addictive authorial pleasure against which he was not able to fight. The narrator seems particularly upset about what he sees as "the most damaging detail" involving Gallus's performance "because it definitely spoke of bad faith and unmanliness": the fact that "he frequently substituted worthless and inferior materials for noble metals and precious stones, replacing platinum with tinplate, gold with brass, and diamonds with quartz crystals or glass" (ibid.: 203). As a substitute for the original, which apparently is valuable just for being the original, the translation can only offer the translator's deceiving replacement, a replacement that misguides those unable to read the original into believing that what they are presented with is the author's authentic material. Just as the translation is a false original, the translator is a spurious author and, as the narrator suggests, also an "unmanly" man (ibid.). In relation to this, it is significant that Kosztolányi's translator character is called "Gallus," a name that is especially meaningful in the context of ancient Roman sexual roles. As "the ultimate scare-figure of Roman masculinity," Gallus was the self-castrated priest who chose to follow the cult of Cybele, the Mother Goddess (Williams 1999: 140). Often referred to as fake women, the *galli* were seen as "figures of unmanliness for having abdicated male responsibilities," among which was the legitimate production of offspring (Endres 2015: 1). Dressed in gaudy women clothes and wearing heavy make-up, the *galli* lived as beggars in the fringes of Roman society. As an obvious trope for ambiguity, infertility, and marginality, the Roman "gallus" helps us understand why Kosztolányi's translator character is portrayed as the clear opposite of his narrator's idealized author figure. From the point of view of Kosztolányi's narrator, who defines himself as a writer of originals, while the figure of the author seems to be associated with what is unambiguously masculine and, therefore, with the ability and the right to produce "legitimate" textual material, the translator, as an "unmaly man," is unable to create original work and is not only a marginal, but also an object of ridicule.

* * *

As I explore the underlying conflict between the conception of the author as the exclusive master of textuality and the interpreter's own authorial will to power in Kosztolányi's plot I am obviously reminded of both Borges's and Kafka's. While Kafka's burrowing animal illustrates the creator's obsession to devise a perfectly invulnerable textual labyrinth, and while Borges's Scharlach and Lönnrot represent the violent struggle for the control over meaning that both separates and brings together authors and interpreters, in Kosztolányi's piece some of the consequences of this conflict are actually made explicit, particularly by the narrator's speculation on the reasons why Gallus seems to have such a peculiar need to take possession of someone else's property. After comparing Gallus's translation to the original, Kosztolányi's narrator continued his "detective work" and prepared a complete list of all the "stolen" items in his quest to solve the true enigma of the thriller represented by Gallus's story: "Where did he put these chattels and real estate, which, after all, existed only on paper, in the realm of the imagination, and what was his purpose in stealing them?" (Kosztolányi 2011: 203). Yet, in spite of his interest, the narrator finally decided to stop thinking about the issue on the grounds that such an investigation might go too far and, instead, chose to simply conclude that the translator was still "a slave to his sinful passion or sickness [and] that there was no hope of a cure, and that he didn't even deserve the support of decent society" (ibid.). The narrator then simply gave up on Gallus and "abandoned him to his fate" (ibid.).

Who or what, one may ask, is the narrator trying to protect in his refusal to further investigate Gallus's "unforgivable" crime? As I myself play the detective in this textual puzzle, I find the basis of a plausible answer in Borges's "The Homeric Versions," according to which the problems posed by any translation do shed some unflattering light on the "modest mystery" that surrounds original writing and literature in particular (Borges 1999: 69, trans. Weinberger). As it addresses a "visible text," rather than an "invaluable labyrinth of past projects," any translation is bound to deconstruct and decanonize originals, revealing perhaps that "the modest mystery" surrounding such writing is nothing but "the fear of confessing mental processes which are dangerously ordinary" (ibid.). From this perspective, it could be argued that what Gallus's creative work stole from "the realm of [the author's] imagination," and which could not be fully understood by Kosztolányi's narrator, is not simply the "mystery" of originality, or the widespread notion that originals are inherently superior to their translations, but, first and foremost, the illusion that authorship could in fact grant writers an exclusive mastery over their texts. Consequently, Gallus's translation also shows that instead of protecting the original and its author's meaning, the translator's task may actually represent a threatening interference, especially when it is recognized to be a flagrant improvement. To the extent that Gallus refuses to be strictly faithful to his mediocre author and ends up exercising his authorial power, he, too, seems to be related to Hermes, the Greek god, also known for his talent as a deceitful, invisible thief. It is from this kind of appropriation, which seriously undermines the traditional hierarchical opposition separating authors from translators, that the story's narrator seems to be defending not merely originals and their authors, but, ultimately, also his own writing and, perhaps, Kosztolányi's as well.

In revealing the conflict that takes place between original writing and translation, the Hungarian narrative is especially efficient in exploring some of the most important implications and consequences associated with the translator's will to power. Though Gallus is not by any means innocent and is in fact "guilty" of being visible and human, Kosztolányi's narrator, as the typical writer who associates original texts with the "sanctity of private ownership," reflects the generally defensive reaction that essentialist views display towards translation, counting on the strategy of blind fidelity as a form of antidote against difference and intervention. Like Kafka's and Borges's stories, Kosztolányi's is eloquent in expressing the violence associated with the will to power that seems to trigger both writing and interpreting. Whereas Kafka's architect and Borges's Scharlach exhibit explicitly murderous behavior towards their competitors or potential enemies, the kind of "crime" we find in Kosztolányi's piece is more easily relatable to the actual world of writers, readers, and translators, as it epitomizes, for instance, the widespread disregard for translation as both a theoretical issue and a legitimate profession. When the narrator gives up investigating the translator's thefts and chooses to marginalize Gallus, he mirrors the kind of treatment translation and translators tend to receive both from the general public and the great majority of academic studies that still revolve around the possibility of establishing some kind of objective control over the translator's agency. In Kosztolányi's storyline, the basically asymmetrical relationship that opposes original writing to translation and author to translator is also reflected in the relationship that involves both the "decent, kindly" editor and the allegedly generous narrator who claims to have tried to be the translator's protector, and Gallus himself. Emblematically, as an illustration of the stereotypes usually associated with translators and their work, Kosztolányi's story treats the translator as someone who ends up translating for lack of "legitimate" employment, rather than a professional who deserves to be respected for the invaluable work that he does.

Finally, like the labyrinth in which Scharlach and Lönnrot will be forever struggling for the impossible, pre-Babelic power to transform words into definite truths, and like the burrow in which Kafka's animal will be forever searching for the absolute control of his ever-changing textual construction, Kosztolányi's plot seems to be directly related to that essential longing for property that Nietzsche associates with the will to power as the primary impulse of life. And if, in the world as text, the search for authorial mastery also drives readers and translators, we are never able to achieve the definitive stability of meaning or the neutralization of difference that could ultimately free us from our own circumstances and end all conflict and all struggle. It is precisely the acceptance of difference and, thus, the acceptance of the interpreter's authorial interference in the processes of reading and translating that, in the wake of Nietzsche's anti-essentialist thought, has begun to change the general plot that has typically captured authors, readers, and translators in the same kind of narrative. In such a context the translator's visibility has ceased to be regarded as an incurable disease or an unforgivable crime that should be repressed at any cost and has begun to constitute an actual object of study. In this sense, unlike Kosztolányi's narrator, we do not have to be discouraged by the complexities that are involved in the undeniable power of translation. Indeed, in recent years, we have begun to chart the almost unknown ground in which writing and interpretation overlap as a result of our attempts to review the old clichés that have underestimated the impact of the translator's task on the shaping of culture and history.

Bibliography

Borges, J. L. (1998) "Death and the Compass," A. Hurley (trans.) *Collected Fictions*, New York: Penguin, 147–156.

—— (1999) "The Homeric Versions," E. Weinberger (trans. and ed.) *Selected Non-Fictions*, New York: Penguin, 69–74.

Brown, N. O. (1969) *Hermes the Thief – The Evolution of a Myth*, New York: Vintage Books.

Deleuze, G. (2006) *Nietzsche and Philosophy*, H. Tomlinson (trans.), New York: Columbia University Press.

Endres, N. (2015) "Galli: Ancient Roman Priests." Available at: www.glbtqarchive.com/ssh/galli_S.pdf (accessed March 24, 2014).

Freud, S. (1983) "Creative Writers and Daydreaming," J. Strachey (trans.), in E. Kurzweil and W. Phillips (eds.) *Literature and Psychoanalysis*, New York: Columbia University Press, 24–28.

Irwin, J. (1994) *The Mystery to a Solution: Poe, Borges, and the Analytic Detective Story*, Baltimore, MD: The Johns Hopkins University Press.

Kafka, F. (1971) "The Burrow," W. and E. Muir (trans.), in N. N. Glatzer (ed.) *Franz Kafka – The Complete Stories*, New York: Schocken, 325–359.

Kofman, S. (1993) *Nietzsche and Metaphor*, D. Large (trans.), Stanford, CA: Stanford University Press.

Kosztolányi, D. (2011) *Kornél Esti – A Novel*, B. Adams (trans.), New York: New Directions.

Lahiji, N. (ed.) (2014) *The Missed Encounter of Radical Philosophy with Architecture*, London: Bloomsbury.

Nehamas, A. (1996) *Nietzsche: Life as Literature*, Cambridge, MA: Harvard University Press.

Nietzsche, F. (1968) *The Will to Power*, W. Kaufmann and R. J. Hollingdale (trans.), W. Kaufmann (ed.), New York: Vintage Books.

—— (1990) *The Twilight of the Idols or How to Philosophize with a Hammer*, R. J. Hollingdale (trans.), M. Tanner (ed.), New York: Penguin.

—— (1999) "On Truth and Lies in a Nonmoral Sense," in D. Breazeale (ed. and trans.) *Philosophy and Truth – Selections from Nietzsche's Notebooks of the Early 1870s*, Amherst, NY: Humanity Books, 79–97.

—— (2005) *The Anti-Christ, Ecce Homo, Twilight of the Idols and Other Writings*, J. Norman (trans.), A. Ridley (ed.), Cambridge: Cambridge University Press.

—— (2006) *Thus Spoke Zarathustra – A Book for All and None*, A. Del Caro (trans.), A. Del Caro and R. B. Pippin (eds.), Cambridge: Cambridge University Press.

—— (2007) *Ecce Homo – How To Become What You Are*, D. Large (trans.), Oxford: Oxford University Press.

Schrift, A. D. (1990) *Nietzsche and the Question of Interpretation – Between Hermeneutics and Deconstruction*, New York: Routledge.

—— (1995) *Nietzsche's French Legacy – A Genealogy of Poststructuralism*, New York: Routledge.

Strong, T. B. (1975) *Friedrich Nietzsche and the Politics of Transfiguration*, Berkeley: University of California Press.

Sussman, H. (1979) *Franz Kafka: Geometrician of Metaphor*, Madison, WI: Coda Press.

Williams, C. A. (1999) *Roman Homosexuality – Ideologies of Masculinity in Classical Antiquity*, Oxford: Oxford University Press.

6 Authorship as the affirmation of masculinity

José Saramago's *The History of the Siege of Lisbon* and Isaac Babel's "Guy de Maupassant"

> Until you attain the truth, / you will not be able to amend it. / But if you do not amend it, / you will not attain it. Meanwhile, / do not resign yourself.
>
> From The Book of Exhortations, José Saramago, *The History of the Siege of Lisbon*, trans. Giovanni Pontiero

> I spoke to her of style, of an army of words, an army in which every type of weapon is deployed. No iron spike can pierce a human heart as icily as a period in the right place.
>
> Isaac Babel, "Guy de Maupassant," trans. Peter Constantine

In his review of José Saramago's *The History of the Siege of Lisbon* (Saramago 1997, trans. G. Pontiero), originally published in 1989, Edmund White finds a striking parallel between the proofreader Raimundo Silva, the novel's protagonist, and Fernando Pessoa, one of the greatest, most remarkable poets ever to write in Portuguese. Like "his near contemporaries Franz Kafka and Constantine Cavafy," Pessoa, with whom, by the way, Saramago's protagonist also identifies, was "a writer and a clerk [who] made his living by translating business letters into Portuguese, but in his spare time [...] wrote poems and prose pieces under many different names and in many styles" (White 1997). As characterized by White, Pessoa constitutes a striking illustration of the typical hierarchy that opposes the creative voice that produces "originals" to the alleged non-creative, mechanical role played by those engaged in activities like proofreading and translation whose main goal should be to simply protect texts and the interests of their authors or those who own them. In Saramago's novel, the clear-cut opposition between the proofreader and the author is closely associated with the novel's enthusiastic celebration of literary power as a direct, almost immediate manifestation of enhanced masculinity, which brings about the concrete possibility of reshaping history as well as the bliss of love and personal happiness. On the other side of the opposition, proofreading is represented as a stereotypically feminine or feminizing task that entails the repression or the absence of creativity and a selfless dedication to someone else's writings. Thus, in order for Raimundo Silva to become the writer he would like to be, the shy, frustrated, virtually emasculated proofreader has to man up, so to speak, and find the courage to act on his own desire both for the power to rewrite history and for the companionship of a woman. Soon after Raimundo manages to consciously intervene in the text he is proofreading in order to register his own take on the siege of Lisbon, a founding narrative in Portuguese history, he meets Maria Sara, originally also a proofreader, whose main role in the narrative will be to help him become an author. In his trajectory from lonely proofreader to aspiring author and Maria Sara's lover, Raimundo reflects the close association between male sexuality and literary power that has been one of the most resistant and recurrent motifs of Western culture, which tends to view the author of originals as "a father, a progenitor, a procreator, an aesthetic patriarch whose pen is an instrument of generative power like his penis" (Gilbert and Gubar 2000: 6). While creative writing is affirmed as an essentially masculine endeavor, proofreading is portrayed as a quintessential ancillary textual practice that not only protects originals, but also enables the aspiring author to pursue his dream and find his voice. Therefore, just as the translation of business letters might have made it possible for Fernando Pessoa to produce exquisite literary pieces in his spare time, proofreading is, for Raimundo, not exactly a vocation or a desirable career choice, but a convenient means to earn a (modest) living while he finds the courage and the incentive to unleash his repressed literary power.

In order to further examine these representations of textual practices, I will also bring to my discussion Isaac Babel's "Guy de Maupassant," a story first published in 1932 (Babel 2002, trans. P. Constantine), and which may remind readers of Borges's "Pierre Menard, Author of the *Quixote*." Like Borges's story, "Guy de Maupassant" offers a captivating reflection on the relationship between original writing and its translations as well as a portrayal of the translator as an aspiring writer who desires to become a great author. In spite of its obvious differences from Saramago's novel, "Guy de Maupassant" can also be read as an exploration of some pivotal associations between gender and creative writing and will allow me to focus on issues more directly related to the actual practice of translation. As we move from Saramago's Lisbon of the 1980s to Babel's Saint Petersburg of 1916, we will also explore the strong link between literary power and masculinity that is also a major theme in the Russian story, which, like the Portuguese novel, explicitly underscores the power of language and its association with the possibility of sexual seduction and authorship. This association is represented by Babel's narrator, a young writer who refuses to become a clerk and manages to seduce the wealthy Raisa Bendersky with his translations of Maupassant's stories. Significantly, what separates Raisa and the gentle Aleksei Kazantsev, the other translator character featured in the story, from the narrator is the latter's language skills and determination to become a writer, traits that are subtly associated with his strong sexual appetite. In contrast, Raisa and Aleksei, who have no ambition to write their own texts, represent a secondary, feminized position as their main role in the story is to nurture and support the narrator's budding writing career.

The main focus of this chapter is to propose readings of Saramago's and Babel's pieces that will enable us to reflect on some consequences associated with the usual hierarchy that separates original writing from "secondary" textual practices, and which is often highlighted by gender metaphors that help shape and contextualize the ways in which such practices tend to be conducted and viewed in Western culture. As Lori Chamberlain argues, while, in our culture, "originality or creativity" has been directly linked to "paternity and authority," and, hence, to the masculine, the figure of the female has been linked to "a variety of secondary roles" such as those associated with translation, often viewed as "an archetypal feminine activity" (Chamberlain 2000: 306, 315). Unsurprisingly, the practice of translation has been typically related, for example, to the supportive roles of secretaries or clerks, that is, roles that are not expected to involve agency or writing skills, but, rather, subservience to somebody else's authority and wishes. As I will be arguing, since the gap established by such distinctions is ultimately traceable to the preposterous notion that females are somehow inferior to men, the hierarchy they propose is not only fallacious, not to mention insulting, but fails to recognize translation and proofreading as professional activities that must also rely on creativity and agency and, more importantly, that should not be defined as a second or third option for those who would like to be authors, but may not dare or are not talented enough to write their own texts.

Multiple histories of the siege of Lisbon

Let us begin with a brief summary of Saramago's storyline. Raimundo Silva is a lonely bachelor in his fifties who works as a proofreader for a publishing house in Lisbon. He devotes his monotonous days to the texts of others and must ignore his distaste for most of what he has to read while repressing his desire to produce his own writing. One day, after an agonizing inner struggle, while proofreading a historian's book on the reconquest of Lisbon in the year 1147 – entitled "The History of the Siege of Lisbon" – he decides to ignore the norms that discipline his profession and adds a "not" to a key sentence originally meant to say that the crusaders will help the Portuguese reclaim Lisbon and, consequently, rewrites the founding narrative of his country's history. As he finally dares to act on his desire to author the text he is expected to simply proofread, his life changes. Soon he starts a romance with Maria Sara, the specialist who is hired to coordinate all the proofreading work done for the publishing house after his "deception" is uncovered. Instead of punishing Raimundo for his uninvited intervention, Maria Sara suggests that he write his own book on the reconquest of Lisbon. Smitten with his new boss, Raimundo begins to work on his own manuscript – a historic novel entitled "The History of the Siege of Lisbon" – in which he attributes to the troops fighting under Alfonso I, the King of Portugal, the victory over the Moors, and not to the foreign crusaders, as the official history would have it.

Saramago's intriguing epigraph to the novel – "Until you attain the truth, / you will not be able to amend it. / But if you do not amend it, / you will not attain it. Meanwhile, / do not resign yourself" – does foreshadow its general theme: the inevitable, endless reconstruction of truth that underlies our attempts at making sense of both the past and the present. Such an ongoing reconstruction, which we might identify as a comprehensive metaphor for processes of interpretation in general, underscores the foundational power of language as the material that makes truth and history possible. Consequently, if we must keep trying to reach and amend that which is not reachable in order to own it, we will be forever interpreting and rewriting truths without ever reaching any level of permanent stability and certitude that could finally stop us and our will to power. In Saramago's narrative, which presents history as a form of writing that cannot be definitely separated from fiction or literature, readers will find the subversion of several other similar, traditional oppositions: the past and the present, the author and the reader, the author and his characters, the narrator and the protagonist. However, this is a perspective that will not be associated with the historian and author figure whose book Raimundo is proofreading but, rather, with the proofreader's actual reading experience while he daydreams of his own version of the siege of Lisbon. In the dialogue that takes place between the proofreader and the historian at the beginning of the novel, while the latter claims that history is comparable to science or "real life," for Raimundo, it is literature, "and nothing else" (Saramago 1997: 8). Elsewhere, Saramago's narrator reinforces the proofreader's position as he ironically defines historians as a "human category which is closer to divinity in its way of looking at things" (ibid.: 161). Hence, generally speaking, Saramago's narrative, which is mostly presented from the proofreader's point of view, will show that what we call history is constructed not just by the historian but by the historian's reader as well.

As someone whose professional life is devoted to the attentive reading of texts, Saramago's protagonist constitutes an emblematic representation of the creative nature of interpretation. As a reader, Raimundo not only fills in the gaps he finds in the narrative that he carefully follows, but also uses what he reads to develop his own version long before he begins to write it down as an actual text. For example, soon after the dialogue with the historian mentioned above, we are presented with a detailed description of an early morning in Moorish Lisbon and introduced to the blind muezzin reminding the faithful that it is time to pray. As the narrator informs us, however, such a description is not to be found in the historian's book, which "simply" stated that:

the muezzin climbed the minaret and from there summoned the faithful to prayer in the mosque, without specifying whether it was morning or noon, or sunset, for certainly in his opinion, such minute detail would be of no historical interest and all the reader needed to know was that the author knew enough about the life of that time to be able to give them due mention.

(Ibid.: 11)

The description that we actually read in Saramago's novel is thus defined by his narrator as "nothing more than vague thoughts in the proof-reader's mind," thoughts that are triggered while he is "reading and correcting" what he might have "surreptitiously missed in the first and second proofs" (ibid.: 14). As the narrator puts it, in a clear reference to Fernando Pessoa's heteronyms, the proofreader becomes multiple while reading: he

heteronomises himself , he is capable of pursuing the path suggested by an image, a simile, or metaphor, often the simple sound of a word repeated in a low voice leads him, by association, to organize polyphonic verbal edifices capable of transforming his tiny study into a space multiplied by itself.

(Ibid.)

(For an introduction to Fernando Pessoa's heteronyms in English, see Sadlier 1998.) As a reader, Raimundo cannot help but reconstruct what he reads in his own terms, thus establishing a relationship with the text that defies traditional oppositions between reader and writer, the original and its interpretation, or even the literary and the historical (Saramago 1997: 17). When the otherwise reliable proofreader finally decides to introduce a "not" into the historian's sentence that says that "the crusaders will help the Portuguese to conquer Lisbon," his intervention, because "it is written," at least for Raimundo, has "come to be accepted as true," and "what we would call false has come to prevail over what we would call true" (ibid.: 40). Consequently, for Raimundo and/or for Saramago's narrator, "someone would have to narrate the history anew" (ibid.), and it is this conclusion that will open up for Raimundo the possibility of channeling his creativity as a reader of history into the actual writing of fiction, a possibility that soon will be made explicit to the proofreader by Maria Sara.

The blurring of the borders separating the reader from the writer, which is one of the most prevalent motifs in the novel, suggests that the proofreader's intervention in the historian's text is not simply the arbitrary result of a whim. Rather, it is associated with a great deal of research through reputed key documents on the crusades and the Portuguese victory over the Moors, research that also suggests how naïve it would be to "ascertain the truth" about the siege of Lisbon once and for all since we cannot really separate what is viewed as fact from its alleged interpretations. After his intervention, the proofreader begins to build up a narrative that offers a plausible explanation on why the crusaders might have refused to help the Portuguese reclaim Lisbon (Saramago 1997: 111). (It is relevant to add that Raimundo's technique seems to mirror Saramago's own writing, which tends to favor hybrid narratives – a composite of historiography and fiction – illustrating the author's overall interest in "placing human experience against a historical background" and in creating stories that embody "past events and contemporary reactions to another age so remote yet tangibly present" [cf. Pontiero 1997: 313].) In this process, the line separating the past from the present is also blurred as Saramago has his protagonist living in a modest apartment located precisely where the Porta de Alfofa used to be, that is, in a location that has been associated with the very wall that quite probably separated the Moors from the Portuguese in the 1140s (Saramago 1997: 65). In such a strategic position, which offers Raimundo an optimal view into what the past might have been like, the aspiring author immerses himself in his project and sets out to look for twelfth-century Lisbon in the landscape of his own city. Furthermore, as this vantage point allows him to bring the past into the present, Raimundo can also imagine the everyday lives of those involved in the conflict and sympathize and identify with both the Muslims and the Christians and, more specifically, with the characters from the different camps that begin to populate his narrative. Thus, sometimes, he "belongs to the besieging army" (ibid.: 59), but he can also "become" a crusader (ibid.: 113) or a "Moorish soldier watching the shadowy forms of the enemy" (ibid.: 118–119). While Raimundo's full immersion in his writing project allows him to live between the past and the present and bond with his characters, the delicate boundary that attempts to mark the limits between his real life and his fiction becomes blurred as well. Just as the proofreader's everyday life is enhanced by his search for the past, his newly found happiness is reflected in the romantic encounter between the main characters he creates – the soldier Mogueime and his beloved Ouroana – an encounter that also stimulates Raimundo's own relationship with Maria Sara. (As we consider the blurring of such limits, we could also speculate on how some recognizable components of Saramago's autobiography may actually have been written into his protagonist's story. It may be worth noting, for example, that Saramago's *The History of the Siege of Lisbon*, which is dedicated to "Pilar," was published in 1989, one year after his marriage to Pilar del Rio, his Spanish translator, whom he met in 1987. Then a thirty-year-old journalist and translator, Pilar wanted to meet the sixty-four-year-old author because she was fascinated by his writing [see Teixeira da Silva 2010].)

Gender roles and the opposition between authoring and reading

While Saramago's narrative challenges most of the usual oppositions, it does not touch the grand dichotomy that traditionally distinguishes a man from a woman, a dichotomy that is not only taken for granted, but treated as an indisputable, ahistorical truth. Thus, whatever roles the opposing elements of such a dichotomy have come to represent or been associated with in the broad cultural context of the West, they have to be unequivocally separated as well. This "separation" is made quite clear, for instance, at the beginning of the novel, in the revealing dialogue between Raimundo and the author of the book he is proofreading, a dialogue that highlights the "indisputable" limits between the two activities they represent. Regardless of the eminently creative character of Raimundo's reading practice and of the blurring of borders taking place between his experience as a reader and his initiation as a writer described throughout the book, the terms in which proofreading and authorship are defined – mostly from the perspective of the author figure personified by the historian who wrote "The History of the Siege of Lisbon" – clearly suggest unequivocal, hierarchical categories. According to him, proofreaders are comparable to "guardian angels" who have "no desire to modify" what they read, while authors "are forever making changes, [...] perpetually dissatisfied" (Saramago 1997: 4). Proofreaders are also selfless, attentive caregivers whose very existence is justified by their "solemn duty to respect and safeguard the original text" (ibid.: 75). Raimundo, for example, reminds the historian of his "caring mother who would comb the parting in [his] hair, over and over again, until it looked as if it had been made with a ruler" (ibid.). This characterization of proofreading as "a vigilant task" (Saramago 1997: 30) is foreshadowed by the very name chosen for Saramago's protagonist. Defined by the narrator as "a name [that] somehow conveys the solemnity of another age" (ibid.: 22), "Raimundo" is related to "Raimund" (Old French) and "Raginmund" (Frankish) and is composed of two elements, *"ragin"* ("counsel, might") and *"mund"* (protection) (see *Online Etymology Dictionary*). It is also relevant to note that the proofreader was named after his godmother, Raimunda, because his parents were expecting that an inheritance from her would help their son (Saramago 1997: 23), a detail that could reinforce the characterization of proofreading as an activity associated with the selfless protectiveness of mothers. (About the significance of names in the novel, it is appropriate to mention that Saramago's narrator is particularly careful when choosing names for his characters as he is eager to explore "what secret links a person to a name, even when that person scarcely matches up to the name itself" [ibid.: 256].)

The proofreader is further described as a disciplined, methodical man, whose subaltern role entails blind respect to the authors whose manuscripts he proofreads: "the first of the ten commandments observed by a proof-reader aspiring to sanctity is that you must always try to avoid upsetting the author" (ibid.: 27). Therefore, Raimundo often "allow[s] the errors of others to pass, when what he is tempted to do, and rightly so, is to fill the margins of the page with a flurry of indignant *deleaturs*" (ibid.: 32). This subordinate attitude also defines his relationship with Costa, the editor to whom Raimundo is initially expected to deliver his work and to whose "insolence" he has grown accustomed (ibid.: 29). As one of the worst paid professions in the world (ibid.: 18), proofreading is for those who enjoy books, but have little education and no talent for literary creation (ibid.: 7). For Raimundo, books are his "whole life, yet [he is] always the outsider, even when [he] correct[s] a printing error or some mistake made by the author, rather like someone strolling in a park who feels obliged to keep the place tidy and lifts any litter in sight" (ibid.: 218). Understandably, "a born proof-reader is an unknown phenomenon" (ibid.: 4) and those who find themselves in the profession have to face "a monotonous and humdrum existence" (ibid.: 31), dealing with "the horror of having to read once, twice, three or four or five times books that, Probably would not even warrant a first reading" (ibid.: 5). Sadly, Raimundo's professional routine is compatible with the loneliness and the isolation to which his personal life has been reduced. As a bachelor in his fifties who has no relatives or close friends, the proofreader leads a life that has been mostly shaped by a persistent negation of the "voluptuary" hiding beneath the humble man of letters who is "all too aware of [his] place in literary circles" (ibid.).

As mentioned, when Raimundo finally finds the courage to express his desire to change the text he is proofreading, the voluptuary outsmarts the guardian angel and the proofreader changes his life. As Raimundo's authorial voice is about to emerge, the narrative that describes his inner conflict begins to divide his world into hierarchical, clear-cut distinctions. Thus, the "titanic struggle" that ensues will be fought by Raimundo's alter egos, or "heteronyms," Mr. Jekyll and Mr. Hyde. Even though the "angelic" Jekyll tries to convince Raimundo to take his work seriously, "respect[ing] tradition, observ[ing] the conventions, and suppress[ing] his private inclinations," the demoniac Hyde will prevail, and the proofreader will dare to infringe on the ethical code that regulates "the actions of proof-readers in relation to the ideas and opinions of authors" (Saramago 1997: 40). When he finally changes the original, the anxiety Raimundo feels in relation to the risk that he has taken does not tarnish the exhilaration he also experiences as he no longer needs to repress his authorial voice. Soon, he is comparing himself to the great Fernando Pessoa (ibid.: 42). Immediately after delivering the altered manuscript to the publishing house, Raimundo decides to stop dyeing his gray hair and frees himself from the "artifice" that used to help him deal with the loss of his youth (ibid.: 47). Without the mask of the hair dye, a supposedly truer Raimundo emerges as a man who is finally ready to pursue his dream. After a few days, the reenergized Raimundo learns that even though the publishing house has found out about his "deception," he is not being punished and can continue to work for them. He is then introduced to Maria Sara, an attractive woman in her thirties who has just been hired to supervise all the proofreading work done at the publishing house and who hands him their new policies on proofreading. Their mutual attraction is immediate and she unexpectedly encourages him to write his own version of "The History of the Siege of Lisbon," reminding him that the "Not [that he] slipped in that day will prove to be the most important act in [his] life" (ibid.: 96). Back in his apartment, while he prepares to start working on his new project, he feels "that his home belongs to someone else, and that he himself is the stranger, and the furniture seems out of place or distorted by means of a perspective governed by other laws" (ibid.: 99–100). Now that his desire to be an author has been made explicit, Raimundo clearly distinguishes the proofreader from the author, a distinction that is reflected, for example, in how he reorganizes his working space. While he does his proofreading of "the work of others [in] the study which has no windows," his own writing is carried out in the bedroom at "a small table which he has placed beside the window" so that he can see the river (ibid.: 160). He writes only "in daylight, the natural light falling on to his hands, on to the sheets of paper, on to any words that might appear and remain, for not all words that appear remain, in their turn casting light on our understanding of things" (ibid.). Fully devoted to his ambitious new endeavor, Raimundo is well aware that Maria Sara's initial interest in him is closely linked to his writing: "Tell me, Have you started to write your *History of the Siege of Lisbon*, Yes, I have, Good, for I'm not sure that I could have gone on liking you if you'd said no" (Saramago 1997: 213).

While Raimundo starts reshaping both his life and the history of Portugal he gets acquainted with the protagonist he creates, that is, the young soldier named Mogueime, whom he begins to admire and who will provide his narrative with a reflection of its own author. Appropriately, what distinguishes Mogueime from his fellow soldiers is "his power of narration" and his "lack of inhibition" (ibid.: 168), qualities that have allowed Raimundo himself to change his path. In Raimundo's storyline, Mogueime leads a successful movement among his fellow soldiers to demand wages that equal the crusaders', having the courage and the composure to defend their case not only to their captain, but all the way to the king (ibid.: 304). Impressed with Mogueime's way with words, Dom Afonso Henriques agrees to pay the soldiers what they demand. "Who taught you to speak with more eloquence than a prelate, The words are there, Sir, in the air, anyone can learn them" (ibid.: 307). Mogueime's valor and powerful voice are also rewarded with the love of Ouroana, the beautiful peasant woman whose master, a German crusader, has perished in the fight for Lisbon (ibid.: 280). As mentioned, the creation of these characters and their relationship mirrors the life and the experiences Raimundo now shares with Maria Sara. As fiction and "reality" become almost indistinguishable for the aspiring author, creative writing – or the ability to use words to shape reality – is once again intimately associated with the almost miraculous power of language, which is, apparently, an exclusive prerogative of strong, daring male figures.

While the radical changes that take place in Raimundo's life clearly equate the emergence of his authorial voice with the reawakening of his masculinity, the appearance of Maria Sara in the plot underscores the representation of proofreading as an activity that is basically associated with the feminine. As suggested, since it primarily involves – or should allegedly involve – the selfless protection of someone else's interests, proofreading has been compared to the kind of selfless care and attention generally associated with the role of mothers. Even though, as the publishing house's head proofreader, Maria Sara is Raimundo's supervisor, and *not*, strictly speaking, his proofreader, her main role in the novel is figuratively associated with the profession: to cherish the budding author and make sure that his writing comes to light and is properly handled. In fact, her nurturing role, which is also reflected in her composite name (both "Maria" and "Sara" are associated with two major Biblical mother figures – Mary, mother of Christ; and Sarah, mother of Isaac), is not just a metaphor. She literally brings Raimundo food supplies and whatever he needs so that he can fully focus on his work. Moreover, even though she has a doctoral degree – she is, after all, "*Dra*. Maria Sara" — and earns more than him, Maria Sara is "only a simple woman" (ibid.: 296) and as such not very different from Raimundo's character Ouroana, the peasant girl who had been snatched from her family and turned into a crusader's concubine before meeting Mogueime. Maria Sara is, in fact, Ouroana, as the narrator often reminds us: "What is your name Raimundo Silva asked Ouroana, and she replied, Maria Sara" (ibid.: 259). Like Ouroana, who inspires Mogueime to be a brave soldier and stand up for his rights, Maria Sara is perfectly happy as Raimundo's guardian angel, lover, and Muse. Hence, metaphorically speaking, paired together as a couple, Raimundo and Maria Sara seem to represent an ideal opposition between authoring and reading: while the author figure does not need to fear competition from his loving reader, the latter is content in her ancillary position.

Predictably, this version of the well-known opposition becomes associated with Raimundo's perspective as the new author, not the proofreader, of "The History of the Siege of Lisbon." If, from the point of view of Raimundo Silva, the emerging author, we could say that Maria Sara is the ideal proofreader – whose function in the plot is also to make sure that the hierarchy between authors and proofreaders is restored after his "deception" – then, Raimundo, as the proofreader, personifies the "other" side of this practice as he not only radically changes the text he is supposed to protect but, also, seizes its topic and title to write his own book. In other words, while Raimundo's proofreading practice can certainly be viewed as a predatory activity from the point of view of the author of "The History of the Siege of Lisbon," it is undoubtedly nurturing when we consider Raimundo's perspective and authorial designs. When he sits down for the first time to work on his own book, Raimundo is well aware of how much he has learned (or taken) from his proofreading practice:

his memory as a proof-reader is filled with snatches of verse and prose, the odd line or fragment, and even whole sentences with meaning, hover in his memory like tranquil and resplendent cells coming from other worlds, the sensation is that of being immersed in the cosmos, of grasping the real meaning of everything, without any mystery.

(ibid.: 160–161)

While the notion that texts are born out of other texts may be quite acceptable to Raimundo, the proofreader, as soon as he sees himself as an aspiring author he takes a very different position. When he hears from Maria Sara that his "History of the Siege of Lisbon" could in fact be published and that he will need a proofreader, he accepts the idea,

> but on one condition. Such as, That I should proof-read my own book. But why, when everyone knows that the author is the last person to be trusted with checking his own work. So that I don't find a *yes* where I've written *not*.

(Ibid.: 269)

Babel's "Guy de Maupassant"

As mentioned, Babel's story features two translator characters besides the unnamed, penniless twenty-year-old narrator who arrives in Saint Petersburg in the winter of 1916 and who seems to reflect some key autobiographical traits relatable to Babel's own beginnings as a writer in the same city (Nilsson 1982: 215), a city that has often been identified as the symbolic home of Imperial Russia's literary masters (Fallen 1974: 18). Aleksei Kazantsev, a teacher of Russian philology, who also does translations from Spanish, offers the narrator shelter in the cold attic where he lives in dire poverty and shares his space with several men and women who find themselves in similar circumstances. The narrator is offered a good position at a major factory, but refuses it as he would rather "suffer hunger, prison, and homelessness than to sit at a clerk's desk ten hours a day" (Babel 2002: 680). As he explains, "the wisdom of [his] forefathers was ingrained" in him and, like them, he was born "to delight in labor, fighting and love" (ibid.). His "forefathers," we might conclude, could very well represent the major literary figures that have been associated, in one way or another, with Saint Petersburg's literary circles: Alexander Pushkin, Nikolai Gogol, Ivan Turgenev, and, of course, Fyodor Dostoyevsky and Leo Tolstoy, against whom Babel's narrator has the habit of ranting. Through Aleksei the narrator starts collaborating with Raisa Bendersky on translations of a few stories by Guy de Maupassant. The Benderskys live on the third floor of a "spuriously majestic, vulgar" building, quite compatible with their bourgeois tastes (Babel 2002: 682). The narrator soon learns that Maupassant is the passion of Raisa's life and as he goes over her translation of "Miss Harriet" he finds it correct but lacking in style. He works on the manuscript and the following morning reads his version out loud to Raisa who becomes "transfixed" with emotion (ibid.: 681). Then they begin to translate "Idylle" ("An Idyll"), another story by the French master. Raisa pays the narrator a generous advance and he celebrates his good fortune with his friends at Aleksei's. He continues to work with Raisa every morning and they begin to develop a closer relationship. One evening the narrator brings her the translation of another story, "L'Aveu" ("The Confession"), and finds out that the Benderskys are having a dinner party. While Raisa's husband and guests leave for the theater she decides to stay home and work with the narrator. She opens a bottle of her husband's finest wine and he reads fragments from the translated story out loud. "The Confession" is about Céleste, the country girl who drives to town twice a week with Polyte, the flirtatious coachman, to sell her farm's goods, and ends up seduced by him. Seduced also by the narrator's reading of the translation, the inebriated Raisa raises a toast to Maupassant and the two stories – Maupassant's and Babel's – begin to merge as Raisa plays Céleste to the narrator's Polyte (ibid.: 685). The narrator leaves Raisa's house just before her husband returns from the theater.

"Miss Harriet," originally published in *Le Gaulois* in 1883, names Maupassant's protagonist, a deeply religious, elderly English lady who was never married (Maupassant 2014a, trans. unnamed). While spending time at an inn in the French countryside, she gets acquainted with Leon Chenal, a young painter who is also staying in the inn. He is "very handsome, very strong, very proud of his physique and very popular with women" (ibid.). Miss Harriet begins to discreetly follow him in his painting expeditions and becomes quite interested in his work. One day she finds the courage to ask him if he would be willing to show her how he paints his pictures. He agrees and she watches him paint for hours. Miss Harriet, who has ignored her sexuality all her life, soon finds herself absurdly smitten with the young man. Incapable of dealing with her frightening new feelings, she tries to avoid Chenal at all costs. One evening, after seeing him kiss one of the young servants in the inn, Miss Harriet jumps into a well. She is found the next day and Chenal personally prepares the body for the funeral and lovingly kisses her lips.

"An Idyll," the second story mentioned in Babel's piece, first published in *Gil Blas* in 1884, is about the encounter between a buxom peasant woman and a slender young man whose dark skin suggests long hours of hard work under the burning sun (Maupassant 1909, trans. Rousseau-Wallach). They are sitting face to face in the last car of a train going from Genoa to Marseilles and from the windows they can appreciate the spring scenery filled with roses. The train stops in every station and both travelers fall asleep. Suddenly she wakes up and retrieves some food from one of her baskets and consumes it with gusto. The young man also wakes up and watches her eat. Feeling a bit uncomfortable, she unbuttons her dress. They begin to talk and find out that they are both from Piedmont. They discover mutual acquaintances and talk about themselves. She is married and has three children that she has left with her sister so that she could go to Marseilles and work for a French lady as a nurse. He is a farm laborer and is also going to Marseille to look for work. The heat becomes more oppressive and the two fall asleep again. They awake at the same time and she does not seem well. She explains that because she has not nursed for a whole day her breasts are very heavy and she is having difficulty breathing. With "an unconscious motion" she bares her chest. Her right breast is swollen and stiff. "Ah, mon Dieu! Mon Dieu! What shall I do?" (ibid.: 386). Hesitant, the young man suggests that he might be able to help her. He kneels down before her and she leans over to him in a maternal gesture. He greedily begins to nurse. He has his arms around her waist and holds her close so as not to lose a drop of milk while her two hands rest on his back as she is "breathing happily, freely, enjoying the perfume of the flowers" (ibid.: 387). He continues to nurse with his eyes closed. After a while, she gently pushes him away. "That's enough. I feel much better now. It has put life into me again." "It is I who thank you, madame, for I hadn't eaten a thing in two days" (ibid.).

"The Confession," published for the first time in *Gil Blass* in 1884, is the last of Maupassant's stories coopted by Isaac Babel (Maupassant 2014b, trans. unnamed). Under the relentless midday sun, two women, mother and daughter from a family of respected farmers, are on their way to milk the cows. When they finish milking the first cow, Céleste, the daughter, suddenly stops, drops her heavy bucket, and begins to cry. After a while she tells her impatient mother that she can no longer carry her bucket and confesses that she may be pregnant. The angry mother insists on hearing the whole story and Céleste clarifies that it might have happened in Polyte's cart. The mother considers that if the man who got her daughter pregnant is rich and respectable, maybe they could make it work. "And who was it that did this to you, you whore?" "I think it was Polyte," the daughter answers (ibid.). The mother starts hitting Céleste, who reasons that, although she may have gotten pregnant, she no longer has to pay for the rides. Céleste, who rides Polyte's cart twice a week to get her produce and poultry to town, explains that one day she asked Polyte if he would consider taking her to town for less money. He jokingly replied that he would certainly do that if he could have "a little fun" with her. When she grasped what he meant, she politely declined. After that, every time he picked her up and, just before she paid him, he would ask: "Is today the day for some fun?" "Not today, thanks, monsieur Polyte, but next Saturday for sure!," she would often reply to humor him (ibid.). And Polyte would say "Saturday it is, my sweet!" (ibid.). After a while, Céleste calculated how much money she would save on the rides and decided to accept his proposal. Her mother hears the whole story and asks Céleste how much she has actually saved. When she hears the answer, the woman starts hitting her daughter again. Suddenly she stops and asks Céleste if she has already told Polyte about the pregnancy. She replies that she has not because she fears that he might make her pay for the rides. After making some calculations of her own, the mother tells her daughter not to say anything to him as they may be able "to get six to eight months out of this" (ibid.). Back to her feet, but swollen and disheveled, Céleste promises her mother she will not say a word.

Gendered portraits of authorship and translation in "Guy de Maupassant"

As a central motif in the story, translation is represented first and foremost as a form of apprenticeship for the narrator, the aspiring young writer who moves back and forth from Aleksei's miserable attic to Raisa's gaudy apartment, and in the process introduces readers to a few stereotypes often associated with translators and their craft (for other readings on the role of translation in the story, see Van de Stadt 2006 and Thiem 1995). Aleksei, who works as a teacher and a translator, could very well be an illustration of the marginality and the precariousness of literary translation as a professional activity, something that is as true today, at least in many Western contexts, as it was in pre-Soviet Russia. In spite of his hard work, Aleksei can barely survive and, yet, he is the happiest of all in the commune into which he has transformed his living quarters, finding solace in the culture and literature of Spain, his adopted "motherland," a country that he has never visited (Babel 2002: 679). Translation is, then, also depicted as a labor of love, in which the unassuming translator helps bring the foreign to his domestic context and, unlike the narrator, does not show any ambition to become a writer and seems content in the position of a humble spectator who is deeply impacted by what he reads and hears. This is a position that Aleksei also occupies in his relationship with the narrator whose fiery rant on why he is determined not to become a clerk brings "horror" and "rapture" to the translator's eyes (ibid.: 680). Most importantly, Aleksei's reaction to the narrator's rhetoric foreshadows Raisa's in her collaboration with the aspiring author. The simple-minded, voluptuous Raisa represents another recurrent stereotype associated with translation: a female dilettante with no financial concerns and who wants to keep herself entertained with some form of intellectual activity. She starts translating Maupassant, "the one passion" of her life, because her husband, a wealthy lawyer who owns a publishing house, has decided to bring out a new edition of the French author's work. Translation is, for her also, a labor of love: just as Aleksei finds solace from his bleak reality in Spanish culture, Raisa seeks in Maupassant's French a refuge from her vulgar, petite bourgeois life and, most of all, from her husband and his questionable business dealings. While both Aleksei and Raisa are immersed in idealized versions of the foreign and do not seem interested in directly intervening in their domestic context, the narrator is very much connected to his surroundings, often searching for material to write about "in morgues and police stations," where he often spends his mornings (ibid.: 679) (see also Rougle 1989: 173).

The narrator's ambition to become a writer is made explicit in the relationship he establishes with Raisa, a relationship that reveals a sheer contrast not only between their aspirations, but their talents as well. A devoted reader of Maupassant, Raisa cannot produce adequate versions of his stories because of her poor writing skills and "lack of style" (Babel 2002: 681). While Raisa's clumsy translations suggest that she can never be more than a seduced reader who writes like a clerk or a bureaucrat, the narrator's fine writing blurs the distinction between author and literary translator and places him in the authorial position of skilled seducer. More specifically, the hierarchical distinction that separates them is first and foremost nurtured in gender stereotypes. The most obvious association between gender and power in the story is the equation established between the narrator's keen interest in sex and his ambition to become an author. He is, as has been observed, a young man "of hedonistic, even predatory erotic impulses" who views all the women crossing his path as sexual prey (Rougle 1989: 172, 174). In contrast, his friend, the impressionable Aleksei, who seems shy and asexual, is, as mentioned, perfectly content as a teacher and translator. While the narrator's rhetorical skills are associated with an aggressive, albeit immature, brand of masculinity – both as sexual energy and combative warfare – his reader, the amateur translator Raisa, is portrayed as a submissive, nurturing female who can barely contain her obvious sexuality. When the narrator reads out to Raisa his revision of her translation of Maupassant's "Miss Harriet," she is more than captivated by the magic of his language: "She sat transfixed as I read to her, her hands clasped together. Her satin arms flowed down toward the ground, her forehead grew pale, and the lace between her struggling breasts swerved and trembled" (Babel 2002: 681). Indeed, his words seem to "permeate her body, at once weakening and stimulating it," producing a response that "exudes physical arousal" (Van de Stadt 2006: 645). As the narrator responds to Raisa's question on how he manages to create such a powerful effect with his language, he further expands this obvious association between male prowess and the effectiveness of his writing with a definition of style that relies on warfare metaphors with obviously phallic overtones – "an army of words, an army in which every type of weapon is deployed. No iron spike can pierce a human heart as icily as a period in the right place" (Babel 2002: 681). This representation of words as weapons and, hence, of writing as a quintessentially aggressive, masculine skill also links Babel's narrator to Raisa's husband, who has profited from his dealings with the military and might even be close to the legendary Rasputin. As a man who has "a lean, powerful body that always seem[s] poised to surge up into the air" (ibid.: 683), Raisa's husband epitomizes male strength and bourgeois success and constitutes a model of sorts for the narrator, even though he apparently despises him and what he represents.

The clear opposition between the narrator's role as creative translator/ aspiring author and Raisa's as inadequate translator/seduced reader is also echoed in the storyline of Maupassant's "Miss Harriet." In spite of the obvious differences in the characterization of Babel's and Maupassant's female figures, Raisa's response to the narrator's literary talent reflects Miss Harriet's reaction to Leon Chenal's sensuous depictions of nature. At the same time, Babel's narrator seems to be a younger version of the handsome painter with whom Miss Harriet falls in love. In both stories artistic power is openly related to male sexuality and the ability to seduce women while the reader and the art lover are portrayed as docile, ignorant females who cannot resist falling for the artists they admire. As Babel's narrator seems to mirror the accomplished Chenal, it could be argued that he does not view himself as a "mere" translator, but as an ambitious author in disguise. Significantly, as we are told, he arrives in Saint Petersburg with false documents and, later on, when he first visits Raisa, he wears "another man's jacket" (ibid.: 680), a jacket that, metaphorically speaking, could very well have been borrowed from Maupassant himself (cf. Van de Stadt 2006: 638). In other words, the young man who introduces himself to Raisa as a translator is actually looking for a path that would lead him to become an author like his imagined literary forefathers. Furthermore, it is this desire to be a full-blown author that he seems to act out in his dealings with Raisa, whose reaction to his retranslation of "Miss Harriet" anticipates what is to come in the plot. It is, after all, in the voice and in the words of the skillful, physically "present" translator that the female reader now enjoys Maupassant's stories.

On the narrator's second visit to Raisa they begin to translate Maupassant's "An Idyll," whose storyline can also be directly associated with Babel's: "Who can forget the tale of the hungry young carpenter sucking milk from the overflowing breasts of the fat wet-nurse" (Babel 2002: 682). Just as Raisa can be compared to the married nurse, the young man in "An Idyll" appropriately echoes Babel's hungry narrator in search of work. Moreover, the ambiguity of Raisa's involvement with the narrator is reflected in the intriguing scene that represents the young man sucking at the nurse's breasts, a scene that seems to synthesize both maternal love and erotic pleasure. At the same time, just as the nurse and the young man on the train find comfort in one another, so do Raisa and the narrator: she is overflowing with love for Maupassant and he is eager to take the place of her beloved author. Therefore, the nurturing milk the young man is offered in Maupassant's story is mirrored in Babel's as the sustenance that the narrator literally and metaphorically receives from Raisa who feeds him breakfast every morning and generously pays for his work. Most importantly, as an impressionable reader, Raisa gives Babel's narrator the opportunity to practice and refine his authorial skills. It is then the practice of translation, to which Babel's narrator has access through Aleksei and Raisa as nurturing, non-competitive reader and translator figures, that allows him to support himself and, at the same time, functions as a form of apprenticeship, fostering his growth both as a man and as a writer.

For Babel's narrator, this process of apprenticeship culminates in the seduction scene that takes place almost at the end of the story when he and Raisa get drunk on her husband's wine while working on the manuscript of Maupassant's "The Confession." This is a story that does not simply mirror Babel's, but which is directly incorporated into "Guy de Maupassant" as the two plots intertwine and Raisa becomes almost indistinguishable from Céleste, who finally agrees to have "some fun" with Polyte, the coachman. While Raisa is Céleste, Babel's narrator is, of course, Polyte and, after making a toast to Maupassant, they begin to have "some fun" themselves, reenacting their own version of the seduction scene from the French story: "Aren't we going to have some fun today, *ma belle*?," asks Babel's narrator as he "reach[es] over to Raisa and kiss[es] her on the lips" (ibid.) She calls him "M'sieur Polyte" and asks him to sit on a nearby armchair. He accidentally stumbles towards it, "knocking over the armchair and bumping into the shelf. Twenty-nine volumes [of Maupassant's collected works] c[o]me tumbling onto the carpet, falling onto their spines, their pages flying wild …" (ibid.). As this fragment seems to suggest, just as the narrator and Raisa are about to become intimate, he is not simply playing Polyte to her Céleste. Rather, as he successfully rewrites Maupassant's stories in Russian and seduces his reader, the narrator, who, as noted, has the habit of ranting against Tolstoy, also "knocks down" the French author and literally takes his place, at least temporarily, as the object of Raisa's desire. In this exemplary, gendered setting for translation, while the male translator's Russian effectively replaces the original French, he also ousts the author, whom he is supposed to represent and to whom he is expected to be faithful, from the female reader's domestic context. Therefore, while the dead Maupassant may be the one passion of Raisa's life, it is with the translator that she actually establishes an intimate rapport when addressing the Russian versions of the French author's stories. Finally, as the above comments suggest, in the patriarchal scenario that shapes the story, Raisa seems to play a double role that synthesizes some of the most recurrent female stereotypes of Western culture. As the main female character in the story, whose composition also draws from the female characters featured in the Maupassant stories interwoven into Babel's, Raisa acts, first, as a comforting mother figure that indirectly fosters the narrator's budding writing career. At the same time, though, she also represents a certain brand of female "fickleness" both as a wife and as a reader: just as she betrays her husband, she also betrays Maupassant, so to speak, when she falls for the translator and his words. In any case, whether viewed as a surrogate mother or as a representative of the "weaker sex," Raisa lacks the intellect and the (male) authorial skills that could equip her to adequately rewrite the French author's stories, a lack that imprisons her in a position of subservience and vulnerability to both the author and the creative, highly visible translator.

Regarding the gendering of textual practices that underscores Babel's story, the "knocking down" of the author in the scene of translation is only the culmination of a process that also involves the manipulation of the Maupassant stories that are incorporated into the plot. Consider, for example, the narrator's reference to "An Idyll," in which the train's original itinerary is changed. While in Maupassant's story the train crosses the border between Italy and France, going from Genoa to Marseille, in the narrator's version it goes from Nice to Marseille. Moreover, in his summary of the story, Babel's narrator omits the fact that the two young people who meet on the train are poor Italian peasants traveling to France in search of work. As mentioned, the woman has left behind her own family in order to work as a wet nurse for a French lady, while the man, described as a "carpenter" in Babel's story, actually works the land and has not had anything to eat in a couple of days. These discrepancies could suggest that, in an attempt at seducing his reader, Babel's narrator chooses to omit some of Maupassant's more naturalistic details and foregrounds the idyllic landscape visible from the train "on a sultry midday in the land of roses, the motherland of roses where flower plantations stretch down to the shores of the sea" (Babel 2002: 682). The narrator's version of the story, just like his version of the train ride, entails, so to speak, a "domestication" of the original, which is appropriated primarily to serve the translator's own goals, not the author's. Similarly, in the narrator's version of Maupassant's "The Confession," the emphasis is placed on details that can be romanticized, such as "*le soleil de France*," which becomes "the hero" of the tale: together with wine and apple cider, the sun "with its steep rays had burnished the face of Polyte, the coachman" (ibid.: 684). Again, what Babel's narrator/translator strategically omits from his version is Maupassant's more disturbing, naturalistic elements such as the revelation that Céleste does not simply fall for Polyte, but is in fact selling herself in order to avoid paying for the rides. While he romanticizes Maupassant's originals in order to make them work for himself in the domestic context of his female reader, the narrator also manages to hide from her the more naturalistic aspects of his own agenda as a translator, which suggests that his interest in the translation of Maupassant's story is not by any means to merely protect or faithfully reproduce the French originals in a foreign environment. Unlike Raisa, Babel's narrator does not simply translate Maupassant out of love for the French author's work. Rather, he seems to join Raisa's translation project mainly because he needs the money as well as the writing practice and the sexual initiation that the experience can provide.

The impossible position of "reproductive" textual practices

As suggested, and particularly if we consider that both Saramago and Babel seem to have written autobiographical elements into their storylines, the pairing of their male protagonists with non-threatening, stereotypically female and feminized figures could betray the longing for a convenient, safe encounter between reading and writing that should foster a complementing rather than a competitive relationship between these practices. In fact, their plots may very well serve as appropriate illustrations of Freud's claim according to which the writing of fiction is often "egocentric" and, therefore, comparable to daydreaming, as it tends to reveal the writer's desire to escape his circumstances and indulge in fantasies of potency and invulnerability. According to Freud, in this kind of fiction there is always a "hero who is the center of interest" and whom the author "seems to place under the protection of a special Providence" (Freud 1983: 26, trans. Strachey). Other typical characteristics of egocentric stories that can be related to Saramago's and Babel's texts include the fact that their protagonists seem to attract the attention of women in an unrealistic manner as well as their reliance on clear-cut oppositions that benefit their "heroes" (ibid.). To the extent that the gendered couplings and encounters that make up the core of Saramago's and Babel's fictions reaffirm writing as an almost magical instrument and equate sexual prowess with textual power, they might also distract the authors or author figures involved from their finitude and, perhaps more importantly, from the ambiguous relationships they have established with their precursors and, therefore, from their influence anxiety as well. After all, let us not forget that Saramago's and Babel's protagonists take over and rewrite the very same texts they are expected to preserve and protect in the name of their legitimate authors: Raimundo Silva sets out to write a novel that has the exact same title of and covers the exact same topic as the history book he has proofread while Babel's narrator, who often rants against Tolstoy and ends up "knocking down" Maupassant, learns to seduce his female reader with subversive translations of the French master's stories, the same stories whose plots and characters are coopted in Babel's. In addition, while Saramago's protagonist disdains the author of the original he decides to rewrite, Babel creates a story that, on one hand, could be viewed as a sort of homage to Maupassant, one of his acknowledged influences, but, on the other, suggests an implicit rivalry between his protagonist and the dead French author (for a detailed discussion on "Guy de Maupassant" as a reflection of Babel's autobiography and influences, see Nilsson 1982 and Van de Stadt 2006).

These complex relationships between aspiring author figures and their precursors could remind readers of Harold Bloom's arguments on influence and literary history that share with Freud's thoughts on egocentric stories the view that creative writing is a prerogative of male authors. For Bloom, literary influence is a "filial relationship" (Bloom 1973: 11), which he describes with the help of notions borrowed from psychoanalysis: every ambitious newcomer who wants to carve a place for himself in the world of letters somehow repeats Oedipus's conflict with his father, Laius, and, hence, must struggle against his most admired precursor in a "battle between strong equals, father and son as mighty opposites" (ibid.: 26). The main difference between Saramago's and Babel's plots and the narrative featured in Bloom's arguments is, obviously, the fact that both Raimundo Silva and Babel's narrator are engaged in textual practices that are often viewed as reproductive or secondary and, as a consequence, they cannot exactly engage in a "battle between strong equals." Since the hierarchical opposition between the writing of originals and activities such as proofreading and translation often involves "productive" versus "reproductive" practices, a view that is often implicitly or explicitly inseparable from issues of gender and power differentials, the kind of influence anxiety we can associate with Saramago's and Babel's protagonists is further complicated by the fact that their precursors are actually the authors of the texts that they appropriate through proofreading or translation. More importantly, to the extent that Saramago's and Babel's pieces incorporate previous texts and feature empowered aspiring male authors whose work threatens to erase the typical distinction between the writing and the reproduction of originals, they seem to implicitly suggest that "secondary" or "reproductive" activities such as translation and proofreading are only safe when treated as non-creative and, consequently, associated with the feminine, or the absence of a powerful pen/penis. Such a conclusion is compatible, for instance, with Lori Chamberlain's claim that one of the implications of the traditional gendering of textual practices is that what the consciously visible male translator "claims for 'himself' is precisely the right to paternity; he claims a phallus because this is the only way, in a patriarchal code, to claim legitimacy for the text" (Chamberlain 2000: 323).

If translators are unquestionably the writers of translated texts and, therefore, if they cannot shy away from making decisions about meaning and word choices as they necessarily take over someone else's original, whether they acknowledge or are aware of their agency or not, the usual view of translation as a merely "reproductive" practice fails to properly account for the mechanism that makes the process of translation possible. Rather, as it tries to ignore the translator's undeniably active role in the composition of the translated text, the metaphor of translation as reproduction seems to reflect the interests of those who claim to possess or control texts and who would like to keep their privileged positions. Indeed, as Chamberlain points out, it is precisely because translations can "masquerade" as originals and, thus, "short-circuit" the system, threatening "to erase the difference between production and reproduction which is essential to the establishment of power," that it has been "so overcoded, so over regulated" (ibid.: 322). Consequently, it could also be argued that the hierarchical opposition between male and female roles as well as the representation of authorship as a form of enhanced masculinity found at the core of Saramago's and Babel's pieces do not simply reflect their authors' fantasies. Rather, the gendering of translation is "a symptom of larger issues of western culture: of the power relations as they divide in terms of gender" (ibid.). If authorship is associated with male prowess and the right to produce creative work, the feminization of textual practices such as translation and proofreading is a necessary consequence, following "the binary logic" that "encourages us to define nurses as female and doctors as male, teachers as female and professors as male, secretaries as female and corporate executives as male" (Chamberlain 2000: 323).

At the same time that Saramago's and Babel's storylines mirror our patriarchal culture's deep-seated fantasies involving the hierarchization of textual practices and their intimate association with stereotypical gender roles, they also destabilize their basis. Perhaps the most revealing passage associated with this destabilization is the touching ending to Babel's story. As the young narrator feels empowered after seducing Raisa Bendersky and, hence, after taking Maupassant's place, so to speak, he spends the rest of the night reading about the French author's tragic biography. He learns that Guy de Maupassant had congenital syphilis and "fought the disease with all the potency and vitality he had" (Babel 2002: 686). In spite of his misery, he "wrote unceasingly" (ibid.). At the age of forty, already widely known as a master of the short story, he cut his throat and was "locked in a madhouse," where he degenerated to an animal state and died at forty-two (ibid.). As the narrator, with his heart "constricted," finishes reading about the French author he feels "touched by a premonition of truth" (ibid.). The "truth" here could very well be related to the fact that authorial power and fame cannot really protect author figures from the fragility of humanity and the inevitability of illness and mortality. As for Saramago's plot, it is worth remembering that Raimundo Silva is well aware of the fact that while authors may desire or try to control how their texts are going to be read they are not in any sense immune to their readers' appropriations. Furthermore, as suggested, while Saramago's and Babel's protagonists may entertain the illusion that authorship – as a "righteous" attribute of strong males – could in some way downplay the active role of readers and translators, they also illustrate the underlying power of intertextuality, that is, how texts shape and are born out of other texts, and, therefore, their plots end up deconstructing the very notion of a forever present, true "original" as well as the opposition that attempts to separate "productive" from "reproductive" textual practices.

Finally, Saramago's and Babel's plots can also be read as cautionary illustrations of the impossible position typically reserved for professionals like translators and proofreaders wherever or whenever the possibility of clearly separating productive from reproductive textual practices is taken for granted. In other words, in contexts in which readers and translators are expected to be neutral, selfless participants in the relationships they must establish with texts and their authors, there is no actual place for creative translators or knowledgeable, imaginative readers who appreciate and are proud of what they do. According to the rationale shaping the characters and the circumstances constituting the storylines analyzed above, proofreading and translation are practices chosen by either those who have no talent for creative endeavors or by those who may be gifted writers, but simply use "reproductive" textual activities as a necessary step towards becoming full-fledged authors. Either way, there is no place in such contexts for creative individuals who can be professionally fulfilled as translators or proofreaders. As shown in Babel's story, for example, a translator like Raisa Bendersky, who cannot write with "style," is unable to do justice to Maupassant's craft, but a translator like the narrator, who allegedly has the writing skills to produce translations that could compete with their originals, is primarily interested in becoming an author himself. From such a perspective, besides bringing us stereotypical representations of gender and productive versus reproductive textual practices, Saramago's and Babel's plots also give us the opportunity to reflect on one of the main consequences of such representations: the degrading notion that translation and proofreading are activities pursued only by those who are not good enough to write originals, a notion that unfortunately is still very much ingrained in the ways in which mainstream narratives tend to view and treat translators and professional readers.

Bibliography

Babel, I. (2002) "Guy de Maupassant," P. Constantine (trans.), in N. Babel (ed.) *The Complete Works of Isaac Babel*, New York: W. W. Norton & Company, 679–686.

Bloom, H. (1973) *The Anxiety of Influence*, New York: Oxford University Press.

Chamberlain, L. (2000) "Gender and the Metaphorics of Translation," in L. Venuti (ed.) *The Translation Studies Reader*, London: Routledge, 314–329.

Fallen, J. E. (1974) *Isaac Babel, Russian Master of the Short Story*, Knoxville: The University of Tennessee Press.

Freud, S. (1983) "Creative Writers and Daydreaming," J. Strachey (trans.), in E. Kurzweil and W. Phillips (eds.) *Literature and Psychoanalysis*, New York: Columbia University Press, 24–28.

Gilbert, S. M. and S. Gubar, (2000) *The Woman Writer and the Nineteenth-Century Literary Imagination*, New Haven, CT: Yale University Press.

Maupassant, G. (1909) "An Idyll," *The Works of Guy de Maupassant*, vols. 9–10, F. Rousseau-Wallach (trans.), New York: National Library Co., 382–387. Available through Google books (accessed March 15, 2014).

—— (2014a) "Miss Harriet," "The Literature Network," trans. unnamed. Available at: www.online-literature.com/maupassant/250/ (accessed March 20, 2014).

—— (2014b) "The Confession," "Guy de Maupassant's Short Stories in English," trans. unnamed. Available at: http://maupassanttranslation.blogspot.com/2014/03/the-confession-laveu.html (accessed March 25, 2014).

Nilsson, N. A. (1982) "Isaac Babel's Story 'Guy de Maupassant'," in N. A. Nilsson (ed.) *Studies in 20th Century Russian Prose*, Stockholm: Almqvist and Wiksell, 213–227.

Online Etymology Dictionary. Available at: www.etymonline.com (accessed November 20, 2015).

Pontiero, G. (1997) "Afterword," in J. Saramago, *The History of the Siege of Lisbon*, G. Pontiero (trans.), Orlando, FL: Harcourt, 313–314.

Rougle, C. (1989) "Art and the Artist in Babel's 'Guy de Maupassant'," *The Russian Review* 48(2), April: 171–180.

Sadlier, D. J. (1998) *An Introduction to Fernando Pessoa: Modernism and the Paradoxes of Authorship*, Gainesville: University Press of Florida.

Saramago, J. (1997) *The History of the Siege of Lisbon*, G. Pontiero (trans.), Orlando, FL: Harcourt.

Teixeira da Silva, H. (2010) "Pilar, a Mulher a quem Saramago se Confiou," *Jornal de Noticias*, June 6. Available at: www.jn.pt/cultura/dossiers/jose-saramago-1922-2010/interior/pilar-a-mulher-a-quem-saramago-se-confiou-1597441.html (accessed November 25, 2015).

Thiem, J. (1995) "The Translator as Hero in Postmodern Fiction," *Translation and Literature* 4(2): 207–218.

Van de Stadt, J. (2006) "The Poetics of Transit: 'Miss Harriet' and 'Guy De Maupassant'," *The Slavic and East European Journal* 50(4),Winter: 635–654.

White, E. (1997) "The Subversive Proofreader," *The New York Times*, July 13. Available at: www.nytimes.com/books/98/10/04/specials/saramago-lisbon.html (accessed October 10, 2015).

7   The gendering of texts
Moacyr Scliar's "Footnotes" and Italo Calvino's *If on a Winter's Night a Traveler*

> In patriarchal Western culture, [...] the text's author is a father, a progenitor, a procreator, an aesthetic patriarch whose pen is an instrument of generative power like his penis. More, his pen's power, like his penis's power, is not just the ability to generate life but the power to create a posterity to which he lays claim [. ...] In this respect, the pen is truly mightier than its phallic counterpart the sword, and in patriarchy more resonantly sexual [. ... A]s the author of an enduring text the writer engages the attention of the future in exactly the same way that a king (or father) "owns" the homage of the present. No sword-wielding general could rule so long or possess so vast a kingdom.
>
> Sandra M. Gilbert and Susan Gubar, *The Madwoman in the Attic*

The quotation above addresses a few statements made by male authors who unequivocally sexualize their roles as writers or artists. A revealing example can be found in a personal letter written by the nineteenth-century English poet Gerard Manley Hopkins, according to whom the "most essential quality" of any artist is "masterly execution, which is a kind of male gift, and especially marks off men from women, the begetting of one's thought on paper, on verse, or whatever the matter is" (Abbott 1935: 133, qtd. in Gilbert and Gubar 1984: 3). In contemporary thought, the general metaphor inspiring this view has been notoriously illustrated, for instance, by Harold Bloom's conception of poetic influence as an issue of masculine rivalry: "a battle between strong equals, father and son as mighty opposites, Laius and Oedipus at the crossroads" (Bloom 1973: 26, qtd. in Gilbert and Gubar 1984: 6). According to Bloom's vision, obviously borrowed from Freud's concept of the Oedipus complex, while the son as the latecomer represents the enamored reader of poetry and aspiring poet, the father or precursor is the revered creator (and owner) of the precious text or texts that endow his privileged position and will define and establish his legacy. In their battle, while the father struggles to retain his status among the greats, the son, who strives to be recognized as a deserving poet rather than just a reader or a disciple, must fight to outsmart and replace his precursor. Just as the battle between Laius and Oedipus, in Freud's appropriation of the Greek myth, ultimately involves the possession of a certain woman, in Bloom's narrative, the "thing" that both the established precursor and the aspiring poet actually fight for can also be implicitly associated with the rightful ownership of a female figure.

If what defines the precursor's position in the world of letters is the writing he owns as a desirable object that needs to be kept under control and protected from others, it is not far-fetched to identify an underlying link between text and woman behind the metaphorical battles that, according to Bloom, shape literary history. As an integral element of this patriarchal scenario, the right to own the text as woman is inseparable from the very conception of authorship and some of its implications. As "an aesthetic patriarch," the privileged author must keep his readers' revering attention at the same time that he must own and possess his beloved text as well as "the subjects of his text, that is to say [...] those figures, scenes, and events – those brain children – he has both incarnated in black and white and 'bound' in cloth or leather" (Gilbert and Gubar 1984: 6). That is, the same "brain children" that should immortalize his name and his greatness. Hence, in order for the author to make sure that this narrative is not in any way subverted and that his position is not challenged, he must make sure that his prized texts and his admiring readers/sons are kept in their places and bound by fidelity vows: while readers shall not desire to replace the author, the text must only say whatever the author wants it to say.

If we take into account that conceptions – or fantasies – of patriarchal power have been crucial for Western definitions of authorship and literary influence, we should also investigate how they may have impacted the ways in which translators and translations are viewed and/or represented. As Lori Chamberlain points out, the sexualization of translation is obviously reflected, for example, in the notion of *"les belles infidèles"* and its comparison of translations to women: "like women, the adage goes, translations should be either beautiful or faithful" (Chamberlain 2000: 315). Coined in the seventeenth century, this tag "owes its longevity" to

> more than phonetic similarity: what gives it the appearance of truth is that it has captured a cultural complicity between the issues of fidelity in translation and in marriage. For *"les belles infidèles"*, fidelity is defined by an implicit contract between translation (as woman) and original (as husband, father, or author).
>
> (Ibid.)

At the same time, however, and especially when the (male) translator's authorial thrust cannot be ignored, and, therefore, when the latter is viewed as the author's rival who inappropriately takes over the original and decides how it is going to be re-presented in the target language and culture, both the original and the translation are likely to be stereotypically associated with the feminine. In this patriarchal scheme, while the inevitably unfaithful translation – the *"belle infidèle"* – may not serve the author's interests, she will likely serve the translator's.

The gendering of texts and the practices that generate them is precisely the focus of this chapter, which will propose readings of two quite different, albeit compatible pieces: the Brazilian Moacyr Scliar's short story "Notas ao pé da página" ("Footnotes") (Scliar 1995, hereafter quoted from my unpublished translation from the Portuguese) and the Italian Italo Calvino's *If on a Winter's Night a Traveler*, a novel originally published in 1979 (Calvino 1981, trans. Weaver). Even though both storylines recognize the authorial vocation of the translator's work, they do rely on clichéd gender roles as the basis for their representations of translation and the writing of originals. While their author and translator characters are predictably male, their desirable female figures are portrayed as modern-day Muses that are also expanded representations of both the original and the translated text as "*belles infidèles*," that is, as desirable objects for which the author and the translator characters will turn into bitter rivals. As I will be arguing, both Scliar's and Calvino's fictions can be productively read as spirited depictions of contemporary notions of text, authorship, and translation that playfully transform key theoretical constructs into characters and the relationships they establish with one another. My probing into the representation of such constructs in Calvino's and Scliar's pieces will also claim that when read as an enactment of theory and, more specifically, of certain conceptions that still seem controversial, fiction can in fact be more revealing than most theoretical narratives as it shines some light on the personal, emotional investments usually associated with the writing and the translation of valued literary texts.

Scliar's "Footnotes": the visible translator, the "dummy" author, and a resourceful *"belle infidèle"*

As its title suggests, Scliar's story is exclusively composed of footnotes, five of them, which appear at the bottom of the five empty pages where the invisible translated original is supposed to be. While the translation, the original, and its author are not accessible to us, readers, it is the translator figure's writing that constitutes the actual text of Scliar's piece. And yet, even though the translator represents the only voice recorded in the story, he is definitely speaking on his own behalf and within the only textual space usually granted to him: the bottom of the page. Even though the footnotes refer to his translation of a poet's diaries and their alleged goal is to clarify some points mentioned in the original narrative, what this translator ends up doing is to bring up inappropriate details from his author's biography. We learn, for example, that the poet, now dead, used to be ungrateful, immensely ambitious, and difficult. We also learn of his eagerness to have his work translated by the translator and of his humiliating efforts to achieve that. The last time they both met, the poet, as usual, overpraised the translator's work and confessed that he even liked his footnotes. More importantly, we are exposed to details associated with the love triangle involving the poet, the translator, and N., the poet's mistress, who left the latter in order to marry the translator. We are also told that at the time N. met the poet in France she was working as a secretary in the small publishing house that finally agreed to publish his first collection of poems. Moreover, "the relative success of this book should be attributed, at least partially, to N." and her willingness to grant the publisher "certain favors" that managed to obtain the latter's "reluctant approval" for an enterprise that "financially speaking was clearly risky" (Scliar 1995: 371). N.'s willingness to please the translator was later on also instrumental in convincing him to accept the task of translating the poet's work.

Before examining the characterization of Scliar's translator and author figures as well as the role played by N. in the love triangle representing the scene of translation that constitutes the story, it is important to emphasize that Scliar's narrator is also the translator figure, placed, from the start, in an unequivocal authorial position. And it is from this position that he confronts us with the undeniable, somewhat uncomfortable fact that, for the readers of a translation, the author's original is indeed invisible and the only access they have to what such an original might be saying is inevitably filtered by the translator's own interests and word choices. Therefore, even though the translator's voice is formally registered only in the "official" space where he is allowed to speak about the original and its author, the blanks found on each page of the story also suggest that the separation between the main text and the footnotes is only a formality and all we can find in the translation is, literally, what the translator tells us about the original. Consequently, despite the widespread, commonplace notion that translators should be invisible in their work and provide us with nothing but a faithful, reliable repetition of their authors' texts, Scliar's story reminds us that what we come to know about the author's identity is also largely shaped by what the translator decides to tell us. In Scliar's story, we learn, for instance, that the dead poet was not only a helpless, lonely man who got desperate about the loss of his mistress – a desperation that may have contributed to his death – but one who also had to credit most of his modest success to the translator's talent and compassion. If we consider that N. might function as a metaphor for the author's original, to which he is particularly attached, but which must often change hands, so to speak, and be re-edited and re-interpreted, we can conclude that, once again, all we know about her and what she represents also comes from the translator's narrative. As a metaphor for both the original and the translation, N. can be viewed as a good-humored version of the *"belle infidèle,"* who is not only the author's down-to-earth Muse, but also represents his writing as a prized possession that, however, cannot remain faithful to him. Even though she is the author's mistress, she must also "serve" the publisher and later on moves in with the translator whom she finally marries. In other words, the author's beloved text cannot belong or attend exclusively to him if he wants to get it/her published. In order for the author to succeed in his mission, his text must also please the publisher and then, if it/she is to be made available in another language, it/she must leave the author behind and surrender to the translator as well.

If N. can be viewed as a *"belle infidèle,"* Scliar's translator figure, who introduces himself as a "friend" to the author, can very well be interpreted as a humorous representation of a peculiar *traduttore traditore*. Although we cannot verify whether his translation actually does justice to the author's original, we do know that he steals the author's mistress and, thus, at least on some level, we also know that we are dealing with a translator who, despite his claims of fidelity to the poet's original, is, nonetheless, a traitor. The allegedly competent translator's betrayal could also be associated with the way in which he blatantly misuses (and virtually abuses) the space that is conventionally ceded to him at the bottom of his translation as he offers us a commentary that is outrageously out of place and mostly malicious. Regardless of his inappropriate behavior, Scliar's empowered translator character is not only the exclusive authorial figure actually speaking in the story, as mentioned, but, also, the dominant male in the love triangle defining the relationship he establishes with N. and with the author. As Scliar's story playfully suggests, in the process of translation, it is the translator who must conquer and (legitimately) possess the woman/text while the "dead" author not only loses his access to her, but also owes his recognition in another language and context to the translator's effort and alleged generosity. Finally, we may also argue that the translator's marriage to N. does not necessarily suggest that they will be forever an exclusive couple. As we are told, when he met the poet's mistress, the translator had just been through a traumatic divorce and needed attention and emotional support. Considering what we know about their history, even though the translator and the woman/text are married at the end of Scliar's story, their marriage is quite probably not going to be everlasting as they may have to part at the prospect of new projects. Just as N., at some point, may attract the attention of another translator, the translator himself will likely become interested in other texts and move on.

By resorting to gendered representations of text and textual practices, the story humorously subverts the underlying power relations that usually underscore the basic, old clichés involving the notions of property, fidelity, and betrayal as they get entangled with conceptions of authorship and translation. Readers who are familiar with contemporary translation theories might associate Scliar's story with some often quoted texts, without implying, though, that the author actually meant to have them illustrated in the story. Lawrence Venuti's texts on the translator's invisibility are probably the first ones that come to mind as his main theoretical focus has been the exploration of the "eclipse of the translator's labor" in a cultural context in which translation continues to be "an invisible practice, everywhere around us, inescapably present, but rarely acknowledged, almost never figured into discussions of the translations we all inevitably read" (Venuti 1992: 1).

Venuti has been notably interested in unveiling the asymmetries involving translation practice, his "overriding assumption" being perhaps "the greatest scandal of translation: asymmetries, inequities, relations of domination and dependence [, which] exist in every act of translating, of putting the translated in the service of the translating culture" (Venuti 1998: 4).

This kind of reflection, which has opened productive lines of inquiry within translation studies in the last few decades, should be understood in the wake of poststructuralist conceptions of language and text that have focused on the inescapably active role performed by readers and interpreters in the construction of meaning. Michel Foucault's and Roland Barthes's explorations of the notions of the "dead" author and the productive reader are suitable examples. In his post-Nietzschean celebration of the "death" of the author and the reader's newly recognized power, Barthes argues that "no vital 'respect' is owed to the Text" as "it can be read without its father's guarantee: the restitution of the intertext paradoxically abolishes the concept of filiation" (Barthes 1977b: 161, trans. Heath). As the Text's "father" becomes an unnecessary presence in the scene of reading, it is the reader's prerogative to decide what to do about the role of the powerless author, who can only "come back" into his Text as a "guest" that the reader may, or may not, wish to entertain: "he becomes, as it were, a paper author: his life is no longer the origin of his fictions but a fiction contributing to his work" (ibid.). Michel Foucault has also reevaluated the role of the once all-powerful Author figure, but, unlike Barthes, has not completely neutralized the thrust of authorship and reconceptualizes it as a "function," that is, as a "certain function principle by which, in our culture, one limits, excludes, and chooses; in short, by which one impedes the free circulation, the free manipulation, the free composition, decomposition, and recomposition of fiction" (Foucault 1979: 159). From Foucault's perspective, the author is viewed as one of the several leads that may guide readers in their task of framing the texts they read. Hence, the author is no longer viewed as the indisputable, uncomplicated origin of his writing and becomes an "ideological figure by which one marks the manner in which we fear the proliferation of meaning" (ibid.). Another appropriate example is Jacques Derrida's reading of Walter Benjamin's "The Task of the Translator" (Benjamin 2000, trans. Zohn), presented in "Des Tours de Babel," in which the French philosopher elaborates on Benjamin's radical revision of the relationship traditionally established between originals and translations (Derrida 1985, trans. Graham). As Derrida deconstructs logocentric conceptions of the original as the indisputable product of its author's conscious "intentions," and as he expands Benjamin's view of translation as a form of survival for the text, he also redefines the notion of "debt" that binds the original to its translation (ibid.: 188). As Derrida argues, the original necessarily "calls for a complement" because "at the origin it was not there without fault, full, complete, total, identical to itself" (ibid.). Consequently, it is the original and its author – "dead or mortal, the dead man, or 'dummy' of the text" (Derrida 1985: 182) – that are actually indebted to the translation and the translator, not the other way around. At the same time, if the "structure" of the text is "survival," and if the original can only survive in difference, the translator's debt "does not involve restitution of a copy or a good image, a faithful representation of the original: the latter, the survivor, is itself in the process of transformation" (ibid.: 182–183).

Would such associations between Scliar's story and poststructuralist notions of text and translation suggest that it somehow accepts or defends the main implications of such notions and is, ultimately, siding with contemporary thought on the reconfiguration of the power relations that define the bond between originals and translations, authors and translators? Therefore, could we argue that, according to the story or, maybe, to Scliar himself, it is acceptable for the empowered translator to take over and for the *belle infidèle* to marry him after leaving the "dummy" author? Should we read "Footnotes" as a mere echo of such ideas? Or is it perhaps teaching us something about texts, writing, and the relationships usually developed between authors and translators that conventional theoretical discourse may not be able to? Before I address these questions, let us reflect on another piece that raises similar issues and further complicates the ways in which we can think about the roles attributed to authors, readers, translators, and texts in the scene of translation: Calvino's *If on a Winter's Night a Traveler* (Calvino 1981).

Calvino's *If on a Winter's Night a Traveler*: a male reader, an impotent author, and a swindler/translator in pursuit of a female reader

In *If on a Winter's Night a Traveler*, a complex novel that has been appropriately described as a "meditation on writing" (Mitchell 2004), we will find another plot that humorously sexualizes the relationships generally established between authors, translators, and their texts, and, in addition, brings to the fore a few reader figures as well. The following is a brief summary of the storyline: because of what seems to be an error in the binding of a new book, entitled "If on a Winter's Night a Traveler," by Italo Calvino, the male protagonist simply referred to as the "Reader" is unable to find the continuation of the narrative that by now has captivated him and returns to the bookstore only to discover that the same problem also affects all the remaining available copies. In his search for the continuation of the interrupted text, the Reader accidentally meets an attractive young woman called Ludmilla who has rushed to the bookstore for the same reason. From then on the storyline revolves around the Reader's pursuit of both the real original and Ludmilla, also referred to as the "Other Reader." In twelve numbered chapters we are invited to follow the narrative thread that tells the story of this pursuit, which introduces the Reader to books that are interrupted and misplaced, other readers and, notably, references to a mysterious "swindler," a translator named Ermes Marana who, among other things, was the founder of "Apocryphal Power" and a representative of the "Organization for the Electronic Production of Homogenized Literary Works," operating from New York. In the ten alternate chapters, which are not numbered but titled, we are presented with the first few pages from each of the unfinished plots the Reader encounters in his quest, plots that have been associated with different styles of twentieth-century fiction represented by authors such as the Russian Bulgakov, the Japanese Kawabata, a few Latin Americans – Borges, Rulfo, Arguedas – and the British Chesterton (cf. Calvino 2013: 501).

In Calvino's novel, as in Scliar's story, we will find a clear association between text and woman as inspiring Muse and object of desire. Moreover, the novel offers insights into the mechanisms of reading, which is mostly represented as the male Reader's active pursuit of the original, a pursuit that coincides with his quest to conquer the desirable female character, the Other Reader. As expected, the Reader is not alone in his pursuit of both the woman and the text as there are at least two other characters drawn to Ludmilla: the Irish novelist Silas Flannery, Calvino's author figure, who is no longer able to produce the popular thrillers for which he is known worldwide and can only write a personal diary; and Ermes Marana, the translator who manipulates authors and misplaces originals and translations and is ultimately responsible for the truncated texts that appear as titled chapters in the novel. Apparently, the most comprehensive topic to be explored behind Calvino's plot is a relentless subversion of traditional notions of authorship that still tends to view authors as the identifiable origin of their writing. This "outdated" view is illustrated, for example, by Mr. Cavedagna, the main editor in the publishing house that has issued the defective copies of the book that the Reader and the Other Reader have bought. The elderly gentleman, who is no longer a reader, is nostalgic for a time when he was able to love and read books and when the "author was an invisible point from which the books came, a void traveled by ghosts, an underground tunnel that put other worlds in communication" (Calvino 1981: 102).

In its labyrinthine narrative, in which texts emerge and are disseminated without the strong presence of any one author figure, *If on a Winter's Night a Traveler* can be viewed as an expanded illustration of the intertextual nature of writing in terms that are comparable to those found in Roland Barthes's association of intertextuality with the "death" of the author and the celebration of the reader as an agent, topics with which Calvino was quite familiar (cf., for example, Bloom 2001: 113):

> A text is made of multiple writings, drawn from many cultures and entering into mutual relations of dialogue, parody, contestation, but there is one place where this multiplicity is focused, and that place is the

reader, not, as was hitherto said, the author. The reader is the space on which all the questions that make up a writing are inscribed without any of them being lost; a text's unity lies not in its origin but in its destination.

(Barthes 1977a: 148, trans. Heath)

In a context that seems to recognize the impossibility of establishing indisputable, simple origins, and in which, as Calvino's narrator explains, "[e]verything has already begun before" (Calvino 1981: 153), "the figure of the author has become plural" (ibid.: 96). It is, thus, fitting that the emblematic author character in the novel is the elderly Silas Flannery, who is no longer able to read or write books and who feels that whatever he writes now "does not belong to [him] any more": "At times I think of the subject matter of the book to be written as of something that already exists: thoughts already thought, dialogue already spoken, stories already happened, places and settings seen" (ibid.: 171). Reduced to a mere shadow and at the mercy of a manipulative translator and, in addition, under the spell of a few reader figures, Flannery can be viewed as a satirical personification of the "dead" author theorized by poststructuralist textual theories. Furthermore, in Calvino's novel, being a "dummy" author also seems to imply some form of textual/sexual impotence as Flannery's difficulty writing is paralleled to his inability to seduce the woman/reader he desires, and whom he can only watch from afar through a (phallic) spyglass: "'[s]he's there every day'," the writer says.

> "Every time I'm about to sit down at my desk I feel the need to look at her. Who knows what she's reading? I know it isn't a book of mine, and instinctively I suffer at the thought, I feel the jealousy of my books, which would like to be read the way she reads."

(Ibid.: 126)

Just as authorship is intimately linked to the pursuit of a desirable female in Calvino's novel, so is the process of translation, which is, thus, acknowledged as a form of writing that also involves agency and desire. Like Flannery, Ermes Marana, the translator figure, is "obsessed by the image of Ludmilla reading" (ibid.: 158). Actually, the Other Reader is also the very reason why the translator has decided to misplace texts and their translations: "the secret spring that set [his machinations] in motion was his jealousy of the invisible rival [, i.e., any author she might read,] who came constantly between him and Ludmilla" (ibid.: 158–159). While Flannery seems to represent the author as an impotent "dummy" who can only watch the woman reader he desires from afar, the unscrupulous Marana, who does not hide or shy away from his authorial/sexual desire, has actually lived with Ludmilla, a detail that may suggest, among other things, that when reading a translation, the reader (and particularly the female reader as a *belle infidèlle*, who cannot or will not remain faithful to any one writer) is clearly in close contact with the translator, not with the author, even if all the translator can offer her is his brand of "mystification" (ibid.: 159). As he imagines being involved in a constant struggle against his potential rivals, the translator character defends the end of authorship as we know it:

> Always, since his taste and talent impelled him in that direction, but more than ever since his relationship with Ludmilla became critical, Ermes Marana dreamed of a literature made entirely of apocrypha, of false attributions, of imitations and counterfeits and pastiches.
>
> (Ibid.)

As a jealous former lover, the translator deeply resents the fact that he has been unable to keep Ludmilla under his spell for very long and, therefore, cannot control what she reads or the relationships she may develop with other writers.

Even though the translator is portrayed as a strong figure that even manages to (temporarily) get the girl, his struggle to overpower not only all authors, but their very function, is inseparable from his mission:

> How is it possible to defeat not the authors but the functions of the author, the idea that behind each book there is someone who guarantees a truth in that world of ghosts and inventions by the mere fact of having invested in his own truth, of having identified himself with that construction of words?
>
> (Ibid.)

Marana is also bothered by the very association that is still established between books and their authors' names:

> What does the name of an author on the jacket matter? Let us move forward in thought to three thousand years from now. Who knows which books from our period will be saved, and who knows which authors' names will be remembered?
>
> (Calvino 1981: 101)

As expected, in Marana's vision of literature, the role played by authors would be radically weakened, not simply in the reception, but, most importantly, in the actual creation of their work. According to him, computers could be programmed, for instance, "to complete the novel Flannery cannot write" (ibid.: 118). Programmers would only need to have access to the beginning of the novel in order to create a viable program that could "develop all the elements of a text with perfect fidelity to the stylistic and conceptual models of the author" (ibid.). In a context that devalued or downplayed authorship, authors and translators would finally be on the same level.

Calvino's storyline also seems to suggest that since the translator is not formally bound to his writing, he is free to lead an adventurous life without actually committing to any single project, anyone or any particular place or tradition. As an agent of unbridled dissemination and globalization, the translator Marana only inhabits texts and their contexts temporarily and, therefore, can be spotted wherever his multiple projects and machinations take him – Japan, South America, Switzerland, New York, Liechtenstein, Africa, or the Middle East. As a representative of the "Mercury and the Muses agency, specializing in the advertising and exploitation of literary and philosophical works" (Calvino 1981: 120), Ermes Marana lives up to the multiple meanings we can relate to his very name: "Ermes," which is also "Hermes," the Greek god ("Mercury," for the Romans), usually associated with interpretation ("hermeneutics") and mediation. More specifically, Hermes has been viewed as "the patron of all occupations that occupy margins or involve mediation: traders, thieves, shepherds, and heralds" (Friedrich 1978: 205) and, as a consequence, has been identified as a "master of cunning and deceit" and, thus, readily associated not only with "theft, [but, also, with] the marginality of illusions and tricks" (ibid.). His ability to move quickly makes him "a creature betwixt and between" (ibid.), between languages, cultures, and traditions and, perhaps more significantly, between authors and readers as well. Finally, "his eroticism is not oriented to fertility or maintaining the family but is basically aphroditic – stealthy, sly, and amoral, a love gained by theft without moral concern for consequences" (ibid.). We can also relate Calvino's translator figure to the central character in "Don Juan de Marana," the play written by Alexandre Dumas, the father, in 1836 (Dumas 2009), and which is recognized as one of the several versions of the widely known fictional lady's man whose emergence in literature is traced back to the seventeenth-century play "El Burlador de Sevilla" ("The Trickster of Seville") by Tirso de Molina (de Molina 1986, trans. G. Edwards). As a translation of multiple translations, the very name "Ermes Marana" functions as a meaningful synthesis of the character it names and that has been described as an archetypal *traduttore traditori* – "a double or triple or quadruple agent, in the service of God knows who and what" (Calvino 1981: 119). Portrayed as a sly, deceitful, predatory manipulator of authors, texts, and women, the translator could never be faithful to anybody or anything.

Like the author and the translator figures in the novel, the Reader cannot separate his interest in literature from his attraction to Ludmilla. His pursuit of her, just as his approach to reading, is relentless, steadfast, and stereotypically masculine. Unlike the "feminine" Ludmilla, the Reader chooses to play an active role in the search for the complete versions of the interrupted narratives he encounters, a search that includes direct confrontations with the publisher, the translator, and the author figures that might be involved in the process. Significantly, the pleasure of reading for the Reader starts with the handling of the unread, "virgin" book with anticipation and excitement, a sensual experience that is obviously relatable to the masculine and, thus, reminiscent of invasion and conquest:

> The pleasures derived from the use of a paper knife are tactile, auditory, visual, and especially mental. [...] Penetrating among the pages from below, the blade vehemently moves upward, opening a vertical cut in a flowing succession of slashes that one by one strike the fibers and mow them down – with a friendly and cheery crackling the good paper receives that first visitor [...] Opening a path for yourself, with a sword's blade, in the barrier of pages becomes linked with the thought of how much the word contains and conceals: you cut your way through your reading as if through a dense forest.
>
> (Ibid.: 42)

However, almost at the end of the book, and in spite of his seemingly proactive approach to reading, the Reader clarifies what he enjoys about books, showing that his attitude towards texts is quite compatible with the traditional view that attributes to authors the power to define the meaning and the limits of what they write:

> I like to read only what is written, and to connect the details with the whole, and to consider certain readings as definitive; and I like to keep one book distinct from the other, each for what it has that is different and new; and I especially like books to be read from beginning to end.
>
> (Ibid.: 256–257)

In spite of his pursuit of texts, the Reader's general vision of reading, which rejects the basic notions associated with intertextuality and what it entails for conceptions of originality and interpretation, is, in the end, what will bring him closer to Ludmilla, to whom he finds himself blissfully married in the last chapter of the novel.

Predictably, what makes Ludmilla especially desirable to Calvino's male characters is, also, her non-aggressive attitude towards reading. As she makes clear, she has no interest in crossing the "boundary line" separating "those who make books" from "those who read them":

> I want to remain one of those who read them, so I take care always to remain on my side of the line. Otherwise, the unsullied pleasure of reading ends, or at least is transformed into something else, which is not what I want.
>
> (Ibid.: 93)

As the Reader explains, Ludmilla fears losing the privileged relationship that she has always established with books and, therefore, "the ability to consider what is written as something finished and definitive, to which there is nothing to be added, from which there is nothing to be removed" (ibid.: 115). According to her sister Lotaria, the latter's approach to books favors "a passive way of reading, escapist and regressive" (ibid.: 185). It is by the way her non-competitive attitude towards reading that distinguishes her from Lotaria, a reader whose comically reductive, computer-assisted methods of literary analysis are associated with the academic world and the university, "where books are analyzed according to all Codes, Conscious and Unconscious, and in which all Taboos are eliminated, the ones imposed by the dominant Sex, Class, and Culture" (ibid.: 45). Lotaria's ridiculously assertive, caricaturally feminist approach sterilizes authors and books as she seems to read them, according to Flannery, "only to find in them what she was already convinced of before reading them" (ibid.: 185). In sheer contrast, for Ludmilla, "the function of books" is "immediate reading; they are not instruments of study or reference or components of a library arranged according to some order" (ibid.: 145). Predictably, while Ludmilla's "feminine" attitude is endearing to the male characters involved in pursuing her, Lotaria's "feminism" repels them. As we are told, for example, Ludmilla always gives her sister's phone number to those people she meets and with whom she may not want to be in contact because Lotaria manages to keep them "at a distance" (ibid.: 45).

Lessons from fiction and beyond theory

As suggested, and in spite of their obvious differences, there is a distinguishable common thread bringing together Scliar's and Calvino's pieces: an apparent subversion of traditional conceptions of authorship and translation, which is illustrated, for example, by the fact that in both plots the desirable female character does not end up married to the author figure. Since the sexualization of texts and textual activities plays such a pivotal role in the two storylines, the marriages of their female characters (to the translator, in Scliar's; and to the Reader, in Calvino's) might suggest that, for Scliar, the translator is the celebrated hero of his story while, for Calvino, it is the male Reader who beats his rivals for the love of Ludmilla. This rationale is mirrored, for instance, in Calvino's Silas Flannery, for whom the ultimate purpose of writing is explicitly to get the girl, a purpose reflected in his idea for a new novel that serves as a blueprint for Calvino's *If on a Winter's Night a Traveler*, but with a different ending. After mentioning the main characters he would create for the novel – the Reader, a young lady Reader, a counterfeiter-translator, and an old writer – Flannery clarifies that he

> wouldn't want the young lady Reader, in escaping the Counterfeiter, to end up in the arms of the Reader. [Instead, he] will see to it that the Reader sets out on the trail of the Counterfeiter, hiding in some very distant country, so the Writer can remain alone with the young lady, the Other Reader.
>
> (Ibid.: 198)

As for the Reader, since his "journey would lose liveliness" without a female character, "he must encounter some other woman on his way. Perhaps the Other Reader could have a sister …" (ibid.).

In Calvino's novel, as in Scliar's story, there is a clear contrast between the theoretical positions on writing and translation that their plots seem to illustrate and what they actually value on a more subtle level. As both texts introduce us to weak author figures whose writing abilities and influence are questioned and to empowered translator characters whose authorial force is shown to shape the very texts we are offered to read, they provide us with a unique opportunity to reflect on typical notions of authorship, reading, and translation. However, in spite of their acknowledged power, Calvino's and Scliar's translator figures are not exactly presented as role models. Calvino's Marana, like Scliar's translator character, is not only visible and powerful, but also morally objectionable. As shown, while Marana's practice is mostly described as a vicious form of theft that involves the manipulation of naïve authors and their manuscripts, Scliar's translator figure obliterates the voice of the poet he translates, steals his Muse and partner, and slanders his legacy in inappropriate footnotes. In order to further reflect on what might be lurking behind the main scenes that constitute these narratives, it will be helpful to focus on them a bit closer and approach them comparatively. Starting with Calvino, we may wonder, for example, whether the myth of the author's domineering paternal authority has really been overthrown in his novel. Moreover, if the author were truly "dead" in *If on a Winter's Night a Traveler* and, thus, if the novel were truly celebrating the Reader's agency and, implicitly, also the translator character's aggressive interference in the production and publication of texts, why does the enterprising Marana have such a bad reputation?

Although Calvino fictionalizes key notions directly associated with post-Nietzschean conceptions of language and interpretation by having, for example, the woman as text become intimately involved with the translator and in the end married to the Reader rather than the author character, such conceptions are clearly undermined by other networks of meaning disseminated throughout the novel. Even though its author character, Silas Flannery, can be viewed as a representation of the "dead" author theorized by poststructuralists, it is Calvino's narrator (or, perhaps, Calvino himself?) who claims to be in control of the plot and never gives up the traditional role of the storyteller as the original creator and owner of his fiction (see, also, Fink 1991: 94). In the very first paragraph of the novel, for example, as Calvino's narrator begins to establish a relationship with the Reader and, consequently, also with us, as we inevitably identify with the "You" to whom the narrative is addressed, we are told how to read his book and how to turn this reading into the very center of our lives:

> You are about to begin reading Italo Calvino's new novel, *If on a Winter's Night a Traveler*. Relax. Concentrate. Dispel every other

thought. Let the world around you fade. Best to close the door; the TV is always on in the next room.

(Calvino 1981: 3)

Calvino's narrator then proceeds to indicate "the most comfortable position" and circumstances in which his book should be read and often interrupts the narrative to reiterate that he is, indeed, the one determining not only what is going to happen in his novel, but also how his Reader is supposed to react to it. In more than one passage, the narrator even warns us against his own strategies and at one point explicitly refers to his "method" of gradually involving his readers in the "trap" of his narrative (ibid.: 12). In an interview that appeared soon after the publication of the English version of the novel, Calvino points out that his game-playing is not accidental and unequivocally sexualizes his authorial pleasure:

> there is always something sadistic in the relationship between writer and reader. In *If on a Winter's Night a Traveler* I may be a more sadistic lover than ever. I constantly play cat and mouse with the reader, letting the reader briefly enjoy the illusion that he's free for a little while, that he's in control. And then I quickly take the rug out from under him; he realizes with a shock that he is not in control, that it is always I, Calvino, who is in total control of the situation.
>
> (Du Plessix Gray 1981: 23)

While the novel's actual author compares the pleasure he finds in the writing of fiction to that of a "sadistic lover," the Reader character in *If on a Winter's Night a Traveler* is only given the illusion that he can take initiatives in the shaping of the storyline. All the latter's initiatives are, in fact, predicted and controlled by the guiding hand of Calvino's omniscient narrator who sees the Reader as a puppet in his hands or, perhaps, as the author himself suggests, as a submissive lover. Mary McCarthy also calls attention to the "permissive" *ars amoris* that seems to underlie the relationship taking place between the Reader and the narrator in the novel (McCarthy 1981: 3). While the whole first chapter seems to function as a prolonged "foreplay," in which we can witness the Reader's anxious "anticipation," the powerful author-lover "withholds consummation" as he offers the Reader a series of ten beginnings, ten novels that break off precisely as they become interesting, a strategy that McCarthy associates with instances of "coitus interruptus" in the art and practice of fiction (ibid.). From this viewpoint we can also explain why the ideal reader in Calvino's novel is not the male Reader, but a rather passive, desirable female who refuses the Reader's invitation to join him in his pursuit of the true original on the grounds that, "on principle," she wants to remain simply a reader who is happy to be guided by the authors of the books she chooses to read (Calvino 1981: 93). In the novel's last chapter, when Calvino's narrator marries the two Readers, there seems to be a suggestion that even though they may represent different approaches to reading, they are in fact quite compatible and equally subject to the author's power and wishes. After all, in the end, what really matters is that both Readers, "now man and wife," are together in their "great double bed" reading "*If on a Winter's Night a Traveler*" (ibid.: 260). Like his author character, Calvino's narrator chooses not to marry the attractive female reader to the translator, but, unlike the helpless Flannery, he makes it emphatically clear that his authorial position resembles that of an all-powerful, god-like patriarch figure who gives himself the right to determine not only the limits and contours of his narrative, but, also, his Readers' desires and even their fate.

In a similar vein we can explain why Marana is characterized both as an authorial figure and a "swindler." As shown, he is directly responsible for the fact that the Reader ends up with the ten incipit novels that constitute about half of Calvino's text. Hence, the creation of an important part of the novel is, figuratively speaking, attributed to the unwelcome interference of the translator who appears to the Reader as "a serpent who injects his malice into the paradise of reading" (ibid.: 125) and disrupts the distinction between his writing and the "real" author's original. But who is the real author and who is the thief? It is also important to note that, besides mirroring Silas Flannery's idea for a new novel, as commented on above, Calvino's strategy in *If on a Winter's Night a Traveler* also echoes the approach devised by Marana in the Sultana's episode. As we learn, in a sultanate of the Persian Gulf, the Sultan's wife "must never remain without books that please her: a clause in the marriage contract is involved, a condition the bride imposed on her august suitor before agreeing to the wedding" (ibid.: 123). Since the Sultan fears, "apparently with reason, a revolutionary plot," as well as a betrayal by his wife (another *belle infidèle?*), he hires Marana to translate all the books the Sultana is about to read so that "if a coded message were hidden in the succession of words or letters of the original, it would be irretrievable" after translation (ibid.: 124). Thus, according to the narrator's rationale, since the process of translation inevitably changes texts and blurs their allegedly original intentions, what the translator can offer his readers is only a "counterfeit" that will disseminate unforeseen meanings and influences. As he accepts the assignment to produce the translations that the Sultana will be allowed to read, Marana proposes to her husband a "stratagem prompted by the literary tradition of the Orient":

[he] will break off this translation at the moment of greatest suspense and will start translating another novel, inserting it into the first through some rudimentary expedient; for example, a character in the first novel opens a book and starts reading. The second novel will also break off to yield to a third, which will not proceed very far before opening into a fourth, and so on ...

(Ibid.: 125)

The translator character emulates, of course, Scheherazade, one of the most powerful authorial figures ever created, whose life-changing narrative skills have been an inspiration to fiction writers for centuries and, we may assume, to Calvino himself as well. Consequently, if Marana's strategy is ultimately also Calvino's and if Marana is a manipulative thief who fakes originals and misguides readers, wouldn't the actual author be guilty of similar sins?

After this incursion into Calvino's novel, it will be easier to contextualize Scliar's take on the conflict that often alienates writers of originals from their translators. Even though "Footnotes," unlike Calvino's text, is apparently written from the perspective of a translator, it actually offers us something else. As we witness the unprofessional manner in which Scliar's narrator treats the author whose work he claims to be faithfully translating, how can we possibly trust him? How can we not sympathize with the dead poet whose mistress the translator ends up marrying? If we take into account the translator's improper use of footnotes and the obliteration of the translated poet's voice, it appears that Scliar's story is subtly siding with the absent, possibly wronged author rather than his inadequately visible translator. Like Ermes Marana, Scliar's character epitomizes a perverse view of the translator's agency, which is simplistically reduced to an objectionable, inappropriate attitude towards originals and their authors. Even though, as suggested, Scliar's and Calvino's plots do acknowledge the translator's authorial role in the rewriting of texts in other languages, they do not treat their translator figures' agency and obvious visibility as part and parcel of the process, but, rather, as symptoms of these characters' supposed lack of scruples, that is, as something that might be avoided, or from which authors could somehow defend themselves.

It is also the sensitive nature of what this kind of defense must protect that is at stake in the conspicuous associations that Calvino's and Scliar's storylines promote between texts and women, suggesting, among other things, that an author's desire to protect his work from any unwelcome interference may be as strong as a true patriarch's desire to keep his women and his property away from the reach or influence of others. Evidently, though, such a suggestion is not merely about concerned authors and potentially predatory translators, but, also, about degrading depictions of women who are trapped in male authors' fantasies and fictions. In such a position, like texts, they are fickle, unstable, and potentially unfaithful entities, and their provisional stability depends on powerful male figures who manage to domesticate them under some form of fidelity agreement, as evoked, for example, by Ludmilla's marriage to the Reader in Calvino's novel and N.'s to the translator in Scliar's story. As shown, since the female characters in these plots are grossly objectified, their impact is solely dependent on their sexual appeal, or lack thereof, and whether they may be compatible with their male counterparts' tastes, or whether they serve their interests. Recall, for instance, Scliar's N., whose influence in getting her lover's poetry published is directly associated with the "favors" she concedes to the publisher (for whom she works as a secretary) and, later, to the translator as well. Or Calvino's Lotaria, who, as mentioned, is portrayed as an undesirable female whose "academic" readings are ridiculed by the same male characters that have chosen her antagonist as their Muse.

The blatantly sexist treatment of female characters exposed in Scliar's and Calvino's pieces does not merely reflect their narrators' perspective on gender, but is, obviously, also symptomatic of Western culture's insistent reliance on hierarchical oppositions not only between male and female roles, but, also, between writing and reading, original and translation, subject and object. As discussed, however, in spite of generally conforming to this cultural framework and, thus, in spite of defending, at least implicitly, the "privileges" of (male) authorship, Calvino's and Scliar's pieces blur the limits between translation and the writing of originals and, as a consequence, do acknowledge the authorial role played by translators in the shaping of translated texts. In fact, it is precisely the difficulty in establishing a clear-cut distinction between these two forms of writing that is at the basis of both narratives, the same difficulty that can be related to their representation of texts as *"belles infidèles"* as well as their characterization of translators as rivals and potential betrayers to their author figures. Since one cannot truly distinguish, in a translated text, what belongs to the author from the translator's contribution, the imagined hierarchy that should separate the author from the translator will have to be anchored elsewhere. As suggested, in the plots analyzed, the "anchor" has been a few age-old stereotypes associated with the traditional opposition between male and female roles, an association that is still deeply inscribed in our culture, and which still allows property rights and authoritative roles to be almost exclusively related to men. In this framework, as the hierarchy between author and translator is grounded on the power that each of them may be either able or allowed to exercise over "feminine" representations of texts, the scene of translation is reduced to a narrative about the rivalry between at least two men over the possession and control of an attractive, potentially unfaithful female.

In spite of their generally mocking tone and their sexist underpinnings, Calvino's and Scliar's pieces convey perceptive representations of the translator's undeniable visibility, representations that are, however, also explicitly tinted with a certain animosity on the part of their author figures and/or narrators vis-à-vis the authorial role played by translators in the shaping of texts and, hence, in the shaping of their authors' legacy as well. This ambivalent attitude towards translators as agents of change, upon whom authors must rely in order to live on in other languages and contexts, can be exemplarily played out in fiction, which offers a plethora of perspectives and angles that cannot be found in other genres. Because of its multiple resources and the "liberties" it is allowed to take in the construction of plots and characters, fiction can portray not only lively interpretations of theoretical constructs, but also emotional reactions to such constructs in a unique combination that often includes elements from the author's biography as well as clashing ideological positions that can be defended in the name of different characters. In *If on a Winter's Night*, as shown, we can find a clear contrast between the recognition, implied by the storyline, that the translator's and the author's roles are practically indistinguishable and the narrator's (or, perhaps, Calvino's own) explicit desire to actually be a typical "aesthetic patriarch" who not only owns and controls his texts and everything inside and about them, but who also manages to trap his readers within his domain and have them read his writing exactly the way he wants them to. Such a desire is conspicuously manifested, for example, in the novel's "happy ending" when the female Reader is finally married to the male Reader and, more importantly, far away from Ermes Marana. As a felicitous counterpoint to the way in which Calvino chose to end his novel, Scliar's short story can be read as an amusing illustration of that which could very well be any patriarchal figure's worst nightmare. As shown, in order for Scliar's author character to have his work translated and live on in another language, he loses his mistress to the treacherous translator who also takes over his text, erases and replaces his words, and drastically changes his legacy. Somewhere between Calvino's "happy ending" and Scliar's "nightmare," we can probably detect a certain reluctance on their part to truly accept that once they acknowledge the translator's inevitable participation in the composition of the translated text, they will have to give up the fantasy of the author as an all-powerful patriarch.

Bibliography

Abbott, C. C. (ed.) (1935) *The Correspondence of Gerard Manley Hopkins and Richard Watson Dixon*, London: Oxford University Press.

Barthes, R. (1977a) "The Death of the Author," S. Heath (trans. and ed.) *Image, Music, Text*, New York: Hill and Wang, 142–148.

—— (1977b) "From Work to Text," S. Heath (trans. and ed.) *Image, Music, Text*, New York: Hill and Wang, 155–164.

—— (1979) "From Work to Text," J. Harari (trans. and ed.) *Textual Strategies – Perspectives in Post-Structuralist Criticism*, Ithaca, NY: Cornell University Press, 73–81.

Benjamin, W. (2000) "The Task of the Translator: An Introduction to the Translation of Baudelaire's *Tableaux Parisiens*," H. Zohn (trans.), in L. Venuti (ed.) *The Translation Studies Reader*, London: Routledge, 75–85.

Bloom, H. (1973) *The Anxiety of Influence*, New York: Oxford University Press.

—— (2001) *Italo Calvino*, Broomall, PA: Chelsea House.

Calvino, I. (1981) *If on a Winter's Night a Traveler*, W. Weaver (trans.), New York: Harcourt Brace and Company.

—— (2013) *Italo Calvino: Letters 1941–1985*, M. McLaughlin (trans.), M. Wood (ed.), Princeton, NJ: Princeton University Press.

Chamberlain, L. (2000) "Gender and the Metaphorics of Translation," in L. Venuti (ed.) *The Translation Studies Reader*, London: Routledge, 314–329.

De Molina, T. (1986) "The Trickster of Seville," G. Edwards (trans.), Liverpool: Liverpool University Press.

Derrida, J. (1985) "Des Tours de Babel," J. F. Graham (trans. and ed.) *Difference in Translation*, Ithaca, NY: Cornell University Press, 165–208.

Dumas, A. (2009) *Don Juan de Marana*, Charleston, SC: Bibliolife.

Du Plessix Gray, F. (1981) "Visiting Italo Calvino," *New York Times Book Review*, June 21, 22–23.

Fink, I. (1991) "The Power Behind the Pronoun: Narrative Games in Calvino's *If on a Winter's Night a Traveler*," *Twentieth Century Literature* 1(37): 93–104.

Foucault, M. (1979) "What Is an Author?" J. Harari (trans. and ed.) *Textual Strategies – Perspectives in Post-Structuralist Criticism*, Ithaca, NY: Cornell University Press, 141–160.

Friedrich, P. (1978) *The Meaning of Aphrodite*, Chicago: University of Chicago Press.

Gilbert, S. M. and S. Gubar (1984) *The Madwoman in the Attic – The Woman Writer and the Nineteenth-Century Literary Imagination*, New Haven, CT: Yale University Press.

McCarthy, M. (1981) "Acts of Love," *The New York Review of Books* 28: 3.

Mitchell, D. (2004) "Enter the Maze," *The Guardian*, May 22, 2004. Available at: www.theguardian.com/books/may/22/fiction.italocalvino (accessed January 15, 2015).

Scliar, M. (1995) "Notas ao pé da página," in *Contos Reunidos*, São Paulo: Companhia das Letras, 371–375.

Venuti, L. (ed.) (1992) *Rethinking Translation – Discourse, Subjectivity, Ideology*, London: Routledge.

—— (1998) *The Scandals of Translation – Towards an Ethics of Difference*, London: Routledge.

8 Translation as transference
"Pierre Menard," Cervantes, Borges, and Whitman

> [Whitman] created this very strange character, Walt Whitman, not to be taken for the writer of the book ... He attempted a very daring experiment, the most daring and the most successful experiment in all literature as far as I know. [...] The central character would be called after the author, Walt Whitman, but he was, firstly, Walt Whitman the human being, the very unhappy man who wrote *Leaves of Grass*.
>
> Jorge Luis Borges in Willis Barnstone, *Borges at Eighty: Conversations*

Jorge Luis Borges inaugurated his writing career at the tender age of nine with the publication of a Spanish translation of Oscar Wilde's "The Happy Prince" in *El País*, a Buenos Aires newspaper (Borges 1987: 26). This precocious interest in translating and in English texts, which flourished into a life-long attraction to the foreign and to the dilemmas of translation, would be an important element in the construction of his literary career and the development of some of the major themes that inspired his writing. A prolific translator of literary figures as diverse as Franz Kafka, Virginia Woolf, James Joyce, William Faulkner, Edgar Allan Poe, Walt Whitman, Hart Crane, G. K. Chesterton, and Nathaniel Hawthorne, among others, Borges has left us some of the most original, thought-provoking ideas available on the implications of translation for literature and on the relationships that are generally established between texts, translators, and authors. As I have argued elsewhere, in his essays on translation first published in the 1930s, "The Homeric Versions" (Borges 1999a, trans. Weinberger) and "The Translators of *The Thousand and One Nights*" (Borges 1999b, trans. Allen), and, more pointedly, in "Pierre Menard, Author of the *Quixote*" (Borges 1998a, trans. Hurley), the story that first came out in 1939, Borges anticipates some of the main tenets of translation theory as it has been redefined in the last few decades under the widespread influence of post-Nietzschean thought (see Chapters One and Four for detailed readings of "Pierre Menard," and Chapter Four for comments on Borges's essays on translation).

It has been widely recognized that Borges viewed translation as an intrinsically performative textual activity, that is, as a form of rewriting that is not in any sense neutral or secondary to the original. If, indeed, both the original and the translated text seem to enjoy a similar status, what kind of exchange might there be between the two? Moreover, if translators cannot, in any sense, be invisible in their translations, and, like authors, at least on some level, do mean what they say, what might it represent, for a translator, at a certain point, to choose a certain text to translate? In order to reflect on such questions posed by Borges's texts on the role of translation as a form of authorial writing, I will be concentrating on the paradigmatic relationship that may be established between Borges's interest in Walt Whitman, the great American poet, the publication of his first poem, "Himno del mar" ("Hymn to the Sea") in 1919 (Borges 1997a), and his version of *Leaves of Grass* (*Hojas de hierba*, Whitman 1969), which was published about fifty years later. In order to learn about the strongly emotional investment that seems to have underscored Borges's early attachment to Whitman and his poetry as well as the role played by translation in such a relationship, I will be turning to "Pierre Menard, Author of the *Quixote*" (Borges 1998a, trans. Hurley), a piece that thoroughly deserves George Steiner's often quoted statement, according to which it is "the most acute, most concentrated commentary anyone has offered on the business of translation" (Steiner 1975: 70). Thus, the exemplary relationship that Pierre Menard establishes with Cervantes and his text, a relationship that one might understand as a form of "influence," "transference," or simply "love," will serve as a mirroring map for the complex, productive encounter that took place between Borges and Whitman at the very outset of the first's literary career, an encounter that would have an impact during most of his life.

Pierre Menard's desire to be someone else

Among the solitary, somewhat maniacal characters that inhabit Borges's fictions, Pierre Menard is the one that best synthesizes the pathos of the typically Borgesian character and his self-imposed, generally unrealizable mission, which often involves a deep interest in a strong precursor and/or a major founding text. Divided between his mediocre "visible" works and the ambitious "invisible" project of rewriting verbatim a few excerpts from Cervantes's *Don Quixote*, Menard dedicated his life "to repeating in a foreign tongue a book that already existed" (Borges 1998a: 95). In order to achieve his "astonishing" goal, involving "perhaps the most significant writing of our time" (ibid.: 90), Menard devised a "method" that "was to be relatively simple": "learn Spanish, return to Catholicism, fight against the Moor or Turk, forget the history of Europe from 1602 to 1918 – *be* Miguel de Cervantes" (ibid.: 91). However, this initial plan was abandoned on the grounds that it was too easy. Besides, "of all the impossible ways of bringing it about, this was the least interesting," and Menard decided to continue being himself and come to the *Quixote* through his own experiences (ibid.).

As I have argued elsewhere, Pierre Menard's "methods" for reproducing *Don Quixote* could be viewed as an ironic criticism of the call for faithfulness and invisibility typically associated with traditional translation theories and practices (see Chapter One for a detailed treatment of this issue). The story is in fact a brilliant illustration of how absurd it is for a translator to claim or even try to be absolutely faithful to someone else's text. What is not made explicit, however, in Borges's plot is the reason, the motivation for Menard's choice: "Why the *Quixote*? My reader may ask. That choice, made by a Spaniard, would not have been incomprehensible, but it no doubt is so when made by a *Symboliste* from Nîmes, a devotee essentially of Poe" (Borges 1998a: 92). Furthermore, even though the *Quixote* "deeply" interested Menard, it did not seem to him "inevitable":

> I cannot imagine the universe without Poe's ejaculation "Ah, bear in mind this garden was enchanted!" or the *Bateau ivre* or the *Ancient Mariner*, but I know myself able to imagine it without the *Quixote*. [...] The *Quixote* is a contingent work; the *Quixote* is not necessary.
>
> (Ibid.)

How could we explain, for example, that in spite of his apparent indifference towards the Spanish author, Menard assumed "the mysterious obligation to reconstruct, word for word, the novel that for [Cervantes] was spontaneous"? (Borges 1998a: 92–93). Also, how could we explain that he was defined precisely by his "invisible" work as a "novelist," and not by the "visible" pieces that he actually wrote, and which Borges's narrator has carefully listed for his readers? (ibid.: 90).

This intriguing association between Menard's "subterranean" efforts and his seeming indifference to the very object that occupied his "scruples and his nights" almost begs a psychoanalytically oriented explanation, in which his secretive work could be associated with the unconscious and its production. In fact, it has been almost a commonplace to view both writing and reading as forms of therapy, especially when such activities clearly reveal an undeniable emotional bond between texts and their authors and/ or texts and their readers. As the basics of Freudian psychoanalysis suggests, while writing (and, notably, the writing of fiction), like daydreaming, allegedly gives writers the illusion that they may actually escape the powerlessness with which they have to deal in reality (cf., for example, Freud 1983a, trans. Strachey), reading, like dreaming, will allow readers to get in touch with unconscious material that they need to address (Freud 1983b, trans. Strachey). More specifically, and borrowing from Shoshana Felman's discussion of the unconscious as theorized by Jacques Lacan and its relationship with reading, one could add that the unconscious "is not simply *that which must be read*, but also, and perhaps primarily, *that which reads*," so much so that "whoever reads, interprets out of his unconscious, is an analysand" (Felman 1987: 21–22). If we note that Menard was so (secretly) enamored of Cervantes's text that he actually dedicated his life to rewriting it, it could be argued that Borges's story somehow anticipates Harold Bloom's widely discussed psychoanalysis-inspired reflection on reading, writing, and influence. To the extent that it proposes that "influence," at least in its initial stages, cannot be distinguished from what we call "love" (Bloom 1975: 12), Bloom's theory might shed some light on Menard's interest in the *Quixote*. Actually, in one of Bloom's statements on the complexities of this peculiar type of love affair ("if we have been ravished by a poem, it will cost us our own poem" [ibid.: 18]), it is not difficult to recognize echoes from an early note in which Borges addresses his reader in the opening of his first collection of poems, *Fervor de Buenos Aires* ("Adoration of Buenos Aires"), published in 1923: "If the pages of this book happen to contain any apt line, may the reader forgive me the discourtesy of having stolen it from you" (Borges 1977: 22, my translation). Moreover, Bloom's definition of influence anxiety as "an anxiety in expectation of *being flooded*" could very well supplement Borges's note:

> The ephebe who fears his precursors as he might fear a flood is taking a vital part for a whole, the whole being everything that constitutes his creative anxiety [. ...] Every good reader properly *desires* to drown, but if the poet drowns, he will become *only a reader*.
>
> (Bloom 1975: 57)

(For more about Bloom and Borges on influence, see Balderston 1985: 170.) At the same time, in spite of Borges's apparent awareness of the ambivalent feelings associated with influence anxiety, he often seems interested in neutralizing, or in playing down the underlying conflict and the aggressive feelings related to rivalry as suggested, for example, by the second part of the note mentioned above: "The circumstances that make you the reader of these exercises and me their writer are trivial and fortuitous" (Borges 1997a: 12, my translation). Borges's interest in avoiding issues associated with rivalry and influence could also help to explain Pierre Menard's ambivalent feelings towards Cervantes and his *Quixote*.

The complexities of the emotional bond that some readers tend to establish with some texts is one of the main issues at stake in "Pierre Menard," as it is an important theme in *Don Quixote* as well. It might be argued, for instance, that Pierre Menard was not only interested in the repetition of Cervantes's text, but was, himself, a repetition of the *Quixote* as the legendary character who became so absorbed in chivalry books that "the lack of sleep and the excess of reading withered his brain, and he went mad" (Cervantes 2001: 26–27, trans. Rutherford). Driven by his obsessive love for books and his desire to make reality conform to the stories that he had read, Don Quixote tried to abandon his uneventful, dull life as a modest *hidalgo* and ended up transforming himself into a pathetic version of his favorite character, a knight in the manner of *Amadís de Gaula* – himself a repetition of, among others, *Tirante el Blanco, Olivante de Laura*, the Italian *Orlando Furioso*, and, of course, *Lancelot and the Knights of the Round Table*. One might also try to understand the mechanisms of this kind of attachment with the aid of Jacques Lacan's conception of "transference," which he understood to be "indistinguishable from love," and which he supported with "the formula of the subject presumed to know": "The person in whom I presume knowledge to exist thereby acquires my love" ("Le Séminaire," Lacan 1975: 64, trans. and qtd. by Felman 1987: 86). In other words, transference is "love directed toward, addressed to, knowledge" (ibid.). "Knowledge" here (and particularly in the kind of relationship that can be established between readers and authors or their texts) may be understood as that special form of power that enables the Other (either as the Text or its Author) to seduce readers. From such a perspective, we might view Cervantes as "the subject presumed to know" chosen by Pierre Menard, despite the latter's resistance to acknowledging the depth of his interest in the Spanish master. After all, what the French translator actually desired, as he himself declared, was not merely to repeat Cervantes's work but, rather, *to be* Cervantes, that is, to own precisely that which distinguishes the author of the *Quixote* (and the father of the modern novel) as one of the greatest, most influential literary figures of all time. Furthermore, if we take into account that transference involves apparently antagonistic feelings, bringing together admiration and aggression, homage and rivalry, we could further explain why Menard's project of replacing Cervantes had to be kept invisible.

For the Quixotic Menard, becoming Cervantes, or taking his authorial place, would also entail having the kind of romanticized, heroic life the Spaniard allegedly had: living in Spain, "the land of Carmen," in the seventeenth century, which "saw the Battle of Lepanto and the plays of Lope de Vega" (Borges 1998a: 93), fighting the Moor or the Turk, and, thus, having the opportunity of being successful both as a man of action and as a man of letters. Appropriately, one of the excerpts from the *Quixote* that Menard tried to rewrite was Chapter XXXVIII, Part I, which mostly deals with the opposition between "arms" and "letters" in Don Quixote's famous speech about these two ways of having an impact on reality. As we attempt to figure out what Menard could be "saying" behind the literal surface of his interest in reproducing Cervantes's chapter, we might argue that, like the Quixote, who abandons his books in search of a more effective way to make a difference in the world, Menard wants to leave behind his mediocre, visible works and tries to become the author of one of the best-known texts ever written. In addition, like the Quixote, who makes it clear that what interests him is the possibility of becoming "eminent," Menard, in his reproduction of the "same" speech, might also be telling us of his desire to be famous and influential (for a detailed reading of the chapters that Menard tried, or might have tried to reproduce, see Arrojo 1993: 163–170). Most of all, for Menard, being the author of the *Quixote* would allow him to escape his geography, his age, his surroundings, his native language, and, of course, himself and his petty bourgeois life as a minor writer and obscure scholar. Moreover, as Menard abandoned his project to become Cervantes and decided to continue being Menard and to come to the *Quixote* anyway, he not only seemed to express his wish to take over Cervantes's privileged position, but, also, to eliminate him from the actual text of the *Quixote*. As we learn, Menard was convinced that it was more "interesting" to come to the *Quixote "through the experiences of Pierre Menard,"* a conviction that "obliged him to leave out the autobiographical foreword to Part II of the novel" (Borges 1998a: 91). As Borges's narrator explains, "including the prologue would have meant creating another character – 'Cervantes' – and also presenting the *Quixote* through that character's eyes, not Pierre Menard's. Menard, of course, spurned that easy solution" (ibid.)

The specificity of Borges's text as a story about translation and transference, or translation *as* transference, or, even, translation as a response to influence (here understood as that special power exerted by "the subject presumed to know" over those he/she seduces) lies in the fact that it tells us of a reader who does not merely try to write his own text after being influenced by another, but who actually sets out to occupy the privileged authorial position of his seducer and to repeat the latter's exact same text. From the perspective of a conception of translation informed by psychoanalysis, which would tend to regard anybody "who devotes great time and effort to conveying someone else's words" as "operating with a strong identification, already wishing to operate as a double" (Gallop 1985: 66), Menard would be an exemplary translator figure. Since the process of translation literally involves the repression of the original and its replacement with a close enough replica in another language, it seems to constitute the perfect scenario for such a transferential plot (cf., also, Forrester 1990: 373, n5). At the same time, since this replacement involves the actual writing of a text that reflects the translator's own decisions, it could be argued that translation necessarily deconstructs traditional notions related to authorship and the production of meaning. Regarding this, it is significant, for example, that the first fragment Menard tried to reproduce from Cervantes's novel is Chapter X, which is precisely about the rather nebulous origin of *Don Quixote*, and, hence, the blurred limits between translation and authorship, the original and the translation. The text of *Don Quixote*, as we are informed, is allegedly the Spanish translation of a manuscript by an Arabic historian found by Cervantes's narrator in some old notebooks bought in Toledo. Consequently, according to the narrator, the *Quixote* is not really his. Indeed, it is a translation that is not exactly reliable and whose accuracy cannot be checked because, as the narrator explains, it was done by a *morisco* who, like the manuscript's supposed author, could not be fully trusted since all Arabs tended to be liars. If we consider the fact that Menard chose to "compose" such a plot, he might also be saying that if the Spanish text was already a dubious translation of an original that could not be trusted, his own version should not in any sense be viewed as inferior to Cervantes's.

In addition, as mentioned, it was Menard's invisible efforts at becoming or replacing Cervantes that defined him as a "novelist" and it was, thus, through translation that the French Symbolist managed to respond to influence and act out his desire to be someone else and conquer what he did not have. Appropriately, the mechanism of this "acting out" is made more efficient with the significant repression of the words "translation" or "translator," never mentioned in connection with Menard's efforts regarding the *Quixote*. As we are told, Menard "did not want to compose *another* Quixote (sic)," that is, "he wanted to compose the Quixote (sic). [...] His admirable ambition was to produce a number of pages which coincided – word for word and line by line – with those of Miguel de Cervantes" (Borges 1998a: 91). Finally, as he secretly tried to take over Cervantes's authorial position, Menard, the translator, also covered up the violence of his transferential desire with the alibi of absolute faithfulness. After all, Borges's text could also be read as a story about the ambivalence of fidelity. As one might claim, even though Menard was interested in replacing Cervantes, no translator ever tried harder than him to be so absolutely faithful both to his original and to his author. As we are informed by Borges's narrator, "those who have insinuated that Menard devoted his life to writing a contemporary *Quixote* besmirch his illustrious memory" (ibid.).

Relations of influence and the alibi of translation

It is not difficult to find echoes of Borges's own biography and interests in the many bookish characters he imprisoned in labyrinthine libraries with the mission of handling impossible writing tasks. It is in "Pierre Menard," however, that Borges's own feelings and impressions on the conflicts involved in reading, writing, translating, and influence relationships, seem to be most clearly laid out (see also de Behar 2003: 9; and Aparicio 1991: 109). The general theme of "Pierre Menard," that is, a radical revision of the relationship generally established between the original and its reproduction, is actually something upon which the young Borges was stimulated to reflect on the basis of his own experience. As he writes, his first acquaintance with Cervantes's masterpiece took place when he was a child and it was through an English version, in a Garnier edition, which belonged to his father's library. Later on, as a young man, when he read the *Quixote* in the original Spanish, it "sounded like a bad translation" (Borges 1987: 25). As he elaborates, the relationship between original and translation, or between what one views as the original and its reproduction, is determined by an emotional investment:

> at some point, my father's library was broken up, and when I read the *Quixote* in another edition I had the feeling that it wasn't the real *Quixote*. Later, I had a friend get me the Garnier, with the same steel

> engravings, the same footnotes, and also the same errata. All those
> things form part of the book for me; this I consider the real *Quixote*.
>
> (Ibid.)

In the same text, Borges describes his very first experiments with fiction
writing and we learn that, as a child, he used to be a somewhat precocious
version of Pierre Menard. At the age of "six or seven," he "tried to imitate
classic writers of Spanish – Miguel de Cervantes, for example," and the first
story he ever wrote was "a rather nonsensical piece after the manner of
Cervantes, an old-fashioned romance called 'La visera fatal' ['The Fatal
Helmet']" (Borges 1987: 26).

Cervantes was, by the way, an appropriate "subject presumed to know"
for the Argentine author if we take into account, for instance, that the
Spanish master was known both as a writer and a soldier, something that
was especially attractive to the young Borges who had learned to revere his
ancestors, among whom there were prominent military men and intellectuals.
In his "Autobiographical Essay," he relates the fact that he had "military
forbears" to his "yearning after that epic destiny which [his] gods denied
[him]," at the same time that he mentions his lonely childhood, his
nearsightedness, his frailty: "as most of my people had been soldiers [...]
and I knew I would never be, I felt ashamed, quite early, to be a bookish
kind of person and not a man of action" (ibid.: 24). He also comments on
the "tradition of literature that ran through [his] father's family" and on
how he knew at a very young age that he was expected to become a writer
(ibid.: 25–26). The opposition "man of letters" versus "man of action"
remained a recurrent motif in his writings. Furthermore, one can identify
echoes of Menard's inglorious achievements in Borges's brief account of his
father's timid writing career: Jorge Guillermo Borges "was such a modest
man that he would have liked being invisible" and, like Menard, he had the
habit of destroying his manuscripts (ibid.: 23). Like Menard's, Borges
Senior's visible literary production never managed to go beyond a few
humble attempts that did not escape the shadow of the authors he admired
(ibid.: 25). As "Pierre Menard" seems to mirror aspects and aspirations that
could be associated not only with Borges's, but also with his own father's
biography, and, as the story's general theme involves the complexities of
influence, it is appropriate to take into account the impact of Borges's
relationship with his father as his first literary mentor. We should note, for
example, the fact that his writing career was actually planned by Borges
Senior who early on made it clear that his son was expected "to fulfill the
literary destiny" that blindness had denied him (ibid.). As Ricardo Piglia has
remarked, "Borges must write *for* his father and with his name. Writing for
his father, that is, in his place, but also thanks to him, thanks to his heritage"
(Piglia 1981: 92, my translation; also qtd. in Woscoboinik 1998: 208). As
Julio Woscoboinik elaborates on such a "debt":

Borges's history, it seems, starts from this pact with his father. [...]
Borges is a man of paradoxes and moves amid the paradoxes of family
myth, rooted, on the one hand, in the heraldic memory of conservative
Argentine aristocracy, and, on the other, in world literature, especially
the English.

(Woscoboinik 1998: 208)

As "the object of the desire of others," and, hence, as "a subjected subject
painfully chained to a destiny," Borges often turned his sensation of being
just "an echo of other echoes" into writing (ibid.). In addition, his father's
library was the "chief event" in his life and it was Borges Senior "who
revealed the power of poetry" to him and who gave him his "first lesson in
philosophy [... ,] the paradoxes of Zeno – Achilles and the tortoise, the
unmoving flight of the arrow, the impossibility of motion [... , and] the
rudiments of idealism" (Borges 1987: 24). Understandably, most of Borges
Senior's interests became his son's: Shelley, Keats, Swinburne, books on
metaphysics and psychology (Berkeley, Hume, Royce, and William James),
as well as writings about the East (Lane, Burton, and Payne) (ibid.: 23).

While we recognize echoes of Borges's biography in the story, it is also
important to bear in mind that he wrote "Pierre Menard" only a few months
after his father's death and as he himself began recovering from a serious
infection that kept him "between life and death" for over a month after an
accident that took place at the end of 1938 (ibid.: 45). According to him, the
story came to play a very special role in this crucial stage of his life and
career. As he was recovering and wondering whether he could ever write
again, he thought of trying something he had never done before because if
he failed at that "it wouldn't be so bad" (ibid.). Since he had previously
written some poetry and short essays, he decided to write a story. "The
result was 'Pierre Menard, Author of *Don Quixote*'" (ibid.). (As Borges
declares elsewhere in the same text, he had in fact written fiction before
"Pierre Menard." According to him, "it was only after a long and roundabout
series of timid experiments in narration [approximately from 1927 to 1933]
that [he] sat down to write real stories" [Borges 1987: 42]. And the first
"outright" story he actually wrote as an adult was "Man on Pink Corner"
[Borges 1998c, trans. Hurley] [Borges 1987: 42]. It is quite significant,
however, that Borges seemed to have "forgotten" that fact as he commented
on "Pierre Menard" and its relationship with the 1938 accident.)

The relationship between the first text Borges wrote after recovering and
the events of 1938 that had such an impact on his life has been acknowledged
by some of his readers. Didier Anzieu, for instance, distinguishes two stages
in Borges's entire literary career, one before and one after the death of his
father and the 1938 accident (1971: 178, qtd. in Woscoboinik 1998: 31).
For Rodríguez Monegal, "the accident dramatized Borges's guilt over
Father's death and his deep, totally unconscious need to be set free at last
from Father's tutelage" (Rodríguez Monegal 1978: 326). Hence, from this

stance, the accident represented "both a death (by suicide) and a rebirth" and Borges emerged from it as a different writer, "a writer this time engendered by himself" (ibid.). Likewise, one might take into account Borges's observation that "Pierre Menard" was written as "a halfway house between the essay and the true tale" (Borges 1987: 45), as well as the fact that, according to the story's narrator, it was a sort of eulogy for the recently dead Menard in order to protect the latter's memory from "Error" (Borges 1998a: 88). As I have observed elsewhere, it is also pertinent to add that Borges's narrator is not exactly kind to Pierre Menard and that his piece, instead of celebrating Menard's work, ends up ridiculing the obvious gap separating the Symbolist's ambitious goal from his actual achievement. Moreover, if one considers the story from the point of view of the ("invisible") struggle that Menard stages against his precursor, in the end Cervantes is still the huge author figure that has inspired Menard and so many others, while the latter's complete body of work is nothing more than the laughable list of texts compiled by the narrator (for further thoughts on the treatment given to Menard in the story, see Chapters One and Four).

As an important milestone in Borges's life, the writing of "Pierre Menard" seems to have symbolized a way of putting to rest the kind of modest literary career somewhat represented by his own, as well as by that of his Menardian father, his first important precursor. Since Borges could not be immune to the consequences of literary influence, in the end he seems to have chosen Cervantes (or what the latter represented as a universally celebrated, influential author) over the Quixotic Menard as a model to imitate. This was probably not an easy choice, no matter how subterranean it might have been, particularly if we take into consideration the complex, delicate network of relationships that seems to be established in "Pierre Menard" between influence and transference. One might think for instance of the relationship between an author's desire to be his own origin (a desire often fraught with guilt) and the debt allegedly owed to both intellectual and biological ancestors. Since Borges's writing grew essentially out of other texts, written by authors that he admired and emulated, it is tempting to endorse Harold Bloom's notion that the Argentinian's "idealization of influence relationships" is bound up with "a dread of what Freud called the family romance and of what might be termed the family romance of literature" (Bloom 1994: 471). From such a perspective, one could further explain not only why Pierre Menard's eagerness in composing Cervantes's masterpiece is associated with the subterranean and the invisible, but also why Borges often tried to downplay any implication of rivalry or competition in his commentaries on the kinds of relationships that are usually established between readers and writers, disciples and masters, including his own relationships with the several authors he turned into role models.

The attempt to neutralize any form of conflict or competition implied in such textual encounters emerges as different "symptoms" in Borges's writings. One of them is his elaboration, in a short essay entitled "Coleridge's

Flower," of the "doctrine," somewhat borrowed from Paul Valéry, according to which "all authors are one author" (Borges 1999c: 242, trans. Levine), a conclusion that would divest the notion of "copying" another writer from any connotation of rivalry. As Borges concludes his essay, "those who carefully copy a writer do so impersonally, because they equate that writer with literature, because they suspect that to depart from him in the slightest is to deviate from reason and orthodoxy" (ibid.). In a similar fashion, in "Kafka and his Precursors," Borges explicitly proposes that the word "precursor," although "indispensable in the vocabulary of criticism," be "purified" from "any connotation of polemic or rivalry" (Borges 1999d: 365, trans. Weinberger). Another manifestation of Borges's desire to neutralize any conflict even remotely related to influence relationships may be his alleged modesty, expressed, for instance, in his recurrent declarations of debt to several precursors. In his "Autobiographical Essay," for example, he refers to his attempts at imitating some of his early influences (Rafael Cansinos Assens, Macedonio Fernández, Francisco de Quevedo, and Diego de Saavedra Fajardo, among others) with verbs and expressions such as "to ape," "to plagiarize," "to mimick," "to crib" (Borges 1987: 33–38), which clearly emphasize the abyssal distance that allegedly separated master from disciple, and in a manner that brings to mind the relationship his narrator in "Pierre Menard" imagined between Cervantes and the French translator. Drawing on Borges's explicit as well as his more subtle statements on relations of influence, we may explore further the seminal role played by the practice of translation in the construction of his literary career. As a supposedly invisible strategy to take over someone else's text and authorial position, the practice of translation seems to have allowed Borges not only to play with the idea of being an-Other, but also to imitate (and even transform) the kind of writing he admired in the works of his favorite authors, and which he felt compelled to supplant with his own (for detailed commentaries on Borges's general translation strategies and the use he made of his translations in the actual composition of his texts, see, for example, Kristal 2002: 88–134 and Costa 2002: 182–193).

A young Borges discovers Walt Whitman

During his years as a teenager living in Europe, Borges was beginning to experiment with poetry writing, a practice that was also significantly related to his interest in foreign languages, especially English, and in major European poets. As he reminisces in his "Autobiographical Essay," before leaving Switzerland in 1919, he had been writing sonnets in English and in French: "The English sonnets were poor imitations of Wordsworth, and the French, in their own watery way, were imitative of symbolist poetry" (Borges 1987: 54). Raised in an aristocratic, bilingual household, which also sheltered his father's now famous library, mainly comprised of English books, and in a peripheral country that used to relate everything British to high culture and civilization, Borges learned to associate the reading of literature with English (for an enlightening reflection on Borges's "bilingualism," see Piglia 1981: 89–90). As he was to write in later years, he felt inevitably divided between English, a language that he often wished had been his "birthright," and which he felt "unworthy to handle," and Spanish, which, as "an Argentine writer, [he had] to cope with," and of whose "shortcomings" he "was only too aware" (Borges 1987: 54). Emotionally and intellectually situated between (at least) two languages, two cultures, and two traditions, Borges was bound to be influenced by foreign literature and to turn translation into an essential vehicle that would allow him to move between the languages that made up his personal history.

Among Borges's acknowledged masters, Walt Whitman played a decisive role in the shaping of his literary career, particularly in his early formative years in Europe as he was preparing to become a writer. He first became acquainted with Whitman's work through a German translation by Johannes Schlaf (*"Als ich in Alabama meinen Morgengang machte"*) of "As I have walk'd in Alabama my morning walk," a fragment from *Leaves of Grass* (Whitman 1996: 56–57), and the impact of this discovery was going to last practically all his life. Indeed, it seems that while Borges learned to overcome his "infatuation" with other important influences such as Carlyle and Swinburne, "he never really got over Whitman" (Rodríguez Monegal 1978: 148). As a close friend described him during his first visit to Spain in 1919, in those days he was completely "drunk with Whitman" (ibid.: 139). Soon the American poet became the ultimate role model after which Borges would take in his own search for poetic expression. As he remarked in a lecture given at the University of Texas at Austin in 1961, when he first read Whitman he was "quite overwhelmed" and felt that he had finally found his supreme master: "when I read Walt Whitman I got the feeling that all poets who had written before him, Homer, and Shakespeare, and Hugo, and Quevedo, and so on, had been trying to and failing to do, what Whitman HAD done" (qtd. in Jaén 1967: 51–52, my translation from the Spanish). Even Borges's interest in German Expressionism, which also produced, according to him, "some of the first, and perhaps the only, translations of a number of Expressionist poets into Spanish" (ibid.: 52, my translation from the Spanish), was then mediated by his devotion to Whitman. As Borges wrote at the time, the main source of Expressionism was "constituted by that athletic and Cyclopean vision that comes from Whitman's rhythms and the plurality of his poetry" (Borges 1997b: 52, trans. and qtd. in Kristal 2002: 43). His critical interest in the American poet is evidenced in two short essays, "El otro Whitman" ("The Other Whitman") (Borges 1980a), and "Nota sobre Walt Whitman" ("Note on Walt Whitman") (Borges 1980b). At the same time, his deep admiration of the American poet and his work seems to have been the underlying motivation behind "Himno del mar," the first poem he published while living in Europe in 1919 (Borges 1997a), and, of course, also behind *Hojas de hierba*, his Spanish version of

Leaves of Grass, whose publication, announced as early as 1927, did not take place until 1969.

While it was his father who had "revealed the power of poetry" to him, it was Whitman who eventually became his ultimate "subject presumed to know" as soon as he started to take his poetry writing more seriously. It was under the spell of the American poet that he published "Himno del mar," which could be read as a somewhat clumsy translation of some of Whitman's best-known motifs. According to Borges, "in the poem, I tried my hardest to be Walt Whitman" (Borges 1987: 31). It is significant to note, also, that Borges never included "Himno del mar" in any of his published poetry collections, which suggests that he was probably aware of the poem's shortcomings, or, perhaps, more importantly, of its obvious connection with Whitman's work. The echoes of Whitman's influence upon his young admirer's first published poem are not difficult to identify, especially if one takes into account the rather vehement, overtly sensuous tone in which Borges's poetic persona celebrates his "beloved" sea, whose "mysterious" strength he finds comforting. "Himno del mar" is embarrassingly similar, for example, to the opening lines from section 22 of Whitman's "Song of Myself":

> You sea! I resign myself to you also – I guess what you mean,
> I behold from the beach your crooked inviting fingers,
> I believe you refuse to go back without feeling of me,
> We must have a turn together, I undress, hurry me out of sight of the
>   land,
> Cushion me soft, rock me in billowy drowse,
> Dash me with amorous wet, I can repay you.
> Sea of stretch'd ground-swells,
> Sea breathing broad and convulsive breaths,
> Sea of the brine of life and of unshovell'd yet always-ready graves,
> Howler and scooper of storms, capricious and dainty sea,
> I am integral with you, I too am of one phase and of all phases.
>
>   (Whitman 1996: 84)

Compare, for instance, Whitman's lines to the following from Borges's "Himno del mar":

> Hermano, Padre, Amado … !
> Entro al jardín enorme de tus aguas y nado lejos de la tierra.
> [...]
> Yo estoy contigo, Mar. Y mi cuerpo tendido como un arco
> lucha contra tus músculos raudos. Sólo tú existes.
> [...]
> Oh mar! oh mito! Oh sol! Oh largo lecho!
> Y sé por qué te amo. Sé que somos muy viejos.
> Que ambos nos conocemos desde siglos.

[...]
Oh proteico, yo he salido de ti.

(Borges 1997a: 24–26)

(Brother, Father, Beloved ... !
I enter the enormous garden of your waters and swim away from the
    shore.
[...]
I am with you, Sea. And my body stretched out like a bow
struggles against your swift muscles. You are the only one.
[...]
Oh sea! Oh myth! Oh sun! Oh great bed!
And I know why I love you. I know that we are both very old.
And that we have known one another for centuries.
[...]
Oh protean, I have sprung from you.
    [My translation (cf. also Cortínez 1985: 75 and Bastos 1986: 222)]])

The sensuous atmosphere that dominates Borges's poem is basically created
by the sexualization of the sea (often addressed as "Mar," with a capital
"M") and of nature in general, a characteristic that is a recurrent motif in
Whitman's poetry, and which seems to be the main inspiration for the
imagery chosen by Borges in his first poem. While Borges's "muscular" sea
is "naked," "athletic," and has "swift hands" (Borges 1997a: 25), Whitman's
has "inviting fingers" (Whitman 1996: 84). While Borges's "virgin beaches"
have "golden breasts" (Borges 1997a: 24), Whitman's "night" is "bare-
bosom'd" and "mad naked," and his "earth" is "voluptuous" and
"cool-breath'd" (Whitman 1996: 84). Like the persona in Whitman's poem,
Borges's establishes a loving relationship with his humanized, sensually
charged sea: as he enters "the enormous garden" of the sea's waters, and
swims away from the shore (Borges 1997a: 24), he experiences an "instant
of magnificent plenitude" (ibid.: 25), a plenitude that also seems to echo
Borges's own life experience. Decades after writing his first poem, he talked
about swimming as one of the few experiences he had that could be
associated with actual "physical happiness" (cf. Cortínez 1985: 76;
Barnstone 1982: 8; and Rodríguez Monegal 1978: 479). Returning to
"Himno del mar," as Borges's persona fights the sea's "swift muscles," he
leaves behind his past amorous encounters and disappointments and offers
them to the wind (Borges 1997a: 24). In order to celebrate the sea, "the only
one" for him, Borges's poetic persona wishes to create a poem that might
reproduce the "Adamic rhythm" of its waves (ibid.). Finally, in the last lines,
he explicitly declares why he loves and identifies with the sea:

Y sé por qué te amo. Sé que somos muy viejos.
Que ambos nos conocemos desde siglos.

[...]
Oh proteico, yo he salido de ti.
Ambos encadenados y nómadas;
Ambos con un sed intensa de estrellas;
Ambos con esperanzas y desengaños;
Ambos, aire, luz, fuerza, oscuridades;
Ambos con nuestro vasto deseo y ambos con nuestra grande miseria!

(Borges 1997a: 26)

(And I know why I love you. I know that we are very old.
That we have known each other for centuries.
[...]
Oh, protean, I have sprung from you.
Both of us shackled and wandering;
Both of us intensely yearning for stars.
Both of us hopeful and disappointed.
Both of us air, light, strength, darkness;
Both of us with our vast desire and both of us with our great misery!

[My translation])

As Borges's persona in "Himno del mar" finds solace in the mirror effect of an idealized identification with the sea, it seems plausible to read it as a veiled celebration of the aspiring poet's own deep attraction to Whitman and his poetry. Hence, the sea (as "Brother," "Father," and "Beloved"), from whom Borges's poetic persona "has sprung," and with whom he finds so much in common, could be representing Whitman as the ultimate Poet himself, that is, that powerful voice enticing readers particularly interested in writing poetry with an irresistible invitation that is presented right at the beginning of "Song of Myself": "Stop this day and night with me and you shall possess the origin of all poems" (Whitman 1996: 25; see also Bastos 1986: 221). And it is certainly significant that the poetic persona in "Himno del mar" wants to celebrate the Sea/Whitman by creating a poem that might reproduce the "Adamic rhythm" of his waves, that is, it is under the influence of the poetry that comes from the sea, and it is in order to celebrate Whitman (and the comfort and the pleasure associated with him), that Borges's persona wishes to create a poem. As the poet who claimed to be "integral" with the sea, the universe and even with all human kind, Whitman must have seemed not only to harbor the secret and the strength of poetry writing, but also to offer his shy, impressionable reader a shelter away from his adolescent disappointments as well as the promise of a harmonious, pleasurable perspective on life, a perspective that was also fully tuned to the exuberant movements of nature.

There is, however, at least one striking difference between Borges's first poem and Whitman's poetry. While Borges's poetic persona in "Himno del mar" looks for the sea in an attempt to leave behind his love disappointments, in Whitman's section 22 of "Song of Myself," it is the sea that "refuses to go back without feeling [him]" (1996: 84). Hence, in contrast with Borges's, Whitman's persona is portrayed as a strong man who is in perfect harmony with all that is inside and around him, and who is not running away from anything. The poem is, in fact, an affirmation of his power to celebrate both "virtue" and "vice," "goodness" and "wickedness" (ibid.: 84–85) (see also Bastos 1986: 222). However, even though "Himno del mar," when compared to Whitman's poem, suggests a less optimistic, less confident outlook on life, it would not be difficult to identify echoes of the American poet's celebration of homoeroticism in Borges's enthusiastic praise of the sea's male power in the poem. In a piece on Borges's alleged "phobic treatment" of homosexuality, Daniel Balderston appropriately relates Borges's "The Other," the story first published in 1975 (Borges 1998b, trans. Hurley), to the latter's interest in Whitman, particularly in his early years as a poet apprentice (Balderston 2004). According to the story, which gives us a revealing glimpse of Borges's young self while the older Borges is visiting Cambridge, Massachusetts, in February of 1969, the latter, as the narrator, has an encounter with the young man he used to be in his early years in Geneva and who is working on his first book of poetry, which he plans to call "Red Anthems – Red Rhythms or Red Songs" (Borges 1998b: 414). This project is also obviously connected to Borges's interest in Whitman, especially as it is supposed to be "a hymn to the brotherhood of all mankind" and address "the great oppressed and outcast masses" (ibid.). (In his "Autobiographical Essay," Borges describes "The Red Psalms or The Red Rhythms," which he "destroyed" in Spain at the end of 1920, as "a collection of poems – perhaps some twenty in all – in free verse and in praise of the Russian Revolution, the brotherhood of man, and pacifism" [Borges 1987: 33]. Significantly, "Himno del Mar" was included in the collection.) In "The Other," as both Borgeses start discussing poetry "on a bench besides the Charles River" (Borges 1998b: 411), the young man "fervently" recites "that short poem in which Whitman recalls a night shared beside the sea – a night when Whitman had been truly happy" (ibid.: 415). While the older Borges is primarily interested in the poetic effect of what is allegedly being narrated in the poem ("If Whitman sang of that night [... ,] it's because he desired it but it never happened. The poem gains in greatness if we sense that it is the expression of a desire, a longing, rather than the narration of an event" [ibid.: 416]), his younger self is moved precisely by what he perceives to be the narration of Whitman's real-life experience ("You don't know him [...] Whitman is incapable of falsehood" [ibid.]). Both Cortínez (1985: 76) and Balderston (2004) claim that Borges is referring to Whitman's "When I Heard at the Close of the Day," whose initial lines read as follows:

> When I heard at the close of the day how my name had been receiv'd
>   with plaudits in the Capitol, still it was not a happy night for me
>   that follow'd,

And else when I carous'd, or when my plans were accomplish'd, still I
    was not happy,
But the day when I rose at dawn from the bed of perfect health,
    refresh'd, singing, inhaling the ripe breath of autumn,
When I saw the full moon in the west grow pale and disappear in the
    morning light,
When I wander'd alone over the beach, and undressing bathed,
    laughing with the cool waters, and saw the sun rise.
And when I thought how my dear friend my lover was on his way
    coming, O then I was happy.

(Whitman 1996: 155)

Whitman's poem can also be related to "Himno del mar," especially if we bear in mind the description of the poetic persona's joy as he bathes in the "cool waters" of the sea (see also Cortínez 1985: 76). There are, however, some fundamental differences between the two texts. While in Whitman's poem, "joy" is explicitly associated with a homosexual encounter, in Borges's, "the instant of magnificent plenitude" experienced by his poetic persona can only be shared in the company of the sea as "Brother," "Father," and "Beloved." While Whitman's persona rejoices in the company of his "dear friend [his] lover," Borges's only finds solace in his solitary swim and in celebrating the sea as his double ("both of us with our vast desire and both of us with our great misery") (Borges 1997a: 26).

Even though this is not the place to speculate on Borges's allegedly phobic treatment of homoeroticism in "The Other," we should take note of the revealing dialogue taking place between a young expatriate persona of Borges and the cosmopolitan, world-renowned Borges, who is being honored by Harvard University, as it suggests not only the extent of Borges's investment in the character and the achievement of Whitman, but also the lasting effect of his transferential bond with the American poet. It seems that for the young Borges portrayed in the story, Whitman, who was "incapable of falsehood," had managed to reconcile an allegedly adventurous, "happy" life with a literary career and, consequently, to successfully translate his own personal experiences into meaningful inspiring poetry. Thus, just as Cervantes was "the subject presumed to know" in Menard's biography, Whitman seemed to represent for the younger Borges the desirable, idealized possibility of a life devoted to writing that did not have to be restricted to the confining limits of his domestic library. At the same time, the older Borges, who no longer seems to believe in the possibility of reconciling the poet's mask with his real, melancholy face, is still trying to come to grips with the direction he chose for his life through an understanding of his relationship with Whitman's literary persona. One may thus conclude that while the younger Borges explicitly wants to emulate his idealized version of Whitman, the older Borges seems interested in turning the American poet into a reflection of himself as he apparently finds comfort in the idea that

Whitman's actual life was perhaps not very different from his own. As Borges wrote in "Nota sobre Walt Whitman" ("Note on Walt Whitman"), "there are two Whitmans": "the 'friendly and eloquent savage' of *Leaves of Grass* and the poor man of letters that invented him. This one was chaste, reserved and rather taciturn; but the other, effusive and orgiastic" (Borges 1980b: 194–195, trans. and qtd. in Alegría 1995: 212–213).

As Fernando Alegría observes, the "chaste, reserved, and rather taciturn" man who wrote *Leaves of Grass* "is very much like" Borges himself (Alegría 1995: 213), and also, one might add, very much like the several bookish characters he introduced in his fictions and essays. But this confinement to an ascetic life fully devoted to books does bring some consolation. As Borges remarks in relation to Whitman, what is most important about the poet from Camden is that "the happy vagabond described in the poems of *Leaves of Grass* would not have been capable himself of writing them" (Borges 1980b: 195, my translation). In the same text, he refers to Whitman as "this friend, who is an old American poet of the nineteenth century, and is also his own legend, and also each one of us and happiness as well" (ibid.: 198, my translation). It is to this dear life-long "friend," to this "eternal Whitman" that Borges often declared his debt throughout his own career as a poet. In an interview given to Willis Barnstone in the early 1980s, Borges further elaborates on his identification with Whitman in a manner that is reminiscent of "Borges and I," the piece he published in 1960 on the alleged division between Borges, the man, and Borges, the well-known author (Borges 1998d, trans. Hurley):

> [Whitman] created this very strange character, Walt Whitman, not to be taken for the writer of the book ... He attempted a very daring experiment, the most daring and the most successful experiment in all literature as far as I know. [...] The central character would be called after the author, Walt Whitman, but he was, firstly, Walt Whitman the human being, the very unhappy man who wrote *Leaves of Grass*.
>
> (Barnstone 1982: 136)

As happens in the story of Pierre Menard's relationship with Cervantes, the workings of transference and the practice of translation underwrite Borges's life-long engagement with Whitman's poetry and literary persona. Although one might conjecture that Borges began his translations from the American poet soon after he became acquainted with his work, the earliest reference to his project of publishing them dates back to February of 1927, when the Argentinean literary journal *Martín Fierro* announced his forthcoming version of *Leaves of Grass* as "an important enterprise" that strictly followed "Borges's design," that is:

> to produce such a close fit with the original and its author's innovative conception that the reader will be in contact with the most genuine

Whitman and his informal style down to his vocabulary in the argot, or low-brow English, of the United States.

(trans. and qtd. in Kristal 2002: 49)

And yet, Borges's attempt at reproducing Whitman in Spanish had to remain practically invisible for more than forty years. It was not until 1969 – the same year in which the older Borges meets his young self in the storyline of "The Other" – that he finally published *Hojas de hierba*, his "selections and translations" of *Leaves of Grass* (Whitman 1969, trans. Borges).

Efraín Kristal attributes the long hiatus between the 1927 announcement and the actual publication of Borges's translation to his "evolving interpretation" of Whitman, which supposedly "dissuaded him from publishing his early version of *Leaves of Grass*" in the 1920s (Kristal 2002: 50). According to Kristal, by 1969 Borges was ready to publish his version as he "had developed a richer and more nuanced view of the matter" and, notably, of the relationship between Whitman, the literary persona of *Leaves of Grass*, and the actual man who wrote the poems (ibid.). While Kristal's general argument seems plausible, I cannot help advancing a more subtle reason why it took so long for Borges to publish his versions of Whitman's poems. Let us remember, for instance, that in 1927 Borges was still struggling to find his poetic voice. As he reminisces in his "Autobiographical Essay," the 1920s were, for him, a period of "great activity, but much of it was perhaps reckless and even pointless" (Borges 1987: 37). By 1927 he had published only two books of poetry. The publication of the first one, *Fervor de Buenos Aires* ("Adoration of Buenos Aires"), in 1923, was a domestic, amateurish production financed by Borges Senior. As Borges explains, "the book was actually printed in five days [...] I had bargained for sixty-four pages, but the manuscript ran too long and at the last minute five poems had to be left out – mercifully. I can't remember a single thing about them" (ibid.: 34). His second book of poetry, *Luna de enfrente* ("Moon Across the Way"), published in 1925, was not worth remembering either. It was, in his words, "a kind of riot of sham local color," and, although some of its poems did get reprinted, in later editions Borges "dropped the worst poems, pruned the eccentricities, and successively – through several reprints – revised and toned down the verses" (ibid.: 39). Therefore, one could further speculate that while he was trying to find his own voice, Borges's translations of Whitman had to remain only an invisible project. We might wonder, for instance, that if he had indeed published *Hojas de hierba* in the 1920s, the comparisons that would have been made between his translations and his own early poetry could have imprisoned him forever in the role of the seduced reader and translator of a major literary master who, like Pierre Menard, could only dream of greater challenges.

Borges continued to write poetry and short essays until the mid-1930s, when he wrote his first distinctively Borgesian story, "The Approach to al-Mu'tasim" (Borges 1998e, trans. Hurley), which he defines as "both a hoax and a pseudo-essay," and which is considered as a precursor to "Pierre Menard" (Borges 1987: 43). By 1942, when he published his first collection of stories, *El jardín de senderos que se bifurcan* ("The Garden of Forking Paths"), he had finally found his own means of literary expression, and decided to be only "a part-time poet" (Rodríguez Monegal 1978: 375). Hence, we may infer, his infatuation with Whitman was no longer the main focus of his literary career. By 1969, when his version of *Leaves of Grass* came out, Borges was already a major author, known worldwide for his unique brand of fiction writing. After being translated into French in the 1950s, he became quite visible both in Argentina and abroad. In 1961 he shared the prestigious Formentor Prize with Samuel Beckett and his books "mushroomed overnight throughout the Western world" (Borges 1987: 52). In the same year, Borges made his first visit to his beloved United States where he was honored as a visiting professor at the University of Texas at Austin. In 1967, his second trip to America took him to Cambridge, Massachusetts, where he held the Charles Eliot Norton Chair of Poetry at Harvard University and

> lectured to well-wishing audiences on 'The Craft of Verse' (ibid.). At the end of his stay in the country, he was greatly honored to have [his] poems read at the Y.M.H.A. Poetry Center in New York, with several of [his] translators reading and a number of poets in the audience.
>
> (Borges 1987: 53)

It seems that by then, as he was widely known both in Spanish and in English, and celebrated both as a storywriter and as a poet, Borges was finally ready to share his translations of Whitman with Spanish-reading audiences.

As an important expression of Borges's life-long interest in the American poet, *Hojas de hierba*, like Pierre Menard's *Quixote*, might help us further reflect not only on the subterranean motivations of his own attempts at "repeating in a foreign tongue a book that already existed" (Borges 1998a: 95), but also on the essentially performative role played by translation as a form of invisible authorship. Even though his long-lasting love affair with Whitman's work and persona was obviously more productive – and had a happier end – than Menard's obsession with Cervantes, in both cases translation seems to have played a fundamental, even therapeutic role in helping these ambitious readers deal with the conflicts of influence and act out their desire to be someone else. While Borges did try his "hardest" to be Whitman in "Himno del mar," it was in his translations of the American poet that he was able to somehow *become* a Spanish version of Whitman's poetic persona and inhabit the highly desirable universe of one of his most important precursors, and, thus, temporarily ignore himself, his superego, and his family romance. In such a safe, privileged authorial position, Borges was able to select the poems he was going to rewrite and actually created versions, which, as one of his readers has pointed out, are "autonomous" poems in Spanish that do not need to be read as "dependent" on Whitman's originals (Aparicio 1991: 133).

As a strategy that might have helped Borges escape Borges, translation seems to have allowed him to pretend to be an-Other and, in the Other's name, write, in his native Spanish, that which he was unable to address in his own texts and in his own name. If in his Whitmanesque "Himno del mar" he could not completely lose himself in the sea of otherness and leave behind a certain melancholy, resigned tone that betrayed the "unhappiness" of which he was allegedly ashamed, in his versions of *Leaves of Grass*, Borges managed to have his poetic persona take over whatever he admired and desired in the American poet's originals, and, therefore, on some level, he *was* the "effusive and orgiastic" Walt Whitman, "a man of adventure and love, indolent, full of life, carefree, a wanderer in America," as he himself refers to Whitman's persona in the opening paragraph of his prologue to *Hojas de hierba* (Whitman 1969: 21). As a consequence, one might also consider that, as he translated *Leaves of Grass*, Borges did not simply imitate Whitman, as he could not keep himself from doing in his first published poem, but felt, perhaps, liberated to appropriate and express what he saw and loved in the American poet's work, and was finally able to be "defined," for instance, by lines such as these: "Walt Whitman, un cosmos, de Manhattan el hijo, / Turbulento, carnal, sensual, comiendo, bebiendo, engendrando" (ibid.: 59) ("Walt Whitman, a kosmos, of Manhattan the son, / Turbulent, fleshy, sensual, eating, drinking and breeding" [Whitman 1996: 86]). The possibility of expressing one's unconfessed desires and fantasies through someone else's words, that is, through reading and translating, was something that the author of "Pierre Menard" obviously knew quite well. As he comments in the prologue to *Hojas de hierba*, the reader, who, as he claims, is an integral part of *Leaves of Grass*, "has always tended to identify with the protagonist of a text; to read Macbeth is in some way to be Macbeth. Walt Whitman, as far as we know, was the first to take advantage of this temporary identification to the fullest" (Whitman 1969: 21, my translation). Thus, and particularly in Borges's own case, if reading Whitman was in some way to be Whitman, translating him was an efficient way not only to rewrite and own what seemed so attractive in his poetry, but also to celebrate and be forever associated with the American poet. As in Menard's relationship with Cervantes, it was possible for Borges, as the translator of *Leaves of Grass*, not only to be the actual writer of *Hojas de hierba*, but also to pay tribute to his "subject presumed to know," while, at the same time, disguising the violence of his possessive love with the "alibi" of fidelity to Whitman and his text. In his typically modest tone, Borges states, in the prologue to *Hojas de hierba*, that he is aware of the "deficiencies" of his work, which "oscillates between personal interpretation and resigned rigor," while he reassures his reader that in spite of the inadequacies that may be found in his translations, the strength of Whitman's poetry will certainly come through (Whitman 1969: 22, my translation) (for other comments on the translations, see Aparicio 1991; Alegría 1995; Valero Garcés 1995; and Kristal 2002).

If we take into account Borges's acknowledged desire to be Whitman, it does seem significant that of all the poems collected in *Leaves of Grass*, the only one he chose to translate in its entirety was "Song of Myself" with its fifty-two sections, a poem that opens with the well-known lines that affirm the strength and the unflinching, unrestricted self-acceptance of Whitman's poetic persona and Borges's idealized "semidivine vagabond": "I celebrate myself, and sing myself, / And what I assume you shall assume, / For every atom belonging to me as good belong to you" (Whitman 1996: 63). Indeed, the general theme of "Song of Myself" is precisely the celebration of a "self" that is in perfect harmony with his body, his fellow men and women, as well as the universe, a "self" that lives life to the fullest:

> Welcome is every organ and attribute of me, and of any man hearty
> and clean,
> Not an inch nor a particle of an inch is vile, and none shall be less
> familiar than the rest.
>
> (Ibid.: 66)

> The atmosphere is not a perfume, it has no taste of distillation, it is
> odorless,
> It is for my mouth forever, I am in love with it.
>
> (Ibid.: 64)

> I am enamour'd of growing out-doors,
> Of men that live among cattle or taste of the ocean or woods.
>
> (Ibid.: 75)

In the cathartic writing exercise provided by translation, the cerebral, shy, and allegedly unhappy Borges, who, like the fictional obsessive men of letters of his stories, spent most of his days and nights surrounded by books, had the opportunity to recreate an "effusive and orgiastic" persona and write lines such as the following:

> Soy el poeta del Cuerpo y soy el poeta del Alma,
> Los goces del cielo están conmigo y los tormentos del infierno están
> conmigo,
> Los primeros los injerto y los multiplico en mi ser, los últimos los
> traduzco a un nuevo idioma.
>
> (Whitman 1969: 55)

I am the poet of the Body and I am the poet of the Soul,
The pleasures of heaven are with me and the pains of hell are with me,
The first I graft and increase upon myself, the latter I translate into a
    new tongue.

(Whitman 1996: 83)

It is also relevant to note that while "Song of Myself" celebrates Whitman's own poetic persona and his passionate love for all that surrounds him, it also proposes an open, generous, productive relationship between authorship and reading. In such a relationship the poet and his reader (the precursor and his follower, the master and his disciple) are not only equals, but are also encouraged to establish a rather close, loving bond as Whitman's persona invites his reader to join him and offers him both "the origin of all poems" and the promise of a partnership that is free from any form of influence anxiety:

Stop this day and night with me and you shall possess the origin of all
    poems,
You shall possess the good of the earth and sun, (there are millions of
    suns left,)
You shall no longer take things at second or third hand, nor look
    through the eyes of the dead, nor feed on the specters in books,
You shall not look through my eyes either, nor take things from me,
You shall listen to all sides and filter them from your self.

(Ibid.: 64–65)

If we recognize Borges's reticence about any possible conflict involved in influence relationships as well as his recurrent concern about being just "an echo of other echoes," we might wonder how attractive and, at the same time, how liberating it must have seemed for him to compose Whitman's text in Spanish. As he wrote *Hojas de hierba*, Borges had the opportunity to (re)create himself as a truly magnanimous authorial figure who could fully express and accept the self he wished to be, and, more importantly, who was also ready to welcome and nurture seduced readers and disciples, and to even protect them from the risk of becoming mere "echoes" of their master and favorite poet.

If we take Borges's lessons on translation and its relationship with original writing to their last consequences, and, hence, if we follow the lead of his narrator's reading strategy in "Pierre Menard," we may want to read both *Hojas de hierba* and "Himno del mar" as poems written by Borges in the wake of his attraction to Whitman. Then, we will likely find that while "Himno del mar" is definitely closer to Borges's style and temperament than any of the poems collected in *Hojas de hierba*, it is also a much weaker, much less original poetic statement than Borges's versions of the American poet's work, at least in Spanish. At the same time, while the "miserable" poetic persona in "Himno del mar" seems to be only a timid "echo" of the huge authorial figure represented by Whitman, the persona in *Hojas de hierba* is self-loving, sensual, and truly unconventional, fully endorsing the American poet's pansexual outlook and explicit celebration of homoeroticism. The rather subtle homoerotic celebration of male strength and companionship that underlies "Himno del mar," for example, gets to be unabashedly visible in poems such as "Cuando supe al declinar del día," Borges's version of "When I Heard at the Close of the Day," which, as I have commented on above, has also been associated both with "Himno del mar" and "The Other," and in which the pleasure and the happiness that Borges's persona derives from his contact with the sea are also directly related to the upcoming visit of his *"querido amigo, [su] amante"* ("dear [male] friend, [his] lover"). (Readers of *Hojas de hierba* have commented on Borges's "fidelity" to the American poet's sexual references. According to Alegría, for example, "it is quite possible that no Hispanic translator has ever equaled Borges in his masterful versions of Whitman's ambiguous sex poems" [Alegría 1991: 214]. [See also Kristal 2002: 56–57].)

And yet, one might also speculate that, in spite of the fact that Borges often defended the possibility of a relationship between reading and writing that could apparently transcend the conflicts involved in transference, he might not have welcomed any comparison between "Himno del mar" and his versions of Whitman's *Leaves of Grass*. As pointed out above, Borges never included "Himno del mar" in any of his published collections and it only appeared in *Textos Recobrados* ("Recovered Texts") more than a decade after his death. Outside the protective limits of translation and of the invisible, "temporary identification" it makes possible, and in spite of his recurrent defense of a conception of authorship that could be devoid of any notion of property or individuality, Borges, like his Pierre Menard, did seem interested in erasing the traces of his obvious attempts at being an-Other, and, also, in protecting himself from the critical eyes of readers who might expose his early texts to a judgmental, perhaps unkind scrutiny. As I pay special attention to Borges's translations of the poems from *Leaves of Grass* that have been connected to "Himno del mar," it seems significant, for example, that in the edition of *Hojas de hierba* I am using there is no poem or section number 22 in *"Canto de mí mismo"* ("Song of Myself"), that is, the very same text that has been identified by a few of his readers as the main source of inspiration for his first published poem. And as I try to find a plausible explanation for the fact that what was originally poem 22 has become the continuation of section 21, I cannot help identifying with Borges's narrator in "Pierre Menard" and his pretension to establish the meaning of a text that Menard "would allow no one to see" (Borges 1998a: 95) and I imagine a scenario in which Borges actually tries to hide the traces of his infatuation with a certain fragment from Whitman's poetry. As I construct my fiction, I think, for example, about "The Other," and, more specifically, about the protective, tender feelings that the older Borges confesses to harbor towards his younger self ("I, who have never been a father, felt a wave of love for that poor young man who was dearer to me than a child of my own flesh and blood" [Borges 1998b: 414]). I also think about Borges's narrator in "The Circular Ruins," who worries about the future of the son he has engendered and wishes he could spare him the "humiliation" of being just a "simulacrum" or the mere echo of another echo (Borges 1998f: 100, trans. Hurley). Alternatively, of course, we might also entertain the possibility that we are dealing here with a typesetter's minor mistake and, like Pierre Menard, would be running the risk of "enrich[ing] the slow and rudimentary art of reading by means of a new technique – the technique of deliberate anachronism and fallacious attribution" (Borges 1998a: 95).

Finally, as I ponder the dangers of reading and some of the invisible struggles that seem to underlie the always delicate and complex relationship that usually takes place between readers and authors, translators and originals, and as I try to come to terms with my own transferential bond with Borges and his texts, and, therefore, as I become aware of my desire not only to learn from his writings, but also to somehow outsmart and frame him, I cannot help but admire his persistent and undoubtedly successful life-long quest to find his own authorial voice and become a widely recognized "subject presumed to know," fully endowed with the power to seduce and inspire readers to study, interpret, translate, emulate, and even criticize him. If we recall, for instance, that the first story he ever wrote, "La visera fatal," was allegedly inspired by his love for the English version of *Don Quixote*, it could not be more appropriate that he is now often remembered together with Cervantes as one of the most influential Hispanic writers of all times.

Bibliography

Alegría, F. (1995) "Borges's 'Song of Myself,'" in E. Greenspan (ed.) *The Cambridge Companion to Walt Whitman*, Cambridge: Cambridge University Press, 208–219.

Anzieu, D. (1971) "Le corps et le code dans les contes de J. L. Borges," *Nouvelle Revue de Psychanalyse*, Paris: Gallimard, 177–210.

Aparicio, F. R. (1991) *Versiones, interpretaciones, creaciones – Instancias de la traducción literaria en Hispanoamérica en el siglo veinte*, Gaithersburg: Ediciones Hispanoamérica.

Arrojo, R. (1993) *Tradução, Desconstrução e Psicanálise*, Rio de Janeiro: Imago.

Balderston, D. (1985) *El precursor velado: R. L. Stevenson en la obra de Borges*, E. P. Leston (trans.), Buenos Aires: Editorial Sudamericana.

—— (2004) "The 'Fecal Dialectic': Homosexual Panic and the Origin of Writing in Borges," *Borges Studies on Line*. J. L. Borges Center for Studies & Documentation. Available at: www.borges.pitt.edu/bsol/bgay.php (accessed September 8, 2004).

Barnstone, W. (ed.) (1982) *Borges at Eighty: Conversations*, Bloomington: Indiana University Press.

—— (1986) "Borges, Poet of Ecstasy," in C. Cortínez (ed.) *Borges the Poet*, Fayetteville: University of Arkansas Press, 134–141.

Bastos, M. L. (1986) "Whitman as Inscribed in Borges," in C. Cortínez (ed.) *Borges the Poet*, Fayetteville: University of Arkansas Press, 219–231.

Bloom, H. (1975) *A Map of Misreading*, Oxford: Oxford University Press.

—— (1994) *The Western Canon: The Books and School of the Ages*, New York: Harcourt.

Borges, J. L. (1977) *Obra poética*, Buenos Aires: Emecé.

—— (1980a) "El otro Whitman," in *Prosa Completa*, vol. I, Barcelona: Editorial Bruguera, 139–142.

—— (1980b) "Nota sobre Walt Whitman," in *Prosa Completa*, vol. I, Barcelona: Editorial Bruguera, 193–198.

—— (1987) "An Autobiographical Essay," in J. Alazraki (ed.) *Critical Essays on Jorge Luis Borges*, Boston, MA: G. K. Hall, 21–55.

—— (1997a) "Himno del mar," in *Textos recobrados, 1919–1929*, Buenos Aires: Emecé, 11–12.

—— (1997b) "Lirica expresionista: Síntesis," in *Textos recobrados, 1919–1929*, Buenos Aires: Emecé, 52.

—— (1998a) "Pierre Menard, Author of the *Quixote*," A. Hurley (trans.) *Collected Fictions*, New York: Penguin, 88–95.

—— (1998b) "The Other," A. Hurley (trans.) *Collected Fictions*, New York: Penguin, 411–417.

—— (1998c) "Man on Pink Corner," A. Hurley (trans.) *Collected Fictions*, New York: Penguin, 45–53.

—— (1998d) "Borges and I," A. Hurley (trans.) *Collected Fictions*, New York: Penguin, 324.

—— (1998e) "The Approach to al-Mu'tasim," A. Hurley (trans.) *Collected Fictions*, New York: Penguin, 82–87.

—— (1998f) "The Circular Ruins," A. Hurley (trans.) *Collected Fictions*, New York: Penguin, 96–100.

—— (1999a) "The Homeric Versions," E. Weinberger (trans. and ed.) *Selected Non-Fictions*, New York: Penguin, 69–74.

—— (1999b) "The Translators of *The Thousand and One Nights*," E. Allen (trans.), in E. Weinberger (ed.) *Selected Non-Fictions*, New York: Penguin, 92–109.

—— (1999c) "Coleridge's Flower," S. J. Levine (trans.), in E. Weinberger (ed.) *Selected Non-Fictions*, New York: Penguin, 240–242.

—— (1999d) "Kafka and His Precursors," in E. Weinberger (trans. and ed.) *Selected Non-Fictions*, New York: Penguin, 363–365.

Cervantes Saavedra, Miguel de (2001) *The Ingenious Hidalgo Don Quixote de la Mancha*, J. Rutherford (trans.), New York: Penguin.

Cortínez, C. (1985) "'Himno del mar': el primer poema de Borges," *Revista Chilena de Literatura* 25 (April): 73–86.

—— (ed.) (1986) *Borges the Poet*, Fayetteville: University of Arkansas Press.

Costa, W. C. (2002) "Borges, the Original of the Translation," in D. Balderston and M. E. Schwartz (eds.) *Voice-overs: Translation and Latin American Literature*, Albany: State University of New York Press, 182–193.

De Behar, L. B. (2003) *Borges – The Passion of an Endless Quotation*, W. Egginton (trans.), Albany: State University of New York Press.

Felman, S. (1987) *Jacques Lacan and the Adventure of Insight: Psychoanalysis in Contemporary Culture*, Cambridge, MA: Harvard University Press.

Forrester, J. (1990) *The Seductions of Psychoanalysis: Freud, Lacan, and Derrida*, Cambridge: Cambridge University Press.

Freud, S. (1983a) "Creative Writers and Daydreaming," J. Strachey (trans.), in E. Kurzweil and W. Phillips (eds.) *Literature and Psychoanalysis*, New York: Columbia University Press, 24–28.

—— (1983b) "The Interpretation of Dreams," J. Strachey (trans.), in E. Kurzweil and W. Phillips (eds.) *Literature and Psychoanalysis*, New York: Columbia University Press, 29–33.

Gallop, J. (1985) *Reading Lacan*, Ithaca, NY: Cornell University Press.

Jaén, T. D. (1967) "Borges y Whitman," *Hispania* 1(1) (March): 49–53.

Kristal, E. (2002) *Invisible Work: Borges and Translation*, Nashville, TN: Vanderbilt University Press.

Lacan, J. (1975) *Le Seminaire*, livre XX, Paris: Seuil.

Piglia, R. (1981) "Ideología y ficción en Borges," in A. M. Barrenechea, J. Rest et al. (eds.) *Borges y la crítica*, Buenos Aires: Centro Editor de América Latina, 87–96.

Rodríguez Monegal, E. (1978) *Jorge Luis Borges: A Literary Biography*, New York: E. P. Dutton.

Steiner, G. (1975) *After Babel: Aspects of Language and Translation*, London: Oxford University Press.

Valero Garcés, C. (1995) "Jorge L. Borges poeta y traductor de Walt Whitman: análisis de las estrategias en la traducción de poesía," *Torre de papel* 3 (Fall): 19–40.

Whitman, W. (1969) *Hojas de hierba*, J. L. Borges (trans.), Buenos Aires: Juárez Editor.

—— (1996) *The Complete Poems*, Francis Murphy (ed.), London: Penguin Classics.

Woscoboinik, J. (1998) *The Secret of Borges: A Psychoanalytic Inquiry into His Work*, D. C. Pozzy (trans.), Lanham, MD: University Press of America.

Germany/German 65–6, 71, 73–4, 85, 89, 162
Gide, A. 24
Glaucon 49–51
globalization 2, 141
God/Gods 49, 74, 99–100, 141, 146
Gogol, N. 118
Grutman, R. 2–3
Guimarães Rosa, J. 2
Guy de Maupassant 109, 118–26, 128–9

Happy Prince, The 151
hermeneutics 2
heteronyms 112, 115
hierarchies 3, 30, 39, 68, 71–2, 108, 110, 114–15, 122, 128; dichotomies 35; opposition 66, 105, 127, 148; originals 48, 50, 53, 57, 63
Himno del mar 152, 162–6, 170–1, 173–4
history 19, 22–3, 43–4, 68, 82–4, 106, 108–14, 116, 152, 156; context 34; literary 59, 71, 126, 132; of philosophy 80
History of the Siege of Lisbon, The 108–16, 125–9
Hojas de hierba 152, 162, 169–71, 173
Homer 49–50, 68–9
Homeric Versions, The 66–7, 105, 151
Hungary/Hungarian 89, 102–3, 105
Huysmans, J. -K. 54

idealization 61, 63, 84, 136, 167
ideology 3–4, 48, 63, 149
If on a Winter's Night a Traveler 133, 137–47, 149
Iliad 68
Immoralist, The 24
impartiality 20
In Cold Blood 43
India 74
inequality 44–5, 67, 77, 136
influence 54, 155, 157–61; anxiety 126–7, 154, 173
interpretation 1, 4, 19, 65, 68–9, 76, 79, 93–4, 101, 104, 111, 153; reinterpretation 69

intertextuality 138
invisibility 5, 36, 38, 42, 44, 46, 84, 134–5, 152–3; introducing theory through fiction 19, 21, 23, 26, 31 *see also* visibility
Iran 73–4
Ireland 72
Irigaray, L. 2
Islam 70, 113
isolation 41
Italy 68, 125, 133

James, W. 22
journalism 43
Judaism 72

Kafka, F. 4, 8–9, 85, 89, 94–8, 104, 106, 108
Kaindl, K. 2
Kennedy, J. G. 55–9
Khatibi, A. 3
Kornél Esti 89, 101–4
Kosztolányi, D. 4, 8–9, 89, 101–4
Kristal, E. 169

La visera fatal 175
labor 35, 38–44, 106, 118, 121, 135
labyrinths 94–101, 104
Lacan, J. 6, 153, 155
Lane, E. 70
language 4–5, 19–20, 22–3, 30, 32, 36, 42, 48, 122, 161; classical 18; modern 18; postmodernism 48; texts as private retreats 90–1, 93–5, 101–2; translation of philosophy into fiction 65–6, 77–9
Latin 73, 75, 79, 81
Latin America 2, 72, 74, 79
Leaves of Grass 152, 162–3, 168–72, 174
legacy 30–2
Letter to a Young Lady in Paris 17–32
linguistics 4, 18
literary history 59, 71, 126, 132
literary power 108
literary texts 1, 61
literature 4–6, 45, 80, 158, 162; bourgeois 43; comparative 5, 18; world 5, 18

Taylor & Francis eBooks

Helping you to choose the right eBooks for your Library

Add Routledge titles to your library's digital collection today. Taylor and Francis ebooks contains over 50,000 titles in the Humanities, Social Sciences, Behavioural Sciences, Built Environment and Law.

Choose from a range of subject packages or create your own!

Benefits for you

» Free MARC records
» COUNTER-compliant usage statistics
» Flexible purchase and pricing options
» All titles DRM-free.

Benefits for your user

» Off-site, anytime access via Athens or referring URL
» Print or copy pages or chapters
» Full content search
» Bookmark, highlight and annotate text
» Access to thousands of pages of quality research at the click of a button.

REQUEST YOUR **FREE** INSTITUTIONAL TRIAL TODAY

Free Trials Available
We offer free trials to qualifying academic, corporate and government customers.

eCollections – Choose from over 30 subject eCollections, including:

Archaeology	Language Learning
Architecture	Law
Asian Studies	Literature
Business & Management	Media & Communication
Classical Studies	Middle East Studies
Construction	Music
Creative & Media Arts	Philosophy
Criminology & Criminal Justice	Planning
Economics	Politics
Education	Psychology & Mental Health
Energy	Religion
Engineering	Security
English Language & Linguistics	Social Work
Environment & Sustainability	Sociology
Geography	Sport
Health Studies	Theatre & Performance
History	Tourism, Hospitality & Events

For more information, pricing enquiries or to order a free trial, please contact your local sales team:
www.tandfebooks.com/page/sales

Routledge
Taylor & Francis Group

The home of
Routledge books

www.tandfebooks.com